Intelligence, Biosecurity and Bioterrorism

Patrick F. Walsh

Intelligence, Biosecurity and Bioterrorism

palgrave
macmillan

Patrick F. Walsh
Australian Graduate School of Policing
   and Security
Charles Sturt University
Manly, Australia

ISBN 978-1-137-51699-2   ISBN 978-1-137-51700-5   (eBook)
https://doi.org/10.1057/978-1-137-51700-5

Library of Congress Control Number: 2018943267

In loving memory of
Gwendoline Phyllis May Walsh
(Mum)
(14th April 1934–23rd November 2015)

Thank you for the gift of life and your unconditional love.

Acknowledgements

I wish to thank a number of people for helping this book come into existence. Starting with the researchers and scholars, I thank you all for your time and insights. In particular, I want to thank sincerely the following scholars, who know more about these issues than myself and from whom I learnt so much: Professor Seth Carus, Associate Professor Greg Koblentz, Dr. Jim Wilson, Professor Uwe Mueller-Doblies, Dr. Kavita Berger, Dr. Matthew Watson, Professor Kathleen Vogel, Dr. Jeremy Littlewood, Dr. Ellen Carlin and Asha George. Thank you all so much! The book does not pretend to be a complete survey of the role of intelligence in managing bio-threats and risks, but nonetheless the interviews I was able to do of both senior intelligence and policy officers, who have extensive expertise in biosecurity, intelligence and bioterrorism issues made the work richer. I know for the most part I cannot name you publicly, but rest assured I remain extremely grateful for your time and insights. I can only hope that the book serves to support the people I interviewed in some small way and those in our intelligence communities whose job it is to help decision-makers make sense of potential and emerging bio-threats and risks. I want to thank Glen and my family for your enduring love and support—a profound debt of gratitude which can never be completely repaid. I also want to thank my employer—Charles Sturt University (Australia), particularly my Executive Dean Professor Tracey Green and Head of School Associate Professor Nick O'Brien for their ongoing support of my research efforts. Finally, thanks also for the University's Faculty of Arts, who provided compact funding which enabled me to travel to the United States and Canada to interview participants.

Contents

About the Author

Patrick F. Walsh, Ph.D. is a former intelligence analyst, and has worked in Australia's national security and law enforcement environments. He is an associate professor in Intelligence and Security Studies, Charles Sturt University, Australia. He has taught widely across Australia and internationally. He is also a consultant to government agencies on intelligence reform and capability issues. His research grants and publications focus on a range of areas related to intelligence capability; including but not limited to: governance, leadership, intelligence and ethics, biosecurity and cyber. His last book, *Intelligence and Intelligence Analysis* (Abingdon, UK; Routledge, 2011), examined a range of intelligence reform issues post-9/11 across Australia, Canada, New Zealand, the United States and the United Kingdom. Patrick is also a member of the editorial board for the journal *Intelligence and National Security.*

1

Introduction

This chapter has three objectives. First, it will demonstrate the role intelligence can play for decision-makers, analysts, investigators and others managing bio-threats and risks. In particular, the chapter shows the importance of good intelligence support to preventing, disrupting, reducing and containing such threats. Second, it will define key terminology used throughout the book, such as 'biosecurity', 'bioterrorism' and 'bio-threats'. Given the diverse nature of the biosecurity and bioterrorism fields, differences exist among scholars and practitioners on the meaning of various terminology: including 'biosecurity' and 'bioterrorism'. Several researchers have tried to address these definitional difficulties (Koblentz 2010; Rappert and Gould 2009: 1–19; Lakoff and Collier 2008). The chapter will build on their work to provide definitions for biosecurity and other terminology. Third, it will provide an overview of the book's approach and an outline of the remaining eight chapters. But before addressing each of these objectives, it is important to provide a brief background of where this book fits into the broader biosecurity literature.

© The Author(s) 2018
P. F. Walsh, *Intelligence, Biosecurity and Bioterrorism,*
https://doi.org/10.1057/978-1-137-51700-5_1

Since 9/11, there has been a growing concern amongst decision-makers and the public about bio-terrorism as well as other biosecurity threats. A key priority for policy makers has been to prevent what many argue to be low probability, yet high impact bio-attack scenarios by terrorists—such as the use of a highly pathogenic weaponised substance like anthrax in a major urban centre (Koblentz 2009: 200–227; Rosenau 2001; Tenet 2007). The 2001 *Amerithrax* attacks on members of the US Congress postal system and some media outlets demonstrated that policy makers had cause for concern about such bio-threat scenarios (Walsh 2011). Though in this case, the mode of delivery (via the mail) was not the highly sophisticated 'WMD' platform some might have expected. Nevertheless, the attack demonstrated the critical role of technology and scientific experience in enabling bio-attacks regardless of their mode of delivery or their impact.

Both the first attack (only one week after 9/11), and the second (in October 2001), became a catalyst for recalibrating many policy maker and intelligence agency's understanding of the nature of bio-threats and their impacts. However, the investigation that followed *Amerithrax* showed that planning such attacks was complex and required a great deal of tacit and technical knowledge—beyond simply down loading a 'recipe' for making a bio-bomb from the internet (Walsh 2014; Vogel 2013).

The attack revealed how difficult it was for even a microbiologist, who worked with anthrax for twenty years to make a highly weaponisable form of the bacteria (Walsh 2014). From another perspective though, the *Amerithrax* case provided more insights to our assessments of threat actors and their capabilities to use biological substances—particularly in acts of terrorism. Yet from another, it became clearer that it was beyond the capability of most terrorists groups to down load 'recipes' from the internet for making and weaponising anthrax despite some trying in the past (Rosenau 2001; Tenet 2007; Walsh 2014).

Despite the technological and logistical difficulties of 'weaponising' a dangerous pathogen, the *Amerithrax* incident was seminal in improving our post 9/11 understanding of other important facets of biosecurity and bioterrorism that remain less clear. These include: the role of intelligence, investigation challenges, multi-agency collaboration (particularly between national security and public health agencies) and the role of technology in driving emerging bio-threats.

The history of biosecurity and bioterrorism goes back centuries (Crawford 2007; McNeil 1998). The modern history of bio-weapons (both state sponsored and terrorism) begins in the twentieth century with changes in the international security environment and advancements in both technology and microbiology. However, these changes in the bio-threat landscape during both world wars and the Cold War (Koblentz 2009, 2010; Geissler and van Courtland Moon 1999; Tucker 2000) have been well surveyed from an international security and bio-terrorism perspective.

The book acknowledges and reviews briefly the bio-threat landscape up to the Cold War (see Chapter 2), but its primary focus is on the analysis of the post 9/11 biosecurity environment. In particular, the book seeks to make a unique contribution to the biosecurity and bio-terrorism literature by focusing *exclusively* from an *intelligence perspective* on the four key objectives listed later in this chapter.

Since 9/11, an increasing amount of literature and several government reports have focused on aspects of the role of intelligence in managing biosecurity threats (e.g. Koblentz 2009; Vogel 2008; SSCI 2004; Butler 2004; Silberman and Robb 2005; NRC 2006). However, the literature has only provided a smaller focus on intelligence issues with the broader attention placed on other aspects of biosecurity and bioterrorism, such as: international security issues, bioterrorism, post 9/11 biosecurity policy-making or intelligence failure post WMD assessments in Iraq. The literature has not examined in detail the role of intelligence—either as *a system of processes* resulting in *products* that support decision making in the bio-threat context; or *as a set of organisational and community frameworks in which intelligence capabilities work* to provide strategic, operational and tactical decision-making support.

Drawing on recent theoretical perspectives from research into intelligence reform post 9/11 (Walsh 2011), this book will provide a deeper, macro understanding of both the opportunities and limitations of intelligence processes and capabilities that has been missing in the post 9/11 biosecurity, bio-terrorism literature. The focus will be broad—spanning across the bio-threat spectrum including bio-crime and bioterrorism issues.

The Audience

This book is primarily for intelligence analysts—regardless of their professional context (national security, law enforcement, military or private sector), who are currently or shortly will work on bio-threats and risks. The second audience is for the broader and diverse array of stakeholders, who also play a role in managing bio-threats and risks. These include: policy makers, public health authorities, first responders, intelligence agencies, investigators, researchers, security managers, compliance officers, and the private sector. All of these stakeholders also need to better understand what the intelligence enterprise can and cannot deliver to support biosecurity threat decision-making. Finally, the book will be of interest to undergraduate and postgraduate students enrolled in a range of cross disciplinary courses relating to biosecurity, bioterrorism and health security.

The book does not assume any prior knowledge about intelligence or biosecurity, hence its introductory and incremental approach will be useful to tertiary and other training courses for security officers, post-graduate intelligence and security programs, public health and other regulatory/compliance training programs relating to biosecurity and bio-terrorism.

The Book's Points of Difference

In addition to focusing exclusively on the role of intelligence in managing bio-threats and risks, a second unique feature of the volume is how it addresses the four central objectives (detailed below) by drawing on interviews from key stakeholders (policy, intelligence, security and researchers). The book includes insights from intelligence and security practitioners and researchers across the 'Five Eyes' countries (Australia, UK, US, Canada and New Zealand), who have had an active role in the biosecurity and bio-terrorism space.

Insights from academics, intelligence and security practitioners have been gathered by adopting a flexible qualitative approach using semi-structured interviews. In total 25 interviews were conducted across the 'Five Eyes' intelligence countries—the bulk completed in the US and Canada. This methodology is a similar one adopted during research for my first book, *Intelligence and Intelligence Analysis (2011)*, which involved interviewing 60 intelligence leaders, managers and analysts across the 'Five Eyes' intelligence communities. The insights and experiences of both producers and consumers of intelligence in the biosecurity and bioterrorism context is essential to include when trying to gauge the role of intelligence in a potentially rapidly evolving threat environment.

In summary, the key benefits of this book is its detailed focus on *intelligence processes and capabilities* and assessing their role in preventing, disrupting and containing contemporary and emerging bio-threats. A third benefit is that the book seeks to build a bridge between the intelligence and biological sciences 'worlds'. It does not pretend to be a treatise of technical and scientific knowledge on the biological sciences. The analysis presented is from an intelligence studies perspective only. Nonetheless it seeks to bring our clinical and scientist colleagues into debates of mutual concern relating to biosecurity and bio-terrorism.

Book Scope and Limitations

The small number of interviews obviously do not constitute either a generalizable sample or complete picture of the role of intelligence in managing bio-threats and risks across all 'Five Eyes' intelligence communities. Further, as most interviews were focused on US and Canadian participants, the analysis in subsequent chapters tends to focus more on developments in these countries rather than the remaining 'Five Eyes' partners (Australia, UK and New Zealand).

Further, doing research in the intelligence capability space always presents challenges given the sensitivities involved, and I was not able to reach out to all the intelligence agencies that might have had useful (unclassified) insights to share. Other limitations include a decision made early not to include the role of the military in each 'Five Eyes' country in managing bio-threats and risk, which has been important historically in most of these countries.

I wanted to make the focus on national security and law enforcement intelligence as it relates to understanding bio-threats and risks. Though, I am aware leaving out the military perspective does narrow down further the conclusions that can be made about the role of intelligence in managing bio-threats and risks across the 'Five Eyes' countries.

Why Intelligence?

Before going on to define key terminology and the objectives of the book, it is first necessary to address an even more fundamental question—why intelligence? Why devote an entire volume to *intelligence* in the broader context of biosecurity and bio-terrorism? The answer is that good intelligence frameworks, processes and products can disrupt threats including reducing uncertainty around emerging ones. The function of intelligence is to provide effective decision-making support so that a policy maker can act to prevent, disrupt or mitigate against threats in the security environment.

Good intelligence provides an important vehicle for understanding current and emerging threats and estimating the risks posed by them. However, intelligence as we shall see later does have its limits generally and particularly in the biosecurity and bio-terrorism contexts. For example, unlike nuclear and chemical weapons that contain technology that is more easily detected, it can be difficult to prevent or disrupt threat actors importing biological equipment to make a 'bio-bomb'—given the dual-use nature of biological substances and biotechnology. The dual use of many biological agents, technology, equipment and knowledge complicates both the reliability and validity of intelligence collected and analysed that may be relevant to a decision-maker.

Additionally, the speed in the uptake of synthetic biology and biotechnology particularly since 9/11—like other technologically enabled threats areas such as cyber—means our slow moving and frequently over-bureaucratic intelligence agencies struggle to know what may be the most important critical threats in time to allow a decision-maker to do something about them.

Some of the problems of understanding and interpreting potentially complex technologically enabled bio-threats as we shall see in subsequent chapters relate to more fundamental organisational capability issues in our intelligence communities. What is important to note at this point is that intelligence does have a role in managing bio-threats, but as we shall see later the extent of that role will vary in different threat contexts. The challenge is how can the role of intelligence be best utilised in these contexts and what role do other stakeholders including the scientific community play in identifying and mitigating against bio-threats? All of these issues will be tackled in the following chapters.

Defining Terminology

The biosecurity and bio-terrorism fields are rich in definitional complexity. Several researchers have discussed the difficulties in defining for example 'biosecurity' in ways that are inclusive and has sufficient meaning for the diverse number of disciplines working in it. There are other key terminology, which will be used frequently in this book such as: *intelligence, bio-terrorism, bio-crime, bio-threat* and *bio-risk*. All of these terms are defined here so that the reader knows how I intend to use them in the remaining chapters. In defining them, it would be tempting to provide an expanded discussion and critique of the increasing volume of definitional literature.

This would be interesting, but it is not the central focus of the book so what follows is a brief synopsis of some of the documented challenges in defining terms like *biosecurity* and *intelligence*—before a short description of how each term will be used is provided. Readers interested in exploring further discourses about how key terminology has been defined can also refer to other authors cited here.

Intelligence

Eminent intelligence scholar and former assistant director of central intelligence for analysis and production Mark Lowenthal spends the entire first chapter of his classic text on intelligence (*Intelligence from Secrets to Policy*) dissecting what intelligence is about. In this chapter,

Lowenthal refers to the 'pursuit of secret information' (Lowenthal 2012: 6). That is certainly a characteristic of intelligence. He also talks about the many different kinds of intelligence: military, political, economic, social, environmental, health and cultural (ibid.). There is also of course the different dimensions of intelligence: foreign, domestic and homeland security, and as we shall see in this book such arbitrary classifiers do not accurately depict the nature of many post 9/11 threats, which have both foreign and domestic characteristics. Lowenthal also makes an important point, which has direct bearing on the nature of complex biosecurity threats and risks. He says: 'intelligence is not truth. If something were known to be true, states would not need intelligence agencies to collect the information or analyse it. Truth he says is such an absolute term that it sets a standard that intelligence rarely would be able to achieve. It is better and more accurate to think of intelligence as proximate reality' (2012: 6–7).

While those working in our intelligence communities would like to strive for 'the truth' Lowenthal's quote is a sobering reminder for them and the policy-makers relying on intelligence, that in most cases such degrees of certainty and accuracy are not reachable. But we can still make our goal more reliable intelligence that can assist policy-makers even in fast moving and complex threat areas like biosecurity. Finally, Lowenthal like other intelligence studies authors also suggest that intelligence can be thought as a *process* (how we acquire and assess information), *a product* (the written and oral analyses) and as *organisation* (the units that carry out its various functions) (2012: 9). Again these three ways of thinking about intelligence are useful and are discussed more fully as they relate to managing bio-threats and risks in subsequent chapters.

Another leading figure of intelligence scholarship—Loch Johnson also discusses Lowenthal's description of intelligence including his three dimensions of intelligence, but for him the focus is squarely on the role of intelligence used by senior officials in supporting national security interests, particularly those related to foreign and defense policies (Johnson and Wirtz 2015: 2). It is true that historically intelligence has played a critical role in the foreign and defence policies of nations, but as we have seen since the end of the Cold War and particularly after

9/11, our understanding of what is a 'national security interest' has broadened out from the traditional state based security issues of war and peace between nations. The growth of transnational security issues and even intra-state security issues such as health, food and water security, has expanded our vision and understanding of what matters may be of national security interest to policy makers.

The broadening out of the national security agenda has resulted in an expansion in all three dimensions of intelligence described by Lowenthal: *processes, products and organisations.* This means in areas such as biosecurity and bio-terrorism, where a diverse cadre of stake-holders are required to manage resulting threats and risks, one cannot think of the kind of intelligence support provided in the traditional military, national security and law enforcement contexts. As we shall see throughout this book, biosecurity and bio-terrorism threats need to be understood by utilising all manner of 'kinds of intelligence', including health and epidemiological intelligence, forensic intelligence, socio-technical intelligence amongst others. The widening post 9/11 national security agenda beyond the exclusive focus on preparing for the potential military conflict between states therefore requires a broader understanding of what intelligence is in this new security environment.

In my 2011 book *Intelligence and Intelligence Analysis*, I define intelligence by attempting to determine what is unique about it compared to other activities such as research, data analysis, information collation and report writing. I argue that while the security environment has changed from the Cold War, Post-Cold War to the now Post 9/11 environment, there are still some fundamental characteristics which define *what intelligence is* regardless of whether one talks about it in a national security, law enforcement or private sector context. In this book, I will adopt these three broad characteristics to define intelligence as together they fit well in describing the emerging nature of the field of 'biosecurity intelligence', which is a mixture of influences from the national security, law enforcement, scientific and private sector worlds. In summary then, I define intelligence as a product and process that must contain three characteristics: *security environment, secrecy* and *surveillance* (Walsh 2011: 31).

By *security environment*, I am referring to the sum total of threats and risks that the intelligence enterprise must strive to understand on behalf of a decision-maker. I define *secrecy* as the second most important defining characteristic of intelligence because the intelligence function would not be able to collect sensitive, privileged information if the source of that information knew that such efforts were being made. Our ability to provide early warning to decision makers of emerging threats and risks would be significantly reduced if all the collection efforts were known by threat actors. Secrecy is of course a relative term. What is 'secret' in an agency like the US national sigint agency—the National Security Agency (NSA) is different in terms of the quality and consequences if that information became public to say information from an agency like the US Internal Revenue Service. But nonetheless in both cases, sensitive information not known to the general public is collected for the purposes of intelligence work. The third defining characteristic of intelligence is *surveillance*, which includes a number of related and inter-dependent activities that we will be discussing in detail in later chapters, including: tasking and coordination, covert collection, analysis and decision-making support. Surveillance whether its physical, technical or electronic is at the core of all intelligence collection and analysis if we are to provide useful, action-focused information to the decision-maker (Walsh 2011: 33–34).

Biosecurity

Debates continue about what constitutes biosecurity and these stretch across the academic, policy and scientific communities (Baker 2009; Koblentz 2010; Ryan and Glarum 2008; Walsh 2011, 2015; Rappert and Gould 2009: 1–19; Lakoff and Collier 2008). These are not mere dry academic debates, but are important to how we frame what is considered a bio-threat and risk and whether a biological agent represents a security and/or a public health issue. As I have discussed elsewhere, 'the intentional or unintentional release of a dangerous pathogen like anthrax may involve health and law enforcement officials, though the mixture of resources required from security/law enforcement or public health is likely to be different if the threat is not a criminally intentional act' (Walsh 2014: 838). The key to defining biosecurity depends to some extent on the extent to which biological agents become 'securitised' and by whom.

Koblentz summarizes the difficulties associated with defining biosecurity, which he argues has 'specific meanings within different disciplines'. He sees four competing definitions of the word (2010: 104). These are: first, threats to animal, plant health and bio-diversity, which he argues at worst may only have an indirect effect on human health (Koblentz 2010: 105). The second definition, he argues, arose in the 1990s 'in response to the threat of biological terrorism' (ibid.). The third relates to monitoring dual use biological research, which is research that has a legitimate scientific purpose (for example vaccine research), but may be misused and therefore present a bio-threat to public health and national security.

The fourth definition listed by Koblentz was developed by the US National Academies of Science and is an amalgamation of the other three. The National Academies of Science defines biosecurity as 'security against the inadvertent, inappropriate, or intentional malicious or malevolent use of potentially dangerous biological agents or biotechnology, including the development, production, stockpiling, or use of biological weapons as well as outbreaks of newly emergent and epidemic disease' (2006: 32).

The National Academies' definition reflects in part the human security agenda that emerged in the mid-1990s, which argued for a broadening of what constitutes 'national security' beyond just the prevention or prosecution of wars *between* states, to also the security of individuals *within* and *between* states (Walsh 2011: 10). Adherents of the human security agenda view 'national security', as including the security of people within states from political violence (terrorism, civil war, state collapse), economic vulnerabilities and even disease and natural disasters (HSC 2005).

What the health security theoretical agenda suggest, is that merely defining biosecurity in a narrow security focused way does not accurately show how bio-threat and risk issues regardless of their 'security dimensions' are also inextricably linked to the broader global health/ health security literature. Perhaps biosecurity can be seen then as the link between those that focus on *criminal exploitation of health* and those that focus on other aspects of the public health security discipline, such as but not limited to pandemic security. Nonetheless, the activities, policy and research we associate with both are by necessity linked.

Bernard refers to a 'tribalism' between the public health and security sectors, which has prevented both understanding each other and perceiving common priorities (Bernard 2013: 157). While there may be some 'tribalism' between public health and security sectors, a greater connectivity and understanding of what each 'tribe' has to offer the other is occurring. By the 1990s and onwards, global infectious diseases such as HIV/AIDS, SARs, Avian Flu and the most recent Ebola outbreak in Western Africa have 'acquired a greater security salience in world politics' (Elbe 2010: 163). In addition, other perspectives—not from the traditional international relations and strategic studies worlds, such as medical sociology also remind those working in the intelligence, national security and law enforcements worlds that while health may have become securitised so too has security to some extent become 'medicalised'. As Elbe rightly points out, 'the task of securing populations cannot rely solely on the traditional institutions of security such as the police, intelligence services and armed forces' (2011: 856). This is one important point we will return to in later chapters.

What is clear from the health security literature is our concept of security is in a flux and continues to mean different things to different discipline audiences (Elbe 2010: 163). Arguably, 'global (public) health security', 'national security', 'human security' and 'biosecurity', while contested terms in themselves may all be components of a broader 'super discipline' of health security. While defining 'biosecurity' remains problematic the health security literature shows that it is inextricably linked to the broader global health literature as much as it connects with the 'traditional' national security and law enforcement contexts. Perhaps biosecurity can be seen then as the link between those that focus on *criminal exploitation of health* and those that focus on other aspects of the public health security discipline, such as but not limited to pandemic security.

One point is clear though, the 'biosecurity label' is really a classifier for what is a broad church of related disciplines: botanists, microbiologists, virologists, vets, physicians, laboratory bio-safety officers and national security analysts/investigators. This cross-disciplinary focus is both a strength and weakness to understanding biosecurity threats. It is a weakness in that multiple players in the biosecurity field can result in a more fragmented understanding and operational response to various biosecurity threats. But it is also a strength in that if intelligence systems are optimal a multi-disciplinary approach allows a combination of expertise to assess and manage the bio-threat or risk.

This is because bio-threats—whether they are intentional or unintentional in origin—can cross multiple dimensions (plant, animal and human health), which in turn requires both a multi-disciplinary interpretation of the 'threat' and treatment of any ensuing risks. This examination of the multiple dimensions of biosecurity across the health spectrum (plant, animal and human health) has been described in policy circles as the 'one health approach' (Walsh 2011: 62).

In summary, there are no optimal definitions of biosecurity agreeable to all disciplines working in this field. For the purposes of this book, I will be using the word biosecurity when referring to threats that include those that are *intentional* (from 'weaponising' dangerous biological material—bacteria, viruses and toxins), the deliberate misuse of dual-use bio-technologies, and other threats that are unintentional from a diverse range of pathogens that threaten the food supply and the environment (Walsh 2011: 47).

While I recognize, that naturally occurring or emerging infectious diseases are a critical part of the bio-threat and health security spectrum, this book will focus exclusively on those bio-threats resulting from the intentional or unintentional (such as bio-safety violations) *use by individuals or groups* of biological agents.

Bioterrorism

In reality there remains a 'lack of professional consensus' on the differences between bio-crimes and bio-terrorism and evolving perceptions of both threat types remain (Inglis et al. 2011: 18). However, there does seem to be some differences between both threat types. Burnette's definition while recognising the use of biological weapons for the commission of crimes is clear to the point. He defines bioterrorism as:

'the threat of use of biological agents as weapons to cause fear, terror, economic and political disruption, and unrest among the populace to achieve political, ideological, social, and /or religious goals is the hallmark of biological terrorism or bioterrorism' (Burnette 2013: 11).

Bio-crime

Other biosecurity issues that have shaped the post 9/11 threat environment have included a litany of 'bio-crimes'. Bio-crimes are a diverse bundle of issues, which have in common the use of biological agents as weapons by non-state actors for extortion, murder or profit rather than politically motivated reasons seen in bio-terrorism (Carus 2001: 6–10). The bio-criminal threat landscape has evolved since the 2001 study by Carus.

There is now growing evidence of more highly organized bio-crimes with multiple victims. One area where complex organized bio-crimes are emerging is in global food supply. Increasing competitive commercial pressures, global environmental degradation and less reliable access to supply chains may tempt less scrupulous food companies or primary producers to 'cut corners' on quality and circumvent public health regulations to sustain profit margins. A number of recent incidents related to food production standards illustrate this sector's vulnerability to criminal exploitation (see for example, Yam 2013; Neville 2013; Trevett 2013).

Similarly, in countries with large primary industry sectors such as Australia and New Zealand, the organized, criminal manipulation of regulations concerning export/import markets, or the criminal introduction of a controlled plant or animal species represent serious biosecurity threats to these economies. We will come back to a number of bio-crimes in Chapter 2.

Bio-risk

The concept of risk and risk management principles remain contested across many disciplines in which intelligence intersects with in the biosecurity and bioterrorism context. For example, in the security field, risk, risk management, risk assessment and risk analysis are used frequently, but without common definitions (Garcia 2006: 510). In this chapter, we will not enter into these debates as they are not germane to the book's objectives.

For the purposes of later discussion in the book we will define risk as: the product of both the likelihood of something happening and the consequences or harmed caused if that threat or event occurred. In particular, we can expand on this general definition of risk by adopting Burnette's definition. Using the *WHO Biorisk Management: Laboratory Biosecurity Guidelines* 2006 Burnette defines bio-risk as the 'probability or chance that a particular adverse event (e.g., accidental infection or unauthorised access, loss, theft, misuse, diversion, or intentional release), possibly leading to harm will occur' (Burnette 2013: 5).

What we shall see in subsequent chapters is that the intelligence enterprise does have a critical role in assessing bio-risk for policy makers and other stakeholders; and an important discussion point in this book is to determine with more precision what role intelligence can play in managing various bio-risks. In particular, using the four steps of security risk management listed by Fisher and Green (1998) (cited in Garcia 2006: 511) as the complexity of the biosecurity threat and risk environment increases, it is important to determine how intelligence can play a role in:

* Identification of risks or specific vulnerabilities.
* Analysis and study of risks, including the likelihood and degree of danger of an event.
* Optimisation of risk management alternatives (avoidance, reduction, spreading, transfer, acceptance, any combination of all).
* Ongoing study of security programs.

Bio-threat

In this book when discussing bio-threats, we are referring to human agents that have either the intent and capability (or both) to use wilfully biological agents for criminal or terrorist objectives. Bio-threats also include human agents, who unintentionally release biological agents into the environment that would in all likelihood cause deaths in a locality, nationally and internationally. The most common example of these unintentional bio-threat actors are individuals working in secure biological facilities that do not follow biosafety protocols correctly, cause accidents and others who unknowingly breach quarantine regulations that result in a public health incident.

The Structure of the Book

In summary, this book will build on our historical understanding of biosecurity and bio-terrorism threats by examining their significance against contemporary and emerging bio-threats. The book will use the 2001 *Amerithrax* attack as a 'stake in the ground' to explore the development of both biosecurity and bio-terrorism in the current and emerging post-post 9/11 period. It investigates what has changed in the threat environment since *Amerithrax*; and what specific role should intelligence play in the prevention, detection, disruption and containment of contemporary and emerging bio-threats? As discussed earlier, what has been missing in the literature, particularly since 9/11 is a comprehensive analysis of the role of intelligence (including both its limitations and applications) to contemporary and emerging bio-threat actors and issues. The book makes a unique contribution to the biosecurity and bioterrorism literature by focusing exclusively from an intelligence perspective on the following four key objectives.

The Book's Four Objectives

1. To provide an assessment of the contemporary (post 2001) and emerging biosecurity and bioterrorism threat environment.
2. Evaluate the role of intelligence in supporting tactical, operational and strategic decision-making in contemporary and emerging bio-threats.
3. Explore the effectiveness of intelligence processes and capabilities for decision-making support on bio-threats.
4. Understand how intelligence can assist in both the management of unfolding and emerging bio-threats.

In order to investigate the objectives, the book is structured into nine chapters. This chapter places the work in the broader biosecurity research agenda, outlines the role of intelligence, defines terminology and lists the four objectives to be addressed. Chapter 2 provides a detailed survey of the contemporary and emerging biosecurity threat environment. It is divided into three sub-sections: *past, present and future*. In each sub-section, threats will be analysed by assessing, to the extent possible, intent/capability and which key drivers (for example, technology, political instability, psycho-social, extremist ideology, research, compliance) enable particular threats.

Chapter 2 provides the necessary scene setting of current and emerging bio-threats and risks before subsequent Chapters 3–5 explore how the intelligence enterprise can play a role in managing them. Together Chapters 3–5 provide a detailed analysis of the *core intelligence processes* (*tasking and coordination, collection, analysis and production*) in providing decision-making support. Each chapter examines how these processes have changed since 9/11, and where the challenges and opportunities reside for biosecurity intelligence practice. Chapter 3 focuses on the most important aspect of all core intelligence processes: who and how is biosecurity intelligence tasked and coordinated? It will explain how effective tasking and coordination processes go hand in hand and is critical to how a decision-maker is able to task their own or other intelligence capabilities.

Chapter 4 surveys intelligence collection activities relevant to the production of biosecurity intelligence across the 'Five Eyes' intelligence countries. The focus will be on intelligence agencies included in the national security and national law enforcement communities. Chapter 5 will outline the many challenges for intelligence analysts working on (particularly emerging) biosecurity threats. These challenges include accessing and retaining in-house analytical skills in biological sciences or public health, organisational cultural issues, and the extent to which various analytical techniques such as structured analytical techniques are helpful in assessing emerging bio-threats (Walsh 2014).

Chapter 6 shifts the focus away from the 'factory floor' or the way intelligence is produced in the bio-threat and risk context to an investigation of the broader, leadership and organisational issues, which facilitate or inhibit effective intelligence support to decision-makers in this threat and risk context. The chapter includes analysis of how some of the structural or key enabling activities within 'Five Eyes' intelligence communities might be addressed to improve intelligence support.

Chapter 7 explores how important stakeholders—both from within the national security and law enforcement communities and those external to it (scientists, clinicians and the private sector) contribute significantly to the understanding of bio-threats and risks. The chapter argues that in many threat and risk contexts, the technical knowledge available within the broader scientific community is indispensable for the prevention, disruption, and treatment of them.

Chapter 8 shifts the focus to other stakeholders that have influence over biosecurity intelligence practice, including the various intelligence oversight and accountability mechanisms operating across the 'Five Eyes' intelligence communities. Given recent changes to some oversight and accountability mechanisms post the 2013 Edward Snowden revelations, this chapter will explore these and the extent to which they impact on improving biosecurity intelligence. Similarly, how dual use research of concern has raised debates over the legitimate pursuit of science and national security concerns will also be explored in terms of how it impacts on intelligence practice and the effective oversight and accountability of it.

Chapter 9 will provide a summary of major themes raised in all sections of the book. It will also evaluate whether the book's four objectives have been addressed.

References

Baker, K. (2009). The Meaning and Practice of Biosecurity. *International Journal of Risk Assessment and Management, 12*(2–4), 121–146.

Bernard, K. (2013). Health and National Security: A Contemporary Collision of Cultures. *Biosecurity and Bioterrorism: Biodefense Strategy, Practice, and Science, 11*(2), 157–162.

Burnette, R. (Ed.). (2013). *Biosecurity Understanding, Assessing, and Preventing the Threat*. Hoboken, NJ: Wiley.

Butler, R. (2004). *Review of Intelligence on Weapons of Mass Destruction: Implementation of Its Conclusions*. London: HMSO.

Carus, S. (2001). *Bioterrorism and Biocrimes: The Illicit Use of Biological Agents Since 1900*. Washington, DC: National Defense University.

Crawford, D. (2007). *Deadly Companions*. Oxford: Oxford University Press.

Elbe, S. (2010). Pandemic Security. In J. Burgess (Ed.), *The Routledge Handbook of New Security Studies* (pp. 163–173). Abingdon: Routledge.

Elbe, S. (2011). Pandemics on the Radar Screen: Health Security, Infectious Disease and the Medicalisation of Insecurity. *Political Studies, 59*, 848–866.

Garcia, M. (2006). Risk Management. In M. Gill (Ed.), *The Handbook of Security* (pp. 509–531). Basingstoke: Palgrave Macmillan.

Geissler, E., & Moon, van Courtland J. (Eds.). (1999). *Biological and Toxin Weapons: Research, Development and Use from the Middle Ages to 1945*. New York: Oxford University Press.

HSC. (2005). The Human Security Centre: Human Security Report. Oxford.

Inglis, T., et al. (2011). Forensic Investigation of Biological Weapons Use. In J. Gall & J. Payne-James (Eds.), *Current Practices in Forensic Medicine* (pp. 17–42). Chichester, UK: Wiley.

Johnson, L., & Wirtz, J. (Eds.). (2015). *Intelligence: The Secret World of Spies*. New York: Oxford University Press.

Koblentz, G. (2009). *Living Weapons*. New York: Cornell University Press.

Koblentz, G. (2010). Biosecurity Reconsidered. *International Security, 34*(4), 96–132.

Lakoff, A., & Collier, S. (Eds.). (2008). *Biosecurity Interventions*. New York: Colombia University Press.

Lowenthal, M. (2012). *Intelligence from Secrets to Policy*. Thousand Oaks, CA: CQ Press.

McNeil, W. (1998). *Plagues and Peoples*. New York: Anchor Books.

NAS. (2006). *Globalization, Biosecurity and the Future of the Life Sciences*. Committee on Advances in Technology and the Prevention of their Application to Next Generation Biodefense Threats. National Research Council. Washington, DC: National Academies Press.

Neville, S. (2013, May 28). Horsemeat Lasagne Scandal Leaves Findus Reputation in Tatters. *The Guardian*. From https://www.theguardian.com/business/2013/feb/08/horsemeat-lasagne-scandal-findus-reputation. Accessed March 15, 2017.

NRC. (2006). *Globalization, Biosecurity and the Future of the Life Sciences*. Washington, DC: Institute of Medicine and National Research Council.

Rappert, B., & Gould, C. (2009). (Eds.). *Biosecurity. Origins, Transformations and Practices*. Basingstoke: Palgrave Macmillan.

Rosenau, W. (2001). Aum Shinrikyo's Biological Weapons Program: Why Did it Fail? *Studies in Conflict and Terrorism, 24,* 283–301.

Ryan, J., & Glarum, J. (2008). *Biosecurity and Bioterrorism*. Burlington, MA: Elsevier.

Silberman, L., & Robb, C. (2005). *Commission on the Intelligence Capabilities of the US Regarding Weapons of Mass Destruction. Report to the President of the United States* (pp. 1–501). Washington, DC.

SSCI. (2004). *Report on the US Intelligence Community's Pre War Intelligence Assessments on Iraq*. Washington, DC: US Senate.

Tenet, G. (2007). *At the Center of the Storm: My Years at the CIA*. New York: Harper Collins.

Trevett, C. (2013, May 28). Fonterra Chief Gets 'Frank and Thorough Grilling'. *New Zealand Herald*.

Tucker, J. (Ed.). (2000). *Toxic Terror: Assessing Terrorist Use of Chemical and Biological Weapons*. Cambridge: Harvard University Press.

Vogel, K. (2008). Biodefense. In A. Lakoff & S. Collier (Eds.), *Biosecurity Interventions* (pp. 227–255). New York: Columbia University.

Vogel, K. (2013). *Phantom Menace or Looming Danger?* Baltimore, MD: The Johns Hopkins University Press.

Walsh, P. F. (2011). *Intelligence and Intelligence Analysis*. Abingdon, UK: Routledge.

Walsh, P. F. (2014). Managing Intelligence and Responding to Emerging Threats: The Case of Biosecurity. In M. Gill (Ed.), *The Handbook of Security* (pp. 837–854). Basingstoke: Palgrave Macmillan.

Walsh, P. F. (2015). Building Better Intelligence Frameworks Through Effective Governance. *International Journal of Intelligence and Counterintelligence, 28*(1), 123–142. https://doi.org/10.1080/08850607.20 14.924816.

Yam, A. (2013, May 28). Memories Still Too Raw for Chinese Parents to Trust Baby Formula. *South China Morning Post*. From http://www.scmp.com/news/china/article/1273375/memories-still-too-raw-chinese-parents-trust-baby-formula. Accessed March 15.

2

The Biosecurity Threat Environment

Before we can really understand the role of intelligence in understanding and managing bio-threats, it is critical first to step back and assess the biosecurity environment. As discussed in Chapter 1, an important defining feature of intelligence—indeed a core function of any intelligence capability (both the human and processes) is how effectively does it 'tap into' the relevant security environment. The security environment can be defined as the sum total of threats and risks that any intelligence capability must understand as fully as possible if it is to reduce uncertainty and provide warning to decision-makers. Depending on the context, the security environment can be made up of a multitudinous and diverse number of threats and risks. For example, if you are a local police officer, your priority is to understand a security environment that most likely is made up of high volume crime issues, domestic violence and small scale drug offences. In contrast, if you are a WMD analyst in the CIA you will clearly not be interested in understanding local community threats and risks. Instead you will be looking at broader and deeper issues related to WMD proliferation, including: countries of concern, treaty compliance and evidence that terrorists groups may have the intent and capability to use WMD.

© The Author(s) 2018
P. F. Walsh, *Intelligence, Biosecurity and Bioterrorism*,
https://doi.org/10.1057/978-1-137-51700-5_2

The purpose of this chapter therefore, is to map both the contemporary and emerging dimensions of the biosecurity environment. By doing so the chapter will address the first key objective of the book: *to provide an assessment of the contemporary (post 2001) and emerging biosecurity and bioterrorism threat environment.* With this achieved, it will provide us with a critical foundation in which to address the book's remaining objectives which seek to evaluate the role of intelligence in supporting decision-making in contemporary and emerging bio-threats, explore the effectiveness of intelligence processes and capabilities and understanding how intelligence can assist in both the management of unfolding and emerging bio-threats.

This chapter will survey the biosecurity threat environment in the following three sub-sections: *past, present and future.* As discussed in Chapter 1, the book's focus is assessing bio-threats from the present (defined as from 2001) to the future. The rationale for this approach is explained shortly, but in order to provide context for a detailed discussion of current and future threats, we will commence our discussion profiling very briefly bio-threats from 1945 to 2001. The brevity of this discussion is not to suggest that the period (1945–2001) was not important to shaping our understanding of bio-threats—indeed they have been crucial, rather it is because this period has been extensively covered already in the literature.

The smaller attention on this period (1945–2001) also does not imply all the complexity of past events and threats have been completely revealed or understood. There remains much to learn about past events that can inform current practice. The intention here though is to provide maximum space to surveying current and emerging threats—given understanding these remains a bigger and more immediate challenge for intelligence and policy-makers.

Defining 'The Biosecurity Threat Environment'

Before I move on to surveying the biosecurity threat environment, an important theoretical issue needs addressing. It is important because as we shall see in discussion below, there are a number of perspectives used in scholarly work on biosecurity, intelligence and national security issues when describing and understanding what is labelled 'a threat'. In this book, I do not take a prescriptive approach to one theoretical perspective over another. Like many other areas in social science disciplines, different perspectives used together often provide a more global understanding of complex socially constructed issues such as what constitutes a 'bio-threat'? So it is important briefly here to reflect on two theoretical perspectives, which I argue are relevant to how scholars, intelligence analysts, and policy makers determine what constitutes a 'bio-threat'.

The two perspectives I will discuss here are realism and constructivism as they seem to have relevance to how intelligence agencies, governments and scholars have thought about how bio-threats are produced, constructed, their implications and management. Naturally, one could argue that there are far more theoretical perspectives relevant to how bio-threats have been constructed such as: liberalists perspectives, critical security studies, and social constructivism, but this is not a book on international relations theory and we will restrict discussions to realism and constructivism.

Classical realists perspectives tend to emphasise that in the absence of any global government it is anarchy, which shapes international relations between states. In a chaotic world—one with few binding laws, states seek security from others. This creates competition for power, which in turn determines the structure of the international system. State survival is therefore inherently a contest between states not internal threats (see Morgenthau 1967; Mearsheimer 2001; Waltz 1979). This approach was later 'softened' somewhat with the emergence of another generation of IR scholars (neo-realists), who while agreeing with their traditional realist colleagues that the international system defines how states behave, also saw domestic factors relevant to how states respond to each other (Burchill et al. 1996: 87–90).

Realist perspectives are useful to some extent in explaining some of the strategic decision-making used to generate state based bio-warfare programs particularly between Cold War opponents the Soviet Union and USA. Though realism is not solely adequate to understand a range of national security policy making on managing evolving bio-threats after the Cold War ended. As noted later in this chapter, the biosecurity threat environment after the Cold War shifted away from an almost exclusive array of potential state based threats to an increasing number of non-state actor ones. This transition requires additional theoretical IR perspectives to make sense of the evolving threats and ensure that national security policy can also adapt to manage this new array of threats. Constructivist perspectives therefore are another useful approach in describing the post-Cold War bio-threat landscape because non-state actors such as bio-terrorists and their impact on the international system is not at its core a competition between states, but rather driven by group social construction and identity for influencing world politics (Wendt 1999).

In summary, many IR theories may be helpful in understanding past, current and emerging bio-threats including both realist and constructivist arguments. Throughout the book other IR theories (e.g. human security) are also used to expand the reader's perspectives on how to understand past and emerging bio-threats. As a result, I do not take a prescriptive view of one theory over another and only suggest the ones discussed here are one of many tools to help us better understand the bio-threat environment and what the intelligence and policy response might be. I will not spend any more time on a detailed analysis of IR theory as this is not germane to the book's objectives outlined in Chapter 1. What is important in applying any theoretical and analytical perspectives is that they need to help intelligence analysts more deeply deconstruct the nature of bio-threats in order to better understand how they may develop. In particular, as we shall see in Chapter 5, effective intelligence analysis (especially at strategic level) requires analysts to weigh both the probability and impact of various drivers for a bio-threat. In other words, an analyst needs to understand the significance of various factors (drivers) that might enable a bio-threat. Depending on the nature of the bio-threat, they need to assess the role of multiple drivers: technology, political instability, psycho-social issues, radicalisation, legislative and policy influences. Theoretical perspectives from IR, security studies and criminology to name only a few can help analysts identify drivers.

Past Biosecurity Threat Environment (1945–2001)

With biosecurity defined, this section will provide a brief historical overview of the threat landscape in the post-World War II and Cold War (1945–1991) period. An analysis of how bio-threats evolved during this period helps explain how the current policy focus arose post 9/11. As I have discussed elsewhere (Walsh 2014: 837–856), starting a survey of bio-threats at 1945 may seem a bit arbitrary given historians and scientists remind us that diseases whether naturally occurring or used as 'weapons' have for centuries had a major impact on the political and cultural history of humans (McNeil 1998; Crawford 2007). The year 1945, however, parallels the development of modern microbiology and the ability by states to use technology to 'industrialize' various biological agents as weapons. Although Germany and Japan during World War I had biological weapons production capabilities, the delivery of such weapons were rudimentary. At the end of World War II, however, developments in industrial microbiology and advances in the aerolisation of biological agents made weaponising them a more accurate and lethal option for states that choose to develop them (Geissler and van Courtland Moon 1999; Walsh 2014; Spiers 2010).

State based biological weapons programmes, particularly those developed by Cold War protagonists—the former USSR and USA from 1945 until 1970s (for the USA), and up to the 1990s for the Soviet Union, dominated policy maker's understanding and framing of the bio-threat environment. Other US allies such as the UK and Canada also had invested heavily in offensive biological weapons programmes (Spiers 2010; Balmer 2001; Regis 1999; Carus 2017). For example, the UK developed its own capability in the 1930s, but abandoned it as a retaliatory option in 1957 (Spiers 2010: 56; Balmer 2001). These were large, industrial programmes that produced vast quantities of dangerous pathogens, such as highly virulent anthrax, plague and tularemia.[1] Prior to President Nixon terminating the US offensive bioweapons program, the US Army had weaponised two lethal agents (*Bacillus anthracis* and *Francisella tularensis*) and three incapacitating biological agents, *Brucella*

suis, Coxiella burnetti, and Venezuelen equine encephalitis virus (VEE).
Supplies of these agents had been mass produced and were stockpiled
at the Army's Directorate of Biological Operations at Pine Bluff Arsenal,
Arkansas (Regis 1999: 210). According to Regis, the production plant
had an overall capacity of 86,000 gallons (ibid.: 211). The Pine Bluff
facility fermenter was smaller than an older Vigo plant in Indiana,
which had a capacity of 240,000 gallons, but nevertheless could produce a substantial amount of agent (Regis 1999: 211). The Soviet
Union built large bioweapons plants in Sverdlovsk (1946), Kirov (1953)
and others such as the one in Stepnogorsk (in Kazakhstan), which was
under the control of the ministry of defence and Biopreparat Group (a
civilian pharmaceutical agency). At the time, US intelligence knew little about the extent of these programmes and it wasn't until the defec-
tion of Ken Alibek (chief scientist and deputy director of Biopreporat)
and biologist Vladamir Pasechnik to Britain in 1989 that the US and
other NATO allies knew the full extent of the Soviet programme
(Spiers 2010: 62). For example, according to Ken Alibek's account of
his time as the chief scientist of the Soviet biological weapons, just one
of its six biological weapons production facilities at Stepnogorsk (in
Kazakhstan) contained ten 20,000 litre fermenters capable of producing
1000 tonnes of anthrax per year (Alibek 1999: 229–301). By the late
1960s at the time that US President Nixon announced a termination
of an offensive American bioweapons programme, the US military had
developed 'a biological arsenal that included numerous bacterial pathogens, toxins and fungal plant pathogens that could be directed against
crops to induce crop failure and famine' (Christopher et al. 1997: 417).
The UK's and later US abandonment of an offensive biological warfare
programme, however, had been based on a calculus by policy makers
in London and Washington that the growing power of atomic weapons
offered a more reliable offensive option than a biological bomb (Balmer
2001: 157). There were a number of drivers influencing a shift away
from an offensive state based biological weapons programme in the US
and UK. Additionally, by 1960s 'the nature of the threat changed as a
complex mixture of technical, economic, political and legal considerations combined to provide for successive changes in outlook' (Balmer
2001: 184). There were variations within policy circles about the

immediacy of the threat from state based biological weapons programs (ibid.: 184) and biological weapons once firmly seen in the same way as chemical and nuclear weapons of mass destruction begun to be seen differently by policy makers. Biological weapons lost the status of offensive weapons of mass destruction and along with this the loss of resources. Concern however, was also raised from 1945, and during the Cold War, that other less stable or rogue states (Iraq, Iran, Syria and North Korea) were seeking to develop biological weapons (Koblentz 2009: 17–18; Spiers 2010: 102–125). Though in some cases, such as Syria information about biological weapons programs was sketchy and lacked specificity (Zanders 2015: 152).

The major exception was Iraq. Iraq in particular showed an early interest (as far back as 1974) in developing biological weapons for their strategic deterrent value. By 1990, the Hussein regime had tested and weaponised anthrax and botulinum toxin using 400 kilogram aerial bombs and Al Hussein warheads. Though thankfully these were not very efficient for disseminating biological weapons and the regime never produced dried, powder agents, which could have covered greater differences and potentially had more lethality (UNMOVIC 2007: 768–790). By the end of the first Gulf War in 1991, as UN weapon teams moved into Iraq, the Iraqi regime destroyed its bulk supply of biological agents and munitions (Walsh 2014).

During the mid-1990s, policy makers started to shift their focus from historical and traditional notions of bio-threats (state sponsored conventional biological weapons programs) to the use of biological agents by non-state actors—primarily terrorists (Koblentz 2009: 200–227). There are a number of policy and changes in the security environment, which underpinned this shift in attention of policy makers away from the traditional state based and military application of biological weapons dominating their attention up until the end of the Cold War. First was a concern that the fall of the Soviet Union and the immediate decline in Russia's economy in the 1990s would see a lot of unemployed bio-weapons scientists as 'guns for hire' by terrorists and other rogue states. Another event (discussed in more detail below) was the 1995 Aum Shinrikyo subway attack in Tokyo, the 1993 attack on the World Trade Center in New York and the 1996 terrorist attack in Oklahoma city all made clear to policy makers, Gronvall argues that the United States was vulnerable to terrorism and the implication that some groups might use biological weapons (Gronvall 2012: Chapter 1). At the same time too, by the late 1990s, increasing developments in biotechnology and the biomedical sciences such as the human genome project raised concerns by some policy makers that such technology in the wrong hands could result in catastrophic bio-attacks (NRC 2004). In particular, the Bush Administration made several announcements that rogue states and terrorists posses bioweapons and are willing to use them (Spiers 2010: 164). The Administration also expressed concerns publicly that advances in biotechnology and life sciences would result in the creation by adversaries of new novel bioweapons that would require 'new detection methods preventive measures and treatments' (Spiers 2010: 156). In April 2005, the Administration said: 'these trends increase the risk for surprise. Anticipating such threats through intelligence efforts is made more difficult by the dual use nature of biotechnologies and infrastructure and the likelihood that adversaries will use denial and deception to conceal their illicit activities' (Spiers 2010: 156). Even after the faulty intelligence on Iraq's possession of WMD which led to the US led invasion of Iraq in 2003 was revealed, other senior US legislators still underlined their assessments that the threat from biological weapons was growing and that genetic modification techniques would 'allow the creation of even worse biological weapons' (Silberman and Robb 2005: 34). Further discussion below and in Chapter 5, argues that the policy pronouncements on the dangers of non-state actors using or developing bio-weapons throughout the period 1999–2009 was not based on 'sophisticated threat assessments' and for many researchers in the field was 'systematically and deliberately being exaggerated' (Leitenberg 2005: 88).

Koblentz (2009) provides a useful summary explaining how 'bio-terrorism' became the policy priority during this period, which in turn redefined the bio-threat space. There is insufficient space to discuss all the events responsible for this shift in policy interest, but we will discuss three significant ones here as they help provide a contextual understanding as to why political leaders started to shift their focus on bio-threat actors away from states to groups and even individuals.

The first event occurred in 1995 when the Japanese doomsday cult Aum Shinrikyo released sarin nerve gas into the Tokyo subway system killing 12 people and injuring 5000 more (Rosenau 2001; Leitenberg 1999: 151–153). As Rosenau notes, 'this attack marked a turning point in the history of terrorism as it was the first time, non-state groups had used chemical weapons against civilians' (2001: 289). While the attack was serious enough, investigations later revealed that the cult had also acquired anthrax and botulinum toxin and was attempting to weaponise it against various Japanese government political, military and public institutions. The cult failed to cultivate sufficiently lethal strains of botulinum toxin and anthrax. Its plans were foiled by other technical challenges, including not being able to disseminate anthrax into the appropriate aerolised and sized spores required to produce mass casualties (Leitenberg 1999). As Rosenau points out, despite the cult having the motivation and resources to use biological agents as weapons, they still lacked the full complement of 'scientific and technological skills that would have helped ensure their success' (Rosenau 2001: 296).

The second event which elevated the importance of bio-terrorism for policy-makers was discoveries by US soldiers post the 2001 invasion of Afghanistan of technical documents and equipment in a biological weapons laboratory under construction near Kandahar. Additional documents were also found in a close by al Qaida training camp—detailing the terrorists groups plans to develop a biological weapons capability. Since 1998, Osama Bin Laden had made statements that the 'acquisition of WMD was a 'religious duty' (Pita and Gunaratna 2009: 10). In his memoirs, former Director of the CIA, George Tenet mentions two individuals (Rauf Ahmad and Yazid Sufaat), who were recruited by al Qaida's second in charge Ayman al-Zawahiri to develop this capability. The documents and searches of the laboratory showed that the al Qaida program was in its early stages and the group had not yet obtained a virulent strain of anthrax or mastered the technique to aerolise it (Tenet 2007: 278–279).

The capture, interrogation or death of most of the key al Qaida operatives associated with its fledgling bio-weapons program constrained further efforts by the group to continue down this pathway. Though throughout the rest of the decade, policy makers and intelligence agencies remained concerned that 'al Qaida central' may have shared what expertise it had developed with its other regional franchises through-out the world. For example, there is some evidence that through Al Qaida's many technical websites aimed at supporting the operational activities of jihadis around the world (e.g. the Mausu'at al-E'adad or the Preparation Encyclopedia) has shared some expertise about making biological weapons. Additionally, after the US led invasion of Iraq, coa-lition forces found a three volume manual outlining steps for conduct-ing chemical and biological experiments in an area previously occupied by Al Qaida affiliate Ansar al-Islam in northern Iraq. There are other reports that Ansar al-Islam were reportedly engaged in the production of ricin, but there is no evidence that it reached a stage of large scale weaponisation that could cause mass casualties (Salama and Hansell 2005: 622). There remains however, little consistently compelling evi-dence that other al Qaida affiliated groups have developed either the intention or capability to develop biological weapons (Salama and Hansell 2005: 618; Tucker 2012).

Concerns also remained over the possibility that al Qaida franchises or 'do it yourself jihadists' would start developing biological weapons from the increasingly available 'recipes' for making them posted on the internet by other jihadists. These recipes were generally crude and unlikely to result in mass-casualties (Koblentz 2009: 223–224; Tucker 2012). In summary, what this second issue demonstrated was although there was a strong desire by al Qaida to develop biological weapons—the capability, particularly the resources, knowledge and skill sets to do so were in short supply. I will return to the importance of *knowledge and skill sets* to understanding biological threats later when discussing emerging threats. Another important aspect of this issue is that there were differences of opinion within the US intelligence community and among biodefense experts on how significant the level of threat and capabilities al Qaida was in bioweapons development pre the 2001 war and post the invasion of Afghanistan (Silberman and Robb 2005; Leitenberg 2005). We will turn back to these variations in analytical assessments in Chapter 5.

In contrast to al Qaida's general lack of advanced knowledge and skills in pursuing biological weapons, the third bio-terror event involved the 2001 release of anthrax spores in the US mail system, and showed the lethality of biological agents when developed by individuals or groups, who do possess expertise to produce and weaponise dangerous pathogens. In September and October 2001, seven envelopes containing a dried powder form of anthrax spores were posted to several media outlets and to the US Senate offices of Senators Thomas Daschle and Patrick Leahy. The letters resulted in 22 cases of anthrax—five of which led to fatal inhalational anthrax. The anthrax letters also resulted in the contamination and closure of several major US postal offices.

In contrast to attempts made by Aum Shinrikyo and al Qaeda to use anthrax as biological weapons, the FBI investigation revealed that the anthrax used in this attack was a highly concentrated, aerolisable 'weapons grade' form of this bacteria. The subsequent seven year investigation was complex and protracted and resulted in the US Department of Justice determining that a single spore batch created by anthrax specialist Dr. Bruce E. Ivins at the US Army Medical Research Institute of Infectious Diseases (USAMRID) was the parent material for the letter spores. In July 2008, Ivins committed suicide before being indicted (Walsh 2011: 49).

Present Biosecurity Threat Environment (2001–Present)

The Ivins case was significant on a number of fronts. While it did not result in mass casualties (the mode of delivery via mail was not optimal for this), it did underline the tremendous skill required to produce biological agents in sufficient pure and aerolised quantities. Ivins had been an anthrax expert for over two decades yet the FBI case against him documents (despite his extensive knowledge and the optimal laboratory conditions), that he was confronted with challenges in producing the anthrax thought responsible for the attack (DOJ 2010). The anthrax incident was unsettling—coming only a week after the 9/11 attacks in New York. Though several facts of the Ivins case, in particular the challenges he faced in producing the anthrax helped re-calibrate some of the assessments being made in the intelligence community about how easy it would be for non-state actors, such as al Qaida to produce and disseminate biological agents as weapons. This may have been comforting to some policy makers, though it did raise another bio-threat scenario—namely that that the terrorists may not be an outsider, but rather an insider—even more concerning a scientist capable of developing a biological weapon.

The fact that the 'attacker' had been a scientist with access to highly controlled dangerous biological agents focused intelligence agencies on the threats and risks associated with *dual-use research and technology*. More time will be spent on the significance of dual use research in the context of emerging bio-threats later on, but briefly dual use research and technology means activities, knowledge and equipment, which is used for legitimate research (for example the development of vaccines), but could also be used inappropriately by those motivated by politics or crime. It is assessing the significance of dual-use research and technology, which came into sharp focus during the *Amerithrax* incident that has dominated discussions about bio-threats in the present period.

Other biosecurity issues that have shaped the post 9/11 threat environment have included a litany of 'bio-crimes'. Bio-crimes as we discussed in Chapter 1 are a diverse bundle of issues, which have in common the use of biological agents as weapons by non-state actors for extortion, murder or profit rather than politically motivated reasons seen in bioterrorism. A 2001 study by Seth Carus attempted to delineate between the motives of bio-terrorists and bio-criminals by surveying major cases of each back to 1900. He concluded that in contrast to bio-terrorism, bio-criminal attacks tend to be aimed at individuals or small groups using crude means of dissemination (for example food contamination, murder of spouses using ricin, or illegal injection of pathogens (HIV) to a victim) (Carus 2001: 6–10). Other authors include politically motivated assassinations such as the famous case of Bulgarian writer and journalist Georgi Markov, who was executed by the Bulgarian secret police in London after he was stabbed in the thigh by an umbrella which discharged a ricin soaked pellet into his leg (Burnette 2013: 35–36). Burnette also includes the *Amerithrax* incident as an example of a bio-crime whereas others see this as an act of bioterrorism (ibid.).

In reality however, there is still a 'lack of professional consensus' on the differences between these two threat classes and as noted earlier 'evolving perceptions of the threat' remain. Inglis and colleagues tend to lump a number of bio-threats across the bio-criminal and bio-terrorists space together. They refer to a 'cluster of malevolent criminal actors (bio-crime, bio-terrorism, deliberate biological release, biological-weapons of mass destruction, murder, homicide and grievous bodily harm with intent' (Inglis et al. 2011: 18).

The bio-criminal threat landscape however, has shifted since the 2011 study by Carus, which focused primarily on small individually motivated bio-attacks by criminals. While bio-criminals will continue to extort money or seek revenge on single victims using biological agents—global food quality, environmental pressures, and companies seeking to 'cut corners' present another layer of more complex bio-criminal threats in the future with potentially greater economic and public health impacts beyond individuals, to groups and nations. For example, an increasing number of recent incidents related to food production illustrate this sector's vulnerability to criminal exploitation. In China there have been several incidents of adulterated infant formula, including the 2008 case where a company used a sub-standard formula that included the industrial chemical melamine—resulting in six deaths and over 300,000 children with kidney disease (Yam 2013). In February, 2013, global food company—Findus—suffered major reputation damage after it was found that some of its ready to eat meat based products were 100% horse (Neville 2013). In August 2013, New Zealand dairy giant, Fonterra had to recall infant formula from Asian markets after it was discovered that some of its whey protein may have been contaminated with botulism (Trevett 2013). Similarly, in countries with large primary industry sectors such as Australia and New Zealand, the organized, criminal manipulation of regulations concerning export/import markets, or the criminal introduction of a controlled plant or animal species represent serious biosecurity threats to these economies.

Finally, a cluster of biosecurity issues, which arguably do not sit neatly under either the 'bio-terrorism' or 'bio-crime' classifiers have begun to capture the focus of policy makers post 9/11. Many of these, such as the

2003 SARS outbreak, the 2009 H1N1 influenza pandemic, the 2014 West African Ebola outbreak and 2015 expansion of the Zika virus into South America are more correctly viewed as public health emergencies, in that they were the result of natural causes and not the intentional or malevolent actions of threat actors.[2] Nevertheless, all these cases, had wider impacts beyond public health. They showed how the pathogen involved was zoonotic (i.e. had the ability to move from one species to another), and each impacted significantly on the global economy and wealth of nations. For example, SARS forced the closure of airports, reduced global travel and resulted increased sick days of many countries.[3] So in the broadest sense of what 'national security' means such pandemics, which can skip species, especially from animals to humans also have profound impacts on the economic security of nations.

As a result of some of these natural pandemics since 9/11, governments in Australia, Canada, New Zealand, the USA and UK also declared that a broader focus and inclusion of other non-bio-terror threats and risks was required. As suggested in Chapter 1, it was becoming clearer that in some cases, the biosecurity response to some of these problems was fragmented. Agricultural scientists, animal and human health specialists tended to only look at the risks posed by zoonotic diseases from their own perspective, but what was needed was a more joined up integrated approach to detecting and managing such pandemics that crossed species. In Australia, Canada and New Zealand, researchers and policy-makers started to refer to this needed policy response as a *one health approach* or *one health continuum* (Walsh 2011: 53–67).

It remains unclear however, the extent to which the rhetoric of a 'one health' response to pandemics has been implemented across agricultural, animal and human health government departments in these and other countries. This is an important discussion which will be developed further in subsequent chapters as it is directly relevant to how we can optimize the role of intelligence in the broader biosecurity context. But what is even less clear, is the extent to which health intelligence or epidemiology gathered about pandemics—which arise from cross species barriers—is fed into the national security intelligence communities of these countries to increase their understanding of naturally occurring pathogens that could be exploited by threat actors.

Emerging Biosecurity Threats (2018–2023)

Given the baseline survey of the post-9/11 bio-threats above, what types of threats and threat actors are likely to emerge over the next five to ten years? There is a great deal of uncertainty around what scientists and security specialist assess as emerging bio-threats. John Caves and Seth Carus' analysis of the future of weapons of mass destruction out to 2030 included a range of perspectives from other experts—many who came to the same conclusion that 'the pace of change is so great in life sciences that they cannot confidently predict where the technology would be in five years much less than in twenty years' (Caves and Carus 2014: 26). Caves and Carus conclude in their study that it is impossible to predict specific biological weapons capabilities available by 2030, but they do assess the growth in biological sciences means what will be possible will be much greater today, 'including in terms of discrimination and the ability to defeat existing defensive counter-measures' (ibid.). Interestingly Caves and Carus assess a number of existing capabilities that been around arguably for decades, which don't involve genetic manipulation or bio-engineering as being potentially exploited by terrorists: including using geo-tagged images from the internet to harvest pathogens from nature of virulent disease, selective culturing to identify strains that are especially virulent or more resistant to existing counter-measures using equipment such as bioreactors available over the internet. They also see the potential exploitation of commonly available agricultural sprayers that can enable high efficiency dissemination of liquid pathogen solutions without special adaptations (ibid.: 26–27). Caves and Carus also briefly discuss the development of new biological weapons, particularly production of viruses such as small pox that are not readily available in nature anymore through the exploitation of molecular modeling and engineering. They argue that the exploitation of this kind of technology will most likely occur in state programs though recognize that terrorists could also utilize it. Their assessment does not indicate which state and non-state actors are likely to exploit emerging bio-technology. It is not possible to provide a full account of all potential emerging bio-threats, so this section will provide a thematic list of major ones. In reality, emerging threats do not fit into neat sub-categories and 'threat areas' can overlap each other. For example, a stolen biological agent from a secure biosafety rated government laboratory may also be a synthetically produced agent with dual-use properties (i.e. it can be used for legitimate scientific reasons but also illegitimate or illegal purposes).

With this caveat in mind, I see the following two biosecurity threat thematic areas as presenting challenges to intelligence agencies, policy makers and first responders in the future. The first theme is *'stolen biological agents'*—and includes material that has been stolen from a supplier, a university, research lab, hospital or animal health facilities. The second theme is *'dual-use research and synthetic biology'*. We will return to a further detailed discussion of these threat thematic areas in subsequent chapters but here we will provide a brief overview of them.

Turning first to 'stolen biological agents', the events of 9/11 and the anthrax letter attack discussed earlier resulted in a number of changes to policy, legislation and codes of ethics aimed at enhancing the control and access to dangerous biological agents and toxins in the USA. Similar policy initiatives have also been developed in other western nations such as Australia, Canada, UK, and the EU. We will come back to a more detailed discussion of policy initiatives in Chapter 8 and their influence on how intelligence supports and is influenced by policy in the biosecurity context. However, a brief discussion of some landmark policy initiatives is important here in order to understand what type of emerging bio-threats may be likely over the next five to ten years. While Chapter 8 will provide a more fulsome discussion of policy and legislative initiatives across other 'Five Eyes' countries, I will restrict the discussion here to key policy changes in the USA. This is because the USA has tended to lead other nations in developing biosecurity oversight policies—partly as a result of 9/11 and the anthrax letter attack.

Both of these events resulted in new policy and legislative provisions, which increased the oversight, control and access to dangerous biological materials. In particular, the enactment of the USA Patriot Act 2001 and the Public Health Security and Bio Terrorism Preparedness and Response Act 2002 required the registration of persons allowed to work with such agents (see in particular, Sections 201 and 351A, of the Act).

Further initiatives such as Biological Surety (US Army 2008), the National Academies Committee on Research Standards and Practices to Prevent the Destructive Application of Biotechnology chaired by Gerald Fink[4] in 2004 also played a role in identifying internal risks posed by those working in secure laboratories (NRC 2004). These initiatives collectively provided guidance on how to improve internal oversight: including background checks on scientists as well, as other safety protocols that appropriately risk managed the access, production and transfer of dangerous pathogens. So it is important to understand how policy, legislative and accountability mechanisms have evolved and whether they decrease or increase vulnerabilities for threat actors to exploit within the biosciences enterprise.

Stolen Biological Agents

Leaving aside the investigation into microbiologist Bruce Ivins and the anthrax postal incident of 2001 discussed earlier, the 'insider threat' to date of a scientist stealing or conspiring to steal a controlled biological agent appears to be both really rare and extremely difficult to detect. Though there have been some cases. For example, a Japanese researcher stole data and material from his host lab (the Mayo Clinic) in 1999 (Cass 1999). Burnette (2013) and Salerno (2015) document others. The increased policy and biosafety regulatory environments that provide guidance on the design, construction and operations of BSL-3 and BSL-4 labs makes it more difficult now than in 2001—both for unintentional accidents in the workplace and the theft of pathogens. BSL-3 and BSL-4 labs are the two most secure bio-safety lab designations. In both cases, strict guidelines prescribe the physical layout, safety equipment and training of scientific staff, who work in them. In BSL-3 and BSL-4 rated labs, scientists work on pathogens that can cause serious or potentially lethal disease. Generally, the most lethal agents, where there is either no vaccine or an unknown risk of transmission are worked on in BSL-4 labs. Debates continue however, within the bureaucracies of western countries about whether biosafety standards for BSL-3 and BSL-4 labs are sufficient (see, for example, GAO 2013). In Chapter 7

(Intelligence and Stakeholders) we will return to a more detailed discussion of biosafety standards and 'the insider threat', but suffice it to say several accidents across 2014 and 2015 in the handling and transportation of dangerous pathogens by the CDC (H5N1 and anthrax) and the US Army (anthrax) involving high containment labs suggest that there is room for improvement in biosafety standards (Schnirring 2014; Burns 2015; Salerno 2015: 191–204). Despite all the new bio-safety measures that have been put in place since 9/11, it remains difficult to predict and detect if someone has the intent and capability to steal a biological agent from a secure lab site for profit, political motivation or due to a mental health issue.

Background checks on scientists may assist in flagging staff, who present security risks *prior* to their appointment—though this process cannot screen out completely individuals whose ethics and intentions change later in their careers in ways that present security challenges. The motivation for individuals to use criminally biological agents from secure labs will likely be different in individual cases. From a bio-criminal perspective, where profit reward is the motive, the intent to commit the theft also depends on the nature of the agent potentially available to the criminal conspirators and how quickly the act can be turned into a 'profit'. In most western countries such as Australia, Canada, New Zealand, UK and the US, stealing a controlled biological agent such as anthrax from a BSL-3 or BSL-4 private or government lab, while not impossible, presents a number of security challenges in terms of physical security barriers and exposure risks for a criminal gang interested in such an enterprise.

There theoretically *may* be some criminals interested in trading controlled biological agents like anthrax, tularemia, or the plague. Though as the 2001 Ivins case revealed, the genetic sequence analysis of the Ames strain of anthrax used in that attack, makes possible the tracing of some of these substances back to their source—enabling investigators to identify which laboratories they came from and ultimately who was working with them. This then becomes a high risk venture for the individual or any organized crime group involved. Even if crime groups have access to scientists or laboratories they may calculate that traditional sources of revenue such as drugs, fraud and money laundering might be in comparison less riskier ways to make money. However, it is possible that for some criminal groups or a scientist working for a biotechnology company, intellectual property theft of new scientific breakthroughs may be more attractive financially, and logistically easier to commit then the theft of a controlled biological substance from a high containment lab. We know there is a long history of economic espionage particularly in the biotechnology sector. For example, there have been theft of trade secrets involving delivery of technologies for small interfering RNA molecules, potential treatment for Alzheimer disease and new immune suppressive drugs and the role of the 'insider' has been key to many of these. Theft of research data has also been common (Elliott 2007: 293; Cass 1999). Another dimension of theft of intellectual property from a research institution or biotechnology company is of course is the theft of data remotely as a type of cybercrime. While making threats to 'use' stolen biological agents as weapons may create the psychological terror sought after by terrorists, exacting harm on an innocent target can still be more efficiently and cheaply achieved using simple homemade devices—such as the kitchen pressure cookers used by the Tsarnaev brothers in the 2013 Boston bombings. Yet we cannot assume there will be no future interest and capability by non-state actors to steal dangerous biological substances or associated data from 'secure' biological facilities. Actual or potential vulnerabilities and attempts by threat actors to steal biological material and information will obviously need careful monitoring for their national security significance. Intelligence agencies need to keep an open mind yet one informed by evidence of whether future cases of theft from facilities might indicate a shift in our understanding of the threat trajectory by non-state actor individuals or groups. We saw during the rise of Islamic State (IS) how IS broke many of the rules that even AQ didn't step over.

While the physical IS Caliphate has largely been dissolved, the endemic instability in Syria and even in Iraq may create opportunities for other non-state actors to procure biological weapons from facilities where biosafety barriers are vulnerable either physically or virtually. We know that up until 2013 the Syrian government had the largest stockpile of chemical weapons in the Middle East and used chemical weapons (Sarin nerve agent) against its own civilians during the civil war though the government in Damascus (Zanders 2015: 150–157). Syria has also still not ratified the 1972 Biological and Toxin Weapons Convention (BTWC), though there is no evidence that the regime has 'set up a full biological weapons program beyond some elementary research' (Zanders 2015: 152). While the ongoing conflict in Syria makes it a hostile location for a non-state actor to pursue the development of biological weapons there, the illicit transfer of scientific knowledge or materials could theoretically be on sale if the price is right.

In summary, the control of laboratories in developing countries *may* be more vulnerable to criminal exploitation if physical security is not optimal or scientists do not perceive that they are adequately remunerated for the research they do (Friedman 2015: 176–180). Vulnerable areas such as the Middle East have few regional institutions that can engage states on biological threats. Friedman provides the example of the Middle East Consortium on Infectious Disease Surveillance (MECIDS) composed of public health experts and ministry of health officials from Israel, Jordon and the Palestinian Authority has made some progress particularly during the 2009 H1N1 pandemic facilitating joint action. However, more efforts need to be made to build capability in the region to counter biological threats from any source—including identifying early signs of threats to physical security in biological facilities and greater cooperation between health and security officials within the region (Freidman 2015: 179).

In addition to difficulties assessing motivation, it is also impossible to measure the consequence of a theft of a Category A pathogen from a BSL-4 lab. Part of this difficulty goes back to motivation. Is the objective of the theft to merely pose a threat to a community or extort funds from a government without the intention to actually use the substance? Or is the intention that the pathogen is weaponised and disseminated at ports, truck stops or airports? Leaving aside issues such as atmospheric temperature, sunlight and choice of dissemination vehicle, there are also other variables at play, which impact on the overall pathogenicity and 'contagion dynamics' of dangerous pathogens into a locality. While there is an active research agenda into epidemiological modeling and surveillance it remains difficult to predict 'the likelihood of a global pandemic, and to mitigate its consequences' (Bombardt 2000; Stattner et al. 2011; Nicolaides et al. 2012: 1; Goncalves et al. 2013; Bravata et al. 2004; May et al. 2009; Lucero et al. 2011). There are also remain a number of challenges at global, regional and local health levels on the storage, real-time sharing and coordination of epidemiologic and laboratory data that can be used for the surveillance of emerging pandemics. Challenges include sufficiently trained personnel to review data, bureaucratic distrusts between different authorities from different sectors and jurisdictions and inadequate laboratory and research capacity to fund pandemic preparedness and surveillance mechanisms. These challenges exist to greater and lesser degrees in developed and developing countries (Edge and Hoffman 2015: 157, 179) and will be discussed further in Chapter 7.

Dual Use Research and Synthetic Biology

Though the theft of well-known and controlled pathogens such as anthrax from a BSL-4 laboratory seems less likely (at least in the 'Five Eyes' countries), debates continue about how dual use research and synthetic biology might create a number of potential emerging threats, risks and vulnerabilities. Such threats may arise from two sources. First there are concerns that highly skilled and trained individuals could use their knowledge to create biological agents under the guise of legitimate research for illegitimate ends. The second source of concern is interested 'outsiders' exploiting legitimate advances in conventional biological research, synthetic biological sciences and bio-technology for illegitimate purposes. Both pathways to potentially new bio-threats underline concerns about dual use technology. Each pathway also defines the key dimensions of 'dual use research', but in reality there are many ways this term has been defined in science, policy and security circles (for example, see, McLeish and Nightingale 2007: 1636; Shea 2006, summary; Tucker 2012; Williams-Jones et al. 2014: 4). While the concept of dual use technology has been around in the arms control and military literature for decades, its application in the biosecurity context is comparably recent. Regardless of what definition of 'dual use research' one adopts, its application in the biosecurity context has largely focused on the research of dangerous biological agents that might be weaponised, and the publication of that research, which theoretically could be disseminated to bio-criminals or terrorists for their own nefarious objectives.

In recent years, the published results of dual use research have captured the concern of the biosecurity policy community and the media—perhaps even more than the experiments the articles describe. Starting in the early 2000s, McLeish and Nightingale argue that the publication of three papers: 'one on the synthesis of polio virus cDNA without a natural template by Cello et al. (2002), the second on how the variola virus (small pox) can invade the immune system by Rosengard et al. (2002), and a third on overcoming resistance to mousepox by Jackson et al. (2001), were widely interpreted as publishing blueprints for terrorists and led to public calls for changes to research and publication procedures' (McLeish and Nightingale 2007: 1636).

Other publications, have followed such as the article detailing the reconstruction of an influenza virus with all the identified gene sequences of the 1918 influenza virus (Tumpey et al. 2005: 77–80), and a 2005 research article describing the potential impact of contaminating the milk supply with botulinum toxin (Wein and Liu 2005). Additionally, two separate articles one in 2012, and the other a letter in August 2013, also raised security concerns about dual use research, and whether the published outcomes of these could be used for illegitimate reasons such as bio-terrorism. The 2012 article showed how scientists were able to identify the genetic changes needed for the avian influenza H5N1 to be efficiently transmitted between ferrets—a surrogate for human to human transmission.

The US National Science Advisory Board for Biosecurity (NSABB) had to determine whether the benefits of such research outweighed the risk of the accidental or intentional release of a lethal new virus. In November 2011, the NSABB recommended that the two articles arising from this research be redacted. The Board also called for the papers data and methods to be shared only with approved scientists and clinicians. This was, as Maher comments, an odd position for US Government to be in as the NSABB was potentially censoring research that the government had funded (Maher 2012: 431).

The NSABB's initial decision was later over-turned with the Board recommending (though not unanimously) that both papers be published in March 2012. The H5N1 research article publication ordeal shows the ongoing challenges in both identifying and oversighting dual use research. The questions of what experiments may be too risky to do and publish and how governments effectively manage this risk remains unclear. In August 2013, twenty-two researchers from labs around the world—some associated with the H5N1 research discussed earlier—submitted a letter to the journals *Nature* and *Science* detailing a proposed set of experiments that would represent a 'gain of function' on the avian influenza virus H7N9. In contrast to the 2012 incident, the scientists, who would be involved in this research are using these letters to gain early support from government scientific oversight bodies by explaining their risk mitigation plans for the research, and clearly explaining the experiments they wish to complete. Their objective is to make more virulent strains of H7N9 that would spread more easily between people so that they can understand how the virus mutates in nature causing pandemics. The experiments would also increase their understanding about how to develop better early warning surveillance of dangerous strains and better vaccines (Fouchier et al. 2013: 612–613).

All of the examples of 'sensitive' dual use research discussed above and others in Chapter 8 illustrate the potential threats and risks associated with synthetic biology and the manipulation of microbial genetics. The manipulation of naturally occurring viruses like H5N1 or horse pox so they can mutate more easily into hyper virulent variants that are more easily passed from animals to humans, or humans to humans—and the creation of dangerous pathogens using chemically synthesized genomes—show that this kind of knowledge can be put on the radar of interested bio-criminals and terrorists. The rapid advances in biotechnology, or what some describe as the 'industrialization of biology' (Center for Biosecurity of UPMC 2011), can result in faster, cheaper and more effective scientific breakthroughs for health, chemical manufacturing, bio-fuels and mining, but it also highlights a number of other newer threat scenarios for criminal or terrorist exploitation.

There are also concerns amongst biosecurity regulators and national security intelligence agencies that it is not just the *knowledge* that is on offer, but some of the *equipment* and *technology* (used chiefly in the past by scientists working on government funded research projects in BSL-3 and BSL-4 labs), that is becoming more available to the wider public. The increasing growth in biotechnology, the growing accessibility of automated biological techniques and relatively in-expensive equipment (such as that used in DNA sequencing and synthesis), makes scientific experimentation accessible in ways it wasn't even a decade ago to 'citizen scientists' or people interested in DIY ('do it yourself') Bio (Center for Biosecurity of UPMC 2011: 7; Caves and Carus 2014: 27). To illustrate this point, the entire human genome was sequenced in 2003. It took a team of scientists 13 years and nearly half a billion dollars to identify the approximately 20, 5000 genes in humans. In contrast today companies such as *Life Technologies* claim that they can decode a human genome sequence in a day for only $1000 using smaller equipment (such as a benchtop Ion Proton Sequencer) that can be ordered from them (Life Technologies 2012). Other DNA sequences from deadly pathogens can also be bought online. For example, in 2006 a journalist from the Guardian was able to purchase online a short sequence of the small pox DNA (Randerson 2006).

A US National Research Council report, *Globalization, Biosecurity and the Future of the Life Sciences* (NRC 2006), provides a detailed summary of both the global drivers and trajectories of advanced life science technologies that raise biosecurity concerns. There is insufficient room here to provide a comprehensive list of all potential threat and risk scenarios in the biotechnology field and interested readers should consult (NAS 2017; NRC 2006; Tucker 2012: 19–45) for a more detailed understanding of the threat environment. In summary though, the list of potential biotechnological threat scenarios may be endless due to the overlapping skills and technologies involved with synthetic biology. The evolving nature of some biotechnology also prevents a full threat and risk assessment of the security issues that may arise out of such technology.

Additionally, part of the difficulty in trying to assess the boundaries of biotechnological threat scenarios is that in many cases insufficient discussion and analysis has taken place between scientists and their national security counterparts as to the rationale for assessing an issue as a threat or risk. This is a theme we will return to in Chapters 4, 5 and 7. To provide however, some context of what threats may be possible, Goodman and Hessel (2013) survey a number of scenarios, including what they refer to as: bad bio-technologists, biological spam, phishing for DNA, identity theft, piracy and spear phishing. I will restrict discussion here to three: bad bio technologists, identity theft, and piracy to illustrate how they assess this threat environment might evolve.

The number of biotech companies have expanded at a steady pace over the last decade. For example, US research and development company Battelle in its sixth biennial report on the biosciences industry estimated that in 2012, 1.62 million people were employed across 73,000 individual businesses working across the range of biosciences such as medical and research laboratories, agriculture, and pharmaceuticals (Battelle 2014: v). This does not include the publicly funded biosciences workforce. So Goodman and Hessel argue that based on statistics alone, the sheer increase in people working in biological engineering, there is likely to be a few 'lunatics' with intentions to cause harm. Their analysis is supported by other biosecurity experts, who see that experts with an intent to cause harm or 'bio Unabombers' as more concerning than amateurish bio-hackers in the suburbs (Center for Biosecurity of UPMC 2011: 16; Ellis 2014: 216). While the stockpiles of 'controlled substances such as anthrax may be relatively secure, the DNA code of many of them Goodman and Hessel argue, exists in public data bases, and advances in synthetic biology allows the building of synthetic organisms—thereby sidestepping current safeguards in place for protecting select agents stockpiled in secure sites'.

The second threat scenario Goodman and Hessel describe (identity theft) is a 'new take' on an old enabler of crime. They argue as countries increase their holdings of DNA in national databases for criminal identification, there will be more opportunities for these to be compromised—resulting in people's identities being stolen to enable identity related and other crimes). Additionally, Goodman and Hessel assess in the future a confluence of situations, whereby genetic identity theft could enable people to circumvent health and employment restrictions based on their genetic data. Genetic cloning or impersonation (leaving another person's DNA at a crime scene) could also frustrate intelligence operations or law enforcement investigations. For example, in 2009, scientists in Israel demonstrated that it was possible to fabricate DNA evidence in a crime scene by fabricating blood and saliva samples containing DNA from a person other than the donor of the blood and saliva (Frumkin et al. 2011: 95–103).

The third interesting threat scenario 'biological piracy' presents a number of security, ethical, policy and legal challenges which remain largely unaddressed. Goodman and Hessel suggest in the future a wide variety of biological and genetic materials will be pirated just like digital media has been. The field of synthetic biology, which is already working towards developing therapies and treatments for cancers and other diseases, provides opportunities for organized crime groups to provide pirated versions (Goodman and Hessel 2013). The recent development in genome editing technology such as Crispr, Finger Nuclease (Zinc) and Talen, which can now manipulate DNA in human germ cells and remove or correct genetic mutations that cause disease might also be manipulated to do the reverse i.e. make people more susceptible to disease or reduce the effect of vaccinations (Corbyn 2015).

Similar to the discussion above of historical and post-9/11 bio-threats, we also need to examine emerging threats by addressing both dimensions of threat assessment—*intention* and *capability*. This is, however, where the challenge begins. The industrialization of biology is happening at such a dynamic and rapid pace, it remains difficult to make reliable estimates of both the future intentions and capabilities of threat actors, who may be interested in exploiting biotechnologies for criminal or terrorist reasons. As one workshop of experts suggested, 'the angles of the attack are almost infinite and very difficult to anticipate' (Center for Biosecurity of UPMC 2012: 15).

Part of the challenge relates to the type of framework used by those in the national security communities and by biosecurity researchers to understand threat and risk. Some frameworks argue for a steady linear increase in biotechnology, and a greater access to skills and technology by bio-criminals and bio-terrorists as a result (Chyba 2006; Carlson 2003; Petro and Carus 2005). In contrast, others have adopted frameworks that estimate a less linear increase in biotechnology. They argue that mere access to technology and even 'know how' does not automatically create either the motivation or ability for bio-criminals or bio-terrorists to exploit biotechnology for harmful purposes. Adherents to this framework suggest that there is a lot more uncertainty in how biotechnologies may develop in the future, as other non-technological variables such as social, economic, and organizational factors will also influence the growth of technology and the extent to which it is exploited by individuals or groups for nefarious reasons (Vogel 2008).

Careful consideration of how the emerging biosecurity threat context will evolve also needs to include an assessment on whether it is likely that we will see more single actor or group threats, and the consequences for policy makers and first responders. For example, as biotechnological knowledge becomes increasingly commoditized and equipment less expensive, will there be an increase in the rhetoric of well-established international terrorists groups (such as one of the Al Qaeda inspired franchises: al Qaeda in the Arabian Peninsula (AQAP), or al Shabab), declaring an intent to use a virus or bacteria that they have synthesized or acquired via a third party? Alternatively, are we going to see intentions being expressed about the desire to use bio-synthetic agents by less established domestic terrorist groups, or even individuals each with different agendas (jihadists, ultra-nationalists, anarchists/bio-hackers or environmentally motivated individuals)?

As discussed previously, there are very few cases of bio-terror attacks—certainly not enough (thankfully) to make analytical generalizations about the specific motivations of various groups or individuals' desire to weaponise conventional biological agents. It is also doubtful the extent to which extrapolations from these cases will assist estimations about threat actor's intentions to use pathogens produced via for example, synthetic genomics. Some profiling of the intentions and operational decisions made by terrorists and criminals using other medium for attack, however, including cyber may provide guidance on how rhetoric becomes operationalised to use a particular weapon over another. An understanding of cyber facilitated intellectual property theft, for example, may provide insights into how bio-criminals or bio-terrorists may seek to access biotechnology in illegal ways. Perman et al.

(2013: 90–110). We continue this discussion of what other disciplines and fields can teach us about improving our analytical understanding of emerging bio-threats in Chapters 5 and 7. Nonetheless, we need to face the reality that 'getting into the heads' of threat actors, who are not yet on the radar of intelligence and law enforcement agencies remains extremely difficult.

It is difficult enough to assess the intentions of threat actors—some who themselves may not have thought about the attractiveness of bio-technology agents. It seems doubly difficult to assess whether bio-criminals and terrorists will have the capabilities to either access or produce harmful biological agents that have been synthesized in a lab. As difficult, indeed near impossible as it is to assess the future intentions of threat actors as we shall see in Chapters 4 and 5, intelligence analysts and the broader intelligence enterprise do need to make efforts to model intentions behavior for possible bio threats. For example, intentions of potential threat actors could be modeled partially to some extent 'from existing case studies in the biomedical and microbiological field in an effort to establish trends in behavior and tactics' Perman et al. (2013: 91–92). Perman discusses how a National Institute of Justice study that was commissioned to better understand the behavioral indicators in attacks on political leaders resulted in the development of the Exceptional Case Study within the US Secret Service. The Exceptional Case Study is a work in progress in continually refining understanding of adversaries and behavioral indicators that can predict threatening behaviors and risks of violence (ibid.: 92). Perman et al. argues that the results of the Exceptional Case Study are applicable to the life sciences as the same kind of behavioral indicators are in play.

In contrast though to the 'intent' side of the threat equation, some intelligence agencies with mandates to assess the threat and risk of bio-weapons have done a lot more work on estimating the capabilities required by an actor(s) in weaponising various biological agents—including those resulting from genetic engineering or biotechnology. Much of this of course, is classified, but the focus is on the level of expertise and equipment required to operationalise different biotechnological based threat scenarios. Part of this work also relates to developing better science, technology, particularly microbial foren-sic analytical skills to detect, and investigate potential bio-criminal and bioterrorism threats (e.g. Murch 2003; Bhattacharjee 2009; Budowle and Williamson 2009; Shea 2006; Inglis et al. 2011). This work seems to be a useful place to start. If agencies continue to have limited visibil-ity on an individuals' intentions (prior to an attack), then re-examining carefully variables related to capability (*knowledge and equipment*), may provide more accurate assessments about the likelihoods of various 'high tech bioterrorism threats' (Suk et al. 2011: 1). If intelligence agencies can develop a more *evidence based* approach to estimating bio-threat capabilities, then they will be in a better place to provide assessments to policy makers, public health, scientists and security managers responsi-ble for developing strategies that mitigate these threats. At the very least, they may be able to provide in some cases more granularity to the analy-sis of which suite of capabilities may be more vulnerable to exploitation by threat actors than others.

The difficulty however, with working on the capability side of the threat formula (knowledge and equipment) is to, as mentioned earlier, potentially either over or under emphasize both the level of expertise, and margins of difficulty in accessing the equipment required to carry out an attack. For example, some authors recognize the various tech-nical steps required to synthesize a dangerous pathogen, yet argue that these may be less difficult to overcome than it may appear for a 'do it yourself' biologist/terrorist (Burr 2012). However, as discussed previ-ously, knowledge is more than reading a book on synthetic genomics, an actor must also develop the skill base and practical tacit knowledge (trial and error in the scientific process) as well.

In summary, a fixation only on the technologies (and equipment) that various actors could exploit can result in a kind of technical deter-minism, which blinds intelligence analysis of potential threats—result-ing in either an under or over-statement of the threat. There are some in the scientific and biosecurity communities, who may be under-stat-ing the capabilities of future threat actors to use synthetic biology and biotechnology in a bio-attack. For example, during a recent over the horizon scanning project conducted by the US Center for Biosecurity of UPMC most of the scientists interviewed stated that there exists simple paths for skilled individuals to making bio-weapons that 'render more technically difficult approaches unattractive and therefore less likely to be pursued' (Center for Biosecurity of UPMC 2011: 16). Or as stated in the project teams' report, perhaps in blunter words: 'the bad guys aren't going to waste their time with sophisticated pie in the eye sky stuff' (ibid.). In most cases, assessing actual capabilities will remain challenging and an evidence based approach is needed to avoid 'over' or under-assessing knowledge, equipment and skills. We will come back to the importance of an evidence based approach for assessing emerging bio-threats in Chapter 5.

Conclusion

In this chapter we have surveyed the historical, contemporary and emerging bio-threat landscape to illustrate the complexity of threats and risks that exist. As this survey suggest, understanding the emerging threat environment in particular is very difficult given with many potential threat scenarios there are a number of drivers at play (technology, psycho-social factors, bio-safety and compliance issues and policy) and it remains difficult to determine the effect of these alone and together in enabling certain threat types over time. Does this difficulty mean that those working in the intelligence enterprise cannot provide any understanding on potential bio-threats for decision-makers? The answer has to be clearly no. There are many other different threat types, for example, cyber where it is difficult to interpret what might be the key emerging threats, but decision-makers still need support in understanding, preventing, disrupting or reducing such threats to the extent that they can be understood.

Intelligence agencies cannot simply say to decision makers 'sorry it's too hard' as this would not be a recipe for continued funding. So the question now to be explored in the next three chapters is given this uncertain and complex bio-threat environment, what role should intelligence play, how has the role of intelligence changed since 9/11 and what challenges and opportunities are there for biosecurity intelligence practice? Chapter 3 will begin to address these questions by exploring how intelligence might be tasked by decision-makers interested in understanding bio-threats and risks and what challenges and opportunities exist for improving each 'Five Eyes' country's response to complex and uncertain bio-threats and risks?

Notes

1. These agents are referred to as 'Category A' bio agents (denoted as such because they have the greatest capacity for harm if used in a bioterrorist attack). The reader should refer to either the World Health Organization (WHO) or the US Center for Disease Control (CDC) websites for good overviews of these agents and others on the Category A list such as small pox, viral hemorrhagic fevers and botulism.
2. SARS or severe acute respiratory syndrome is a corona virus originally sourced to China's Guangdong province. It causes severe life threatening pneumonia. It is highly contagious and the 2003 outbreak resulted in the deaths of 8000 people globally. HINI virus results in a highly contagious flu for humans. It is closely related to a number of animal influenza sources. Early outbreaks started in North America and by June 2009, the WHO declared it a pandemic after the virus spread globally-killing over 16,000 people.
3. Global investment company, Morgan Stanley, predicted in 2003 that the SARs virus would shave more than $15 billion off the output of Asian economies; while the WHO predicted that the global cost could be more than $30 billion. See Watts and Stewart (2003).
4. The National Academies committee produced a report in 2004 called, 'Biotechnology Research in an Age of Terrorism' (sometimes also referred to as the 'Fink Report). The Report contained seven recommendations to ensure responsible oversight for biotechnology research with potential bioterrorism applications. One of these was to create a National Science Advisory Board for Biodefense to provide advice, guidance, and leadership for a system of review and oversight of experiments of concern.

References

Alibek, K. (1999). *Biohazard: The Chilling True Story of the Largest Covert Biological Weapons Program in the World—Told from the Inside by the Man Who Ran It*. New York: Random House.

Balmer, B. (2001). *Britain and Biological Warfare. Expert Advice and Science Policy, 1930–65*. Basingstoke, UK: Palgrave Macmillan.

Battelle. (2014). *Battelle/Bio State Bioscience, Jobs, Investments and Innovation*. Columbus, OH: Battelle.

Bhattacharjee, Y. (2009). News of the Week. Paul Keim on His Life with the FBI During the Amerithrax Investigation. *American Association for the Advancement of Science, 323*, 1416.

Bombardt, J. (2000). *Contagious Disease Dynamics for Biological Warfare and Bioterrorism Casualty Assessments*. Alexandria, VA: US Department of Defense.

Bravata, D., et al. (2004). Systematic Review: Surveillance Systems for Early Detection of Bioterrorism Related Diseases. *Annals of Internal Medicine, 40*(11), 910–924.

Budowle, B., & Williamson, P. C. (2009). *Microbial Forensics Wiley Encyclopaedia of Forensic Science*. John Wiley & Sons, Ltd.

Burchill, S., et al. (Eds.). (1996). *Theories of International Relations*. Basingstoke, UK: Palgrave Macmillan.

Burnette, R. (Ed.). (2013). *Biosecurity Understanding, Assessing, and Preventing the Threat*. Hoboken, NJ: Wiley.

Burns, R. (2015). US Military Says It Mistakenly Shipped Live Anthrax Samples. From http://www.nbcnewyork.com/news/national-international/Pentagon-Shipped-Live-Anthrax-Samples–305221031.html.   Accessed March 13, 2017.

Burr, J. (2012). The Mad (and Not So Mad) Scientist Next Door: A Holistic Approach to Addressing Do-it-Yourself Biology. *Journal of Biosecurity, Biosafety and Biodefense Law, 3*(1), ISSN (Online) 2154–3186. https://doi.org/10.1515/2154-3186.1035.

Carlson, R. (2003). The Pace and Proliferation of Biological Technologies. *Biosecurity and Bioterrorism: Biodefense Strategy, Practice, and Science, 1*(3), 203–214. https://doi.org/10.1089/153871303769201851.

Carus, S. (2001). *Bioterrorism and Biocrimes: The Illicit Use of Biological Agents Since 1900*. Washington, DC: National Defense University.

Carus, S. (2017). Occasional Paper 12. A Short History of Biological Warfare: From Pre-history to the Twenty-First Century. *Center for the Study of Weapons of Mass Destruction*. Washington, DC: National Defense University.

Cass, S. (1999). Researcher Charged with Data Theft. *Nature Medicine, 5*, 474. https://doi.org/10.1038/8350.

Caves, J., & Carus, W. (2014). The Future of Weapons of Mass Destruction: Their Nature and Role in 2030 (Occasional Paper No 10, pp. 1–75). *Center for the Study of Weapons of Mass Destruction*. Washington, DC: National Defense University.

Center for Biosecurity of UPMC. (2011). Center for Biosecurity. US Government Judgments on the Threat of Biological Weapons: Official Assessments, 2004–2011 (pp. 1–26). Baltimore, MD: Center for Biosecurity of UPMC.

Center for Biosecurity of UPMC. (2012). *The Industrialization of Biology and its Impact on National Security*. Baltimore, MD: Center for Biosecurity of UPMC.

Christopher, G., et al. (1997). Biological Warfare: A Historical Perspective. *Journal of the American Medical Association, 278*(5), 412–417.

Chyba, C. (2006). Biotechnology and the Challenge to Arms Control. *Arms Control Today, 36*, 11–17.

Corbyn, Z. (2015, 10 May). *Crispr: Is It a Good Idea to Upgrade? The Observer*. Retrieved from http://newsrule.com/crispr-is-it-a-good-idea-to-upgrade-our-dna/.

Crawford, D. (2007). *Deadly Companions*. Oxford: Oxford University Press.

DOJ. (2010). *The United States Department of Justice. Amerithrax Investigative Summary*. Washington, DC.

Edge, J., & Hoffman, S. (2015). Strengthening National Health Systems Capacity to Respond to Future Global Pandemics. In S. Davies & J. Youde (Eds.), *The Politics of Surveillance and the Response to Disease Outbreaks* (pp. 157–179). Surrey, UK: Ashgate.

Elliott, S. (2007). The Threat from Within: Trade Secret Theft by Employees. *Nature Biotechnology, 25*(3), 293–295. https://doi.org/10.1038/nbt0307-293.

Ellis, P. D. (2014). Lone Wolf Terrorism and Weapons of Mass Destruction: An Examination of Capabilities and Countermeasures. *Terrorism and Political Violence, 26*(1), 211–225. https://doi.org/10.1080/09546553.2014.849935.

Fouchier, R., et al. (2013). Gain-of-Function Experiments on H7N9. *Science*. https://doi.org/10.1126/science.1243325.

Friedman, D. (2015). Towards WMDFZ in the Middle East: Biological Confidence Building Measures. In H. Muller & D. Muller (Eds.), *WMD Arms Control in the Middle East. Prospects, Obstacles and Options* (pp. 176–180). Farnham, UK: Ashgate.

Frumkin, D., Wasserstrom, A., Budowle, B., & Davidson, A. (2011). DNA Methylation-based Forensic Tissue Identification. *Forensic Science International: Genetics, 5*(5), 517–524. http://dx.doi.org/10.1016/j.fsigen.2010.12.001.

GAO. (2013). High Containment Laboratories: Assessment of the Nation's Need Is Missing. *Testimony Before The Subcommittee Emergency Preparedness, Response and Communications, Biosurveillance Observations on the Cancellation of Biowatch Gen-3 and Future Considerations for the Program,* 18 (2014).

Geissler, E., & van Courtland Moon, J. E. (Eds.). (1999). *Biological and Toxin Weapons: Research, Development and Use from the Middle Ages to 1945.* New York: Oxford University Press.

Goodman, M., & Hessel, A. (2013). The Bio-crime Prophecy: DNA Hacking the Biggest Opportunity since Cyber Attacks. *Wired.* From http://www.wired.co.uk/article/the-bio-crime-prophecy. Accessed March 14, 2017.

Gronvall, G. (2012). *Preparing for Bioterrorism.* Baltimore, MD: Center for Biosecurity of UPMC.

Inglis, T., et al. (2011). Forensic Investigation of Biological Weapons Use. In J. Gall & J. Payne-James (Eds.), *Current Practices in Forensic Medicine* (pp. 17–42). Chichester, UK: Wiley.

Koblentz, G. (2009). *Living Weapons.* New York: Cornell University Press.

Lucero, C., et al. (2011). Biosurveillance Applications. *BMC Medical Informatics, 11,* 1–12.

Leitenberg, M. (1999). Aum Shinrikyo's Efforts to Produce Biological Weapons: A Case Study in the Serial Propagation of Misinformation. *Terrorism and Political Violence, 11*(4), 149–158. https://doi.org/10.1080/09546559908427537.

Leitenberg, M. (2005). *Assessing the Biological Weapons and Bioterrorism Threat.* Carlisle, PA: Strategic Studies Institute of the US, Army War College.

Life Technologies. (2012, 10 January). *Life Technologies Introduces the Benchtop Ion ProtonTM Sequencer; Designed to Decode a Human Life Genome in One Day for $1,000.* Press release at http://www.lifetechnologies.com/content/lifetech/us/en/home/about-us/news-gallery/press-releases/2012/life-techologies-itroduces-the-bechtop-io-proto.html.

Maher, B. (2012). The Biosecurity Oversight. *Nature, 485*, 431–434.

May, L., et al. (2009). Beyond Traditional Surveillance: Applying Syndromic Surveillance to Developing Settings—Opportunities and Challenges. *BMC Public Health, 9*(1), 242. https://doi.org/10.1186/1471-2458-9-242.

McLeish, C., & Nightingale, P. (2007). Biosecurity, Bioterrorism and the Governance of Science: The Increasing Convergence of Science and Security Policy. *Research Policy, 36*(10), 1635–1654. https://doi.org/10.1016/j.respol.2007.10.003.

McNeil, W. (1998). *Plagues and Peoples*. New York: Anchor Books.

Mearsheimer, J. (2001). *The Tragedy of Great Global Power Politics*. New York: Norton.

Morgenthau, H. (1967). *Politics Among Nations* (4th ed.). New York: Knopf.

Murch, R. (2003). Microbial Forensics: Building a National Capacity to Investigate Bioterrorism. *Biosecurity and Bioterrorism: Biodefense Strategy, Practice, and Science, 1*(2), 1–5.

NAS. (2017). *A Proposed Framework for Identifying Potential Biodefense Vulnerabilities Posed by Synthetic Biology: Interim Report*. Washington, DC: National Academy of Sciences.

Neville, S. (2013, May 28). Horsemeat Lasagne Scandal Leaves Findus Reputation in Tatters. *The Guardian*. From https://www.theguardian.com/business/2013/feb/08/horsemeat-lasagne-scandal-findus-reputation. Accessed March 15, 2017.

Nicolaides, C., et al. (2012). A Metric of Influential Spreading During Contagion Dynamics Through the Air Transportation Network. *PLOS One, 7*(7), 1–10.

NRC. (2004). *Biotechnology Research in an Age of Terrorism*. Washington, DC: National Academies.

NRC. (2006). *Globalization, Biosecurity and the Future of the Life Sciences*. Washington, DC: Institute of Medicine and National Research Council.

Perman, B., et al. (2013). Basic Principles of Threat Assessment. In R. Burnette (Ed.), *Biosecurity: Understanding, Assessing, and Preventing the Threat* (pp. 89–90). Hoboken, NJ: Wiley.

Petro, J., & Carus, S. (2005). Biological Threat Characterisation Research: A Critical Component of National Biodefense, Biosecurity, and Bioterrorism. *Biodefense Strategy, Practice and Science, 3*, 295–308.

Pita, R., & Gunaratna, R. (2009). Revisiting Al-Qaeda's Anthrax Program. *CTC Sentinel, 2*(5), 10–13.

Randerson, J. (2006, May 28). Revealed: The Lax Laws that Could Allow the Assembly of Deadly Virus DNA. *The Guardian*. From https://www.theguardian.com/world/2006/jun/14/terrorism.topstories3. Accessed March 15, 2017.

Regis, E. (1999). *The Biology of Doom. The History of America's Secret Germ Warfare Project*. New York: Henry Holt and Company.

Rosenau, W. (2001). Aum Shinrikyo's Biological Weapons Program: Why Did It Fail? *Studies in Conflict and Terrorism, 24*, 283–301.

Salama, S., & Hansell, L. (2005). Does Intent Equal Capability? Al Qaeda and Weapons of Mass Destruction. *Nonproliferation Review, 12*(3), 615–653.

Salerno, R. (2015). Three Recent Case Studies: The Role of Biorisk Management. In R. Salerno, J. Gaudioso, (Eds.), *Laboratory Biorisk Management. Biosafety and Biosecurity* (pp. 191–202). Boca Raton, FL: CRC Press.

Schnirring, L. (2014, August 15). CDC Probe of H5N1 Cross Contamination Reveals Protocol Lapses, Reporting Delays. *CIDRAP*. From http://www.cidrap.umn.edu/news-perspective/2014/08/cdc-probe-h5n1-cross-contamination-reveals-protocol-lapses-reporting-delays. Accessed March 15, 2017.

Shea, D. (2006). The National Biodefense Analysis and Countermeasure Center: Issues for Congress *CRS Report* (Vol. RL32891). Washington, DC: Congressional Research Service, The Library of Congress.

Silberman, L., & Robb, C. (2005). *Commission on the Intelligence Capabilities of the US Regarding Weapons of Mass Destruction. Report to the President of the United States* (pp. 1–501). Washington, DC.

Spiers, E. (2010). *A History of Chemical and Biological Weapons*. London: Reaktion Books.

Stattner, E., et al. (2011). Diffusion in Dynamic Social Networks: Application in Epidemiology. In A. Hameurlain et al. (Eds.), *Database and Expert Systems Applications* (pp. 559–573). Heidelberg: Springer-Verlag GMBH.

Suk, J., et al. (2011). Dual Use Research and Technological Diffusion. Reconsidering the Bioterrorism Threat Spectrum. *PLOS Pathogens, 7*(1), 1–3.

Tenet, G. (2007). *At the Center of the Storm: My Years at the CIA*. New York: HarperCollins.

Trevett, C. (2013, May 28). Fonterra Chief Gets 'Frank and Thorough Grilling'. *New Zealand Herald*.

Tucker, J. (Ed.). (2012). *Innovation, Dual Use and Security*. Cambridge, MA: The MIT Press.

Tumpey, T. M., et al. (2005). Characterization of the Reconstructed 1918 Spanish Influenza Pandemic Virus. *Science, 310*(5745), 77–80. https://doi.org/10.1126/science.1119392.

UNMOVIC. (2007). Compendium of Iraq's Prescribed Weapons Programmes in the Chemical, Biological and Missile Areas (pp. 765–1030). New York, UN.

US Army. (2008). *Army Regulation 50–1. Biological Surety*. Washington, DC: US Department of Defense.

Vogel, K. (2008). Biodefense. In A. Lakoff (Eds.), *Biosecurity Interventions* (pp. 227–255). New York: Columbia University.

Walsh, P. F. (2011). *Intelligence and Intelligence Analysis.* Abingdon, UK: Routledge.

Walsh, P. F. (2014). Managing Intelligence and Responding to Emerging Threats: The Case of Biosecurity. In M. Gill (Ed.), *The Handbook of Security* (pp. 837–854). Basingstoke: Palgrave Macmillan.

Waltz, K. (1979). *Theory of International Politics.* New York: Random House.

Watts, J., & Stewart, H. (2003, April 22). Asia Unable to Mask SARS Cost. *The Guardian.*

Wein, L., & Liu, Y. (2005). Analyzing a Bioterror Attack on the Food Supply: The Case of Botulinum Toxin in Milk. *Proceedings of the National Academy of Sciences of the United States of America, 102*(28), 9984–9989. https://doi.org/10.1073/pnas.0408526102.

Wendt, A. (1999). *Social Theory of International Politics.* Cambridge: Cambridge University Press.

Williams-Jones, B., Olivier, C., & Smith, E. (2014). Governing 'Dual-Use' Research in Canada: A Policy Review. *Science and Public Policy, 41*(1), 76–93. https://doi.org/10.1093/scipol/sct038.

Yam, A. (2013, May 28). Memories Still Too Raw for Chinese Parents to Trust Baby Formula. *South China Morning Post.* From http://www.scmp.com/news/china/article/1273375/memories-still-too-raw-chinese-parents-trust-baby-formula. Accessed March 15.

Zanders, J. (2015). Biological and Chemical Weapons and the Prospective Disarmament Process in the Middle East. In H. Muller (Eds.), *WMD Arms Control in the Middle East* (pp. 149–157). Surrey, UK: Ashgate.

3

Intelligence Tasking and Coordination

Biosecurity and Intelligence

In this chapter, we move our attention away from an assessment of the biosecurity environment to a detailed analysis of the core intelligence processes (tasking and coordination, collection, and analysis). In other words, Chapters 3–5 examine what role intelligence should play in responding to the emerging threats discussed in Chapter 2. In the biosecurity context, as in any other, intelligence is a 'service industry' whose sole aim ought to be to interpret the threat and risk environment for a decision-maker in order that they can either disrupt threats or put in place mitigation strategies. Put another way, national security intelligence and law enforcement agencies play a role both in reducing uncertainty around the biosecurity environment, and the impact of threats and risks associated with it. The degree to which intelligence can interpret emerging bio-threats will depend on the issue, and the extent to which intelligence agencies are able to provide 'value added' information in a timely manner for decision-makers. On this point, history shows that intelligence agencies have had a mixed record in assessing bio-threats accurately

© The Author(s) 2018
P. F. Walsh, *Intelligence, Biosecurity and Bioterrorism*,
https://doi.org/10.1057/978-1-137-51700-5_3

during the Cold War, and perhaps most spectacularly on the extent to which Iraq still had a bio-weapons program in 2003 prior to the second Gulf War (Koblentz 2009: 141–199; Vogel 2013).

The dynamic, evolving and dual use nature of emerging bio-threats, present multiple collection and analytical challenges for intelligence agencies. While it may be possible to track some steps along a planned attack, for example, irregular financial transactions, or detecting a series of suspicious supply orders for equipment—it may be even more diffi-cult (despite advances in microbial forensics) to link this to an individ-ual or groups. The choice of biological weapon may also be an agent that agencies have never 'red teamed' previously with fewer predicate operational steps. It may not be the 'classical anthrax attack' that has defined much of the Cold War and early post-Cold War period threat perception. The bio-attack could be as simple as the planned, system-atic food poisoning of multiple trans-Atlantic flights over a one week period. If the terrorist group or individual has never been under surveil-lance; collection and analytical efforts may only lead to their 'footprints' in the best case just prior or worse after the attack.

Such a complex threat and risk environment provides multiple chal-lenges for decision-makers in how they task intelligence agencies and communities effectively. The rapid advances in the biological sciences and biotechnology as discussed in Chapter 2 suggest that particularly at the strategic end, but also at the tactical and operational levels decision-mak-ers are not necessarily the most well equipped to task our intelligence communities on what bio-threats and risks they most want to know about. Similarly, the pace in the advances of biological sciences that could be potentially 'weaponised' or 'criminalised' also challenge both the intel-ligence and scientific communities' ability to fully keep pace with how potential threats and risks may develop during the next decade. Despite the innate difficulties in decision-makers and intelligence communi-ties understanding where potential bio-threats and risks will occur, the intelligence production process does require some focus, which in turn means decisions need to be made about where limited collection and ana-lytical resources will be applied. This means that the political leadership and intelligence communities themselves need to delineate specific task-ing areas for further action. This chapter will draw on a combination of interviews of senior intelligence officers and secondary sources to identify, to the extent that this is possible, what decision-makers across the 'Five Eyes' intelligence communities are saying are their biosecurity tasking priorities and how are the coordinated. There can be no effective tasking without specific requirements being coordinated across the tasked agency or community so our tasking discussion below will also include how the political leadership tasks are coordinated across 'Five Eyes' intelligence communities. Are coordination efforts optimal and if not where do the challenges remain and what can be done about them?

While much of the specifics of actual tasking requirements are classified, it is possible to gain a broad overview (rather than an exhaustive list) of some priority tasking areas. A sample of tasking requirements will be discussed at their strategic, operational and tactical levels to illustrate how in reality tasking at one level (for example strategic) has tasking implications at other levels of decision-making (operational and tactical). And as mentioned earlier, political leaders cannot be expected to understand fully the complex suite of biosecurity threat and risk trajectories that may unfold over the next decade. Hence, intelligence communities themselves, as they have often done in the past will need to 'manage upwards' to help political decision-makers identify and make better tasking decisions. The chapter, will therefore, examine how in some 'Five Eye's' settings intelligence agencies and communities manage up to alert their political leadership on the nature of both actual and potential biosecurity threats. The third objective of this chapter is to examine what role the intelligence communities' understanding of concepts of bio-threat and bio-risk play in the tasking of intelligence; and whether risk and threat assessment methodologies are sufficiently effective in steering tasking and coordination efforts.

Biosecurity Intelligence Tasking Priorities

As noted in Chapter 2, the biosecurity threat and risk spectrum is diverse and difficult to pin down given the pace at which advancements in the biological sciences and uptake of technology is taking place. Each of the 'Five Eyes' countries has a national intelligence priority setting process set by the executive branch of government, which broadly outlines the key national security issues that the government considers priorities for guiding its prosecution of national security policy making. This 'list' of national intelligence priorities provides the bare bones of what the national political leadership needs to know about and it then becomes the responsibility of the intelligence community to both collect and assess a range of sensitive and open source information in a way that services those priorities. National intelligence priorities are a statement of what the nation's executive consumers of intelligence are most interested in the intelligence community spending collection and analytical resources on.

In the United States, the priorities list is called the National Intelligence Priorities Framework and is signed off by the President in consultation with the national security principal's committee. The principals being senior administration officials such as the Secretaries of Defence and State amongst others. Although the National Intelligence Priorities Framework could be seen as a top down driven process, it also completed in coordination with advice from officials within the National Intelligence Council (NIC). The NIC is controlled by the Office of the Director, National Intelligence. It is made up of national intelligence officers and is primarily responsible for producing national intelligence estimates on emerging or complex issues.

Similarly in Australia, Canada and the UK, a centralized national security priority setting process exists. In the case of Australia, the National Intelligence Priorities are set by the highest national security policy making body of the Government—the National Security Committee of Cabinet. While in the US, the ODNI has the responsibility to ensure that collection and analytical activities across the intelligence community are meeting priorities set in the framework, in Australia it is the responsibility of high level committees (e.g. the National Intelligence Coordination Committee and the National Intelligence Collection Management Committee) within the Department of Prime Minister and Cabinet to ensure collection and assessment priorities as set out in the national intelligence priorities are being addressed by the Australian intelligence community. At the time of writing however, changes are underway in the coordination of

Australia's intelligence community with the creation of a new Office of National Intelligence which may alter some of the mechanisms in how intelligence priorities are set and coordinated.

Similarly in the US since 9/11, and to some extent in the other 'Five Eyes' countries there have been a series of 'flag ship' policy declarations on biosecurity and bio-terrorism, which have also provided specific guidance and recommendations to intelligence communities on how to improve their capabilities in dealing with biosecurity threats and risks. Other policy statements have sought to provide broader strategic guidance to communities. Some of these have been executive policy initiatives, while others have been parliamentary or special reviews by legislators, which have provided specific recommendations for improving the intelligence response to bio-threats and risks. For example, the Silberman and Robb Commission Report to the Bush Administration in response to the failures of the intelligence community's prewar judgements on Iraq's WMD capability and concern over *Amerithrax* devoted an entire chapter (Chapter 13) that dealt with how tasking, coordination, collection and analysis of bio-threats and risks could be improved across the intelligence community (Silberman and Robb 2005). More recently other policy declarations such as the Obama Administration's 2009 *National Strategy for Countering Biological Threats* provided the US intelligence community broad strategic guidance on the role the intelligence community could play, along with other public health and international cooperation strategies in the prevention of 'bio-attacks' (both natural pandemics and those caused by threat actors).

Understanding, how intelligence agencies have been tasked on both the collection and analysis of bio-threats and risks since 9/11, therefore, also requires knowledge of what policy initiatives 'Five Eyes' governments have implemented to improve intelligence decision-making support across the evolving bio-threat and risks spectrum.

The national intelligence priorities setting frameworks of all 'Five Eyes' countries use an alpha or numeric category system to denote which priorities decision-makers want the intelligence communities to collect and assess more on. While there is a potentially endless and diverse range of threats and risks (e.g. terrorism, cyber, organized crime and state based threats), resources are limited as is the attention span of the political leadership to deal with all issues as equal priorities. The US National Intelligence Priorities Framework uses a matrix, which rates the highest priorities and interest to the leadership as Tier 1 and the lowest as Tier 5. The US framework also links intelligence issues to specific geographic targets, organisations and issues. All national intelligence priority setting frameworks across the 'Five Eyes' are classified for obvious reasons, though various public policy declarations on national security issued by their governments make it reasonably clear what the relative priority of certain issues would be on their classified lists (see for example, DNI Clapper's 2016 World Wide Threat Assessment, Australia's 2015 Counter-Terrorism Strategy or national cyber strategies in each 'Five Eyes' country).

It is clear for example in Washington DC, London, Ottawa, Wellington and Canberra that governments are concerned with state based threats such as: China's role in the twenty-first century, North Korea's WMD proliferation, the resurgence of Russia, and instability in Pakistan, Afghanistan, Syria, Iraq and Libya. It is also clear that leaders are concerned with non-state actor issues, particularly terrorism and issues, which can be either enabled or exploited by state and non-state actors such as cyber-attacks. Priority frameworks also include broad guidance on what issues under each subject decision-makers are particularly interested in. So for China or North Korea, there would be interest in leadership dynamics in these countries and how they impact on national security announcements and actions by the leadership. Since the Cold War to the present, the broad subject area of weapons of mass destruction (WMD) have long been of top priority for 'Five Eyes' countries. As noted in Chapter 2, state based industrial biological weapons programs of the former Soviet Union during the Cold War and other more modest programs of rogue countries (during a similar time frame 1945–1990) such as Iraq, Libya, Iran, North Korea, Rhodesia and South Africa demonstrate that biological weapons capable of mass destruction were a top intelligence collection and analytical priority. Though the other categories of WMD—nuclear and chemical have traditionally been given more collection and analytical attention. And in the current post 9/11 environment, biological aspects of WMD are seen by many in the 'Five Eyes' intelligence communities as 'the poor man's cousins' in terms of collection and analytical priority. This is partly, as noted in Chapter 1, because monitoring nuclear proliferation from an intelligence perspective is easier than assessing whether dual use biotechnology is being weaponized, and also due to except in a few circumstances (*Amerithrax*, Iraq's WMD)—decision-maker's interest in biological weapons has not been consistently high over successive governments across the 'Five Eyes'.

Indeed it is true that from the Bush Administration's early post 9/11 focus on *Amerithrax* and the potential that either terrorists or Iraq would use biological weapons, 'classical bio' (WMD) became a top intelligence priority for the US intelligence community. As Koblentz notes in particular the intelligence support was critical to a range of bio-defense programs the Bush Administration initiated. However, since the Bush Administration the priority given to intelligence support for classical bio (WMD) seems to have reduced. If one looks at the Obama Administration's 2010 National Security Strategy, it made clear that 'the spread of nuclear weapons is a top priority' and nearly 1 and a half pages were devoted to it compared to one paragraph on biological weapons (Obama 2010). While President Obama's renewed focus on global health security is also mentioned towards the end of the document, there is no discussion about the criticality of the role of intelligence in working with other important stakeholders such as public health officials or the scientific community. A year after the West Africa Ebola epidemic erupted, President Obama's 2015 National Security Strategy— focused a lot more on improving the global health security agenda to manage health security threats—particularly through capacity building for prevention and detection. Though again there was no mention specifically of the role of intelligence in this greater emphasis on pandemics and infectious diseases. Like the 2010 statement, the 2015 version also detailed the high priority the Administration placed in containing nuclear and chemical proliferation. Concern about biological weapons is reduced to the inclusion of just two words 'biological weapons' towards the end of section on WMD issues (p. 11). It does seem that the nuclear and increasingly the chemical proliferation dimensions of WMD (particularly since finding chemical weapons in Libya (2014) and Syria in (2013) and more recently) were more a focus for senior officials in the

Obama Administration. Other potential non-WMD bio-threats or risks, with the exception of more recent concerns raised in 2016 about the gene editing tool CRISPR also don't seem to be grasping the attention of the leadership of 'Five Eyes' countries. One US senior official said in a discussion with me in 2016 that 'we should be doing more on this (bio-threats and risks) but it's difficult and there are multiple other challenges' (terrorism, cyber, China and Russia). Another senior US official also indicated that non-WMD bio-threats and risks (presumably including potential threats from dual-use biology) would be at the lowest priority level of the intelligence framework, i.e. Tier 5 if they appear at all.

It would be wrong to suggest that a reduction in the number of para-graphs allocated to discussing bio-threats and risks in public versions of flagship policy documents such as National Security Statements means the Obama Administration did not see these issues as no longer intelli-gence priorities. Indeed my discussions in the US with key senior intel-ligence staff, who have been engaged in biosecurity threat and risk issues from the Bush and Obama Administrations suggest that bio-threats and risks are still priority issues for the intelligence community. Though some of these same intelligence staff implied that the US did not view bio-threats and risks at the same level as other threats such as 'conven-tional (non WMD) terrorism', cyber or North Korea.

However, it is clear if one examines both the Bush and Obama's Administration's biosecurity policy making that how bio-threats and risks were perceived and the priority placed on them has changed since 9/11—thereby impacting on the way the US intelligence community was tasked on these issues. As Koblentz notes, the Bush Administration's bio-defense policy making was primarily engaged in defending against domestic threats posed by disease outbreaks caused by terrorists and state actors. Koblentz suggest that 'up to 40 percent (or $23.6 billion) spent on biodefense (from 2001 to 2009) was for research and develop-ment of counter measures, diagnostics and sensors and the construction of high containment labs' (2012: 136–137).

As we shall see in the following two chapters (Chapters 4 and 5), var-ious US intelligence agencies had a role in helping develop support for such bio-defense measures including the FBI and DHS. The bio-defense focus of the Bush Administration also of course included the ability of the DOD to improve its warfare detection of biological weapons, but under the Bush Administration global health and bio-defense issues were kept separate which impacted (particularly early in the Administration) on the way the intelligence community was tasked and how it worked with the public health agencies also working on bio-risks and threats. One senior US official working in the biosecurity area did suggest to me, however that although the Bush Administration was focused on bio-defense, by the mid 2005s the pendulum started to swing back to public health issues that may not be caused by states or terrorists. This evolving focus by the Bush Administration on a global health agenda became a prelude to arguably an even larger focus on global health by the Obama Administration. Though as the pendulum started moving away from bio-defense it became unclear what coherent role the US intelligence community would play in global health and preventive measures against pandemics.

The Obama Administration while continuing many of the bio-defense measures introduced by President Bush shifted the focus to prevention (i.e. laboratory bio-safety, export controls and biological threat reduction programs overseas) (Koblentz 2012: 136–137). The policy interest was also more on a one health approach, and the need to develop global health security measures—not just domestic ones to prevent, detect and rapidly respond to increasing biological threats like Ebola and Zika.

It is clear from the above discussion that intelligence priority setting or tasking of the 'Five Eyes' intelligence communities has changed since 9/11 as the perceived bio-risks threats and interests of decision-makers evolve. Additionally, while biosecurity intelligence tasking as noted earlier, is officially set at the cabinet level of each 'Five Eyes country', tasking regularly occurs at principal's level (ministers or in the case of the US secretary level), deputy-principal level (sub-cabinet level), head of agency and then at lower levels within a range of agencies (both intelligence and non-intelligence) that have some remit for managing bio-threats and risks. The US with 17 agencies has the largest intelligence community, while New Zealand is at the other end of the scale with just three core agencies officially included. The scale and number of intelligence agencies therefore will impact on both how government set intelligence priorities in the biosecurity area and how they are operationalized.

In addition, and as discussed further in Chapters 4 and 5, different member agencies of each country's intelligence communities have distinct functions. Some like the CIA have a foreign intelligence focus, while others such as the Australian Security Intelligence Organisation (ASIO) are more focused on domestic security intelligence collection. Some agencies such as the National Security Agency (NSA) (in the US) or the Government Communications Headquarters Communication (GCHQ) (in the UK) have a collection remit—while others such as the Office of National Assessments (Australia) and the National Assessments Bureau (New Zealand) have an all source assessment responsibility. Similarly some agencies have a hybrid collection and assessment responsibility, particularly agencies such as ASIO, the Canadian Security Intelligence Service (CSIS) or MI5. Further away from the traditional 'inner circle' of traditional intelligence agencies others such as national law enforcement/investigations agencies such as: the Australian Federal Police (AFP), the FBI or the Royal Canadian Mounted Police (RCMP) have both a collection, assessment and prosecution function.

Even further afield from the national intelligence communities of 'Five Eyes' countries there are agencies, which may have some collection and analytical roles in managing bio-risks and threats; including but not limited to: immigration/customs/border protection, agriculture and food safety, public health and animal health authorities.

The potentially large number of government agencies involved in the collection and assessment of bio-threats and risks across each 'Five Eyes' country makes it difficult to take an accurate snapshot in time on how each agency would be involved in managing such threats; including how they would be tasked on these or task others. The tasking processes involved in all cases will be different from agency to agency—depending on the priority that an agency ascribes to supporting any national intelligence effort against a bio-threat or risk. The kind of tasking would as indicated above also be contingent on what unique collection or analytical assets the agency could bring to understand a current or emerging bio-threat/risk. For example, in a sudden yet suspicious disease outbreak tasking a national public health authority with the appropriate epidemiological intelligence staff to collect relevant data along with an investigatory agency such as the FBI might well be more appropriate then deploying less useful intelligence assets (at least initially) such as sigint collection.

It is not possible therefore to clearly delineate in every case how intelligence is being tasked by decision-makers to arrive at a complete picture of current or emerging bio-threats and risks priorities. It is equally not possible to describe with accuracy in every circumstance which decision-makers are doing the tasking. In reality, although national intelligence communities are tasked with priorities to work on, the tasking process tends to be more dynamic, fluid and even adhoc. Bio-threats and risks can change in real-time and they are of course more difficult to assess the further they are away from the present. In these respects, they are no different from any other threats and risks (e.g. terrorism, cyber, organized crime, WMD, state based threats) in the security environment. For example, we have seen how the threat from Islamic terrorism has evolved and splintered into various new groups and manifestations from Al Qaeda central to Al Shabab (East Africa), Al Qaeda in the Islamic Maghreb (North West Africa) to Islamic State (in Syria and Iraq) and the growth in lone actor (wolf) attacks in the West.

Additionally, since 9/11 there has been a greater blurring across the old lines of domestic and, foreign threats. This has been particularly been the case with transnational threats such as terrorism, drug trafficking and arms trading. Globalisation and the fast pace changes in digital communications have created a more fluid threat and risk space. Al Qaeda and IS may have international dimensions yet the threat and risk posed by them is also regional, national and even local if one thinks about how they (particularly the latter) have inspired lone actor attacks in the last decade.

If such threats are manifesting themselves at different yet inter-connected dimensions (transnational, regional, national and local), intelligence tasking has since 9/11 also become more clearly focused at dealing with threats at these different levels.

Despite the inherent challenges identified above in understanding how intelligence tasking is being done in the dynamic post 9/11 security environment, it is nonetheless possible to gain some insights into tasking and coordination processes. All intelligence tasking is influenced by two major factors: the time frame required in which a decision needs to be made and the kind of decision that needs to be made. Time frames for decision-making will always be government, community or agency dependent. For example, the military may require intelligence on potential new bio-threats from dual-use technology that they might need to prepare vaccines against over the next 5–10 years. In contrast, a suspicious white powder left on the subway in a major city will likely require intelligence support almost immediately from a city police force. Both situations will involve decision-makers seeking different kinds of intelligence support. Tasking of intelligence therefore happens in different time periods and involves different levels of decision-makers. So while it is difficult to discern exactly in every case 'who', 'by', and 'how' intelligence is tasked it's clear that tasking occurs at the strategic, operational and tactical levels.

Strategic tasking is normally thought of as that which has an 'emerging' or 'over the horizon' focus. Operational tasking is normally, weeks or a year—while a tactical focus is usually the present or out to about a week. These are rough timeframes and as noted above, the actual time frames denoted for each decision-making category are dependent on the threat/risk context and the agencies involved. The development of a threat over a year could, in some agencies, be considered a strategic tasking matter, while in the military this may be considered an operational threat space.

In our scenario of a suspicious white powder being left at three subway stations scenario tasking at the tactical, operational and strategic level might look quite different. At the tactical level, local law enforcement and other first responders (fire department/HAZMAT) would immediately respond to the incident. Immediately on the ground police commanders will be wanting to collect intelligence from any surveillance tapes and start interviewing witnesses. It would be unusual if the discovery of white powder across each site (subway station) would be found and reported to police at the exact same time; so initial tactical intelligence may not immediately show the significance of one incident or how it is connected to the other two. As further information is available, public health officials and national law enforcement agencies with specialized investigative capabilities would become involved and the depth and breadth of intelligence available and required to support this kind of investigation would be more detailed and service a broader range of decision-makers—including the local and state governments and likely at this stage the national government. Later the same day, bio-forensic testing of the substance may confirm that the powder is live Anthrax and the investigation would now become even broader and rely on the collection and assessment of intelligence further afield from the incident site.

At some stage, a witness statement and the forensic analysis of the substance may provide further information on person(s) of interest. Again a wider number of agencies across the intelligence community would then collect and assess further intelligence on the persons of interest to assess their identity, motivations and capabilities. Foreign intelligence collection assets (sigint, humint) and liaison with other 'Five Eyes' partners may also be tasked to assess if the persons of interest were working domestically or if there was international dimensions to the threat. Let's say in our hypothetical scenario, the investigation concludes a lone-actor terrorist is involved. Accordingly towards the end of the investigation, cabinet level decision-makers will be seeking intelligence support to determine if this attack represents a major shift in terrorist's tactics away from more simpler methods such as IEDs—or whether the attack represents an increased interest or willingness to use bio-weapons and a greater capability across a particular group. At this level, presidents and prime ministers along with their senior cabinet members would be tasking higher level intelligence assessments to understand what strategic drivers have come into play that resulted in individuals or perhaps even a terrorist group being interested in procuring and using anthrax for a bio-weapon. There would be a number of strategic level questions national government decision-makers would want to know about such a scenario. Do more individuals or groups have the in-house capability to produce anthrax? Is it being stolen from BSL3 and 4 labs? How? Is it being produced in a fragile state with poor biosafety controls, where the terrorist group operates and likely has sympathizers?

Coordination

Tasking alone will not ensure that a decision-maker at whatever level they are located along the decision-making process (tactical, operational and strategic) will receive the kind of intelligence support they need at the time it is required. There can be no effective tasking without a system(s) that helps ensure that both the collection and analytical response to that tasking is well coordinated. There is no one way tasks are coordinated for all biosecurity threats and risks. Much depends on the nature of the bio-threat and risk (plant, animal, human), and whether it is unintentional or intentional. The former (unintentional) suggests less national security intelligence or law enforcement intelligence agencies would be involved with a greater responsibility for public health agencies. For example, in the case of the 2015 and 2016 outbreak of Zika virus across the US one would expect an almost exclusive response from CDC and state and local health authorities. However, a sudden, unexplained outbreak of Foot and Mouth Disease in areas where it has previously not occurred might at least initially draw in the interest of the FBI, DHS, local law enforcement along with animal health and agricultural authorities at least until more is known about the threat.

Different threat/risk profiles therefore, will bring in different health authorities, scientists and agencies with a range of intelligence capabilities to bring to the task. Does this present problems? Not necessarily. Not all biosecurity tasking needs to follow the same processes, but what is important is that coordination can occur as much as possible in an integrated manner across all three levels of decision-making: strategic, operational and tactical. Such integration is an ongoing challenge for 'Five Eyes' intelligence communities in all intelligence tasking not just in the biosecurity area. Since 9/11, there have been major improvements in the way for example tasking for terrorism has been better coordinated so that senior decision-makers have confidence that the intelligence they use has been drawn and assessed from multiple sources, and is joined together in a way where the validity of key analytical judgements have been contested and peer reviewed. The setting up of national terrorism fusion centres such as the US National Counter Terrorism Center (NCTC) or the UK Joint Terrorism Analysis Centre (JTAC) have vastly improved the coordination of collection and analytical efforts of terrorism related intelligence.

Despite such improvements, different information communications technology platforms, legislation, organizational cultural attitudes and governance issues still conspire against a seamlessly integrated coordinated response to terrorism issues across the 'Five Eyes' (Walsh 2015). As noted earlier, the sheer size of the US intelligence community makes coordination of intelligence efforts difficult. Similarly, further away from the core national security intelligence agencies, the size and diversity of law enforcement and other agencies that might have a role in collection or analyzing relevant intelligence on terrorism is large—making coordination difficult. If such coordination issues still exist for a top priority issue such as terrorism, they also exist and arguably more so for biosecurity related issues, which are less of a priority. Again some efforts have been made both from the collection and analytical perspective, particularly in the US to provide better coordination of biosecurity tasking. These efforts have occurred at the ODNI—the details of which are discussed in Chapters 4 and 5. However, interviews of senior intelligence leaders suggest that there needs to be better coordination of intelligence efforts across intelligence agencies in 'Five Eyes' countries—as well as better coordination of non-national security sources of intelligence such as scientific research/expertise and epidemiology intelligence. Further evidence is required though on how best 'Five Eyes' intelligence communities can improve intelligence coordination of biosecurity intelligence. However, given the absence of any major attack since *Amerithrax*, political masters remain largely disinterested in bio-threats and risks including overseeing better coordination of intelligence efforts in this area. They seem content to receive periodic intelligence on potential, emerging threats that may in some cases not have been produced by the intelligence community in a coordinated manner. This can result in the delivery to the decision-maker of a less comprehensively developed picture of a particular bio-threat/risk.

It is not just the coordination processes or lack thereof that can result in poor tasking results for a decision-maker. It is also true in many cases, the complexities of bio-risks and threats are difficult for many decision-makers or even their advisors to understand. This results in either no tasking or vague requests that may not reflect actual or even potentially relevant bio-threats or risks. Intelligence agencies may find themselves unnecessarily going down rabbit holes wasting limited resources due to a decision-maker not understanding what they are tasking for. Though it might be easy to apportion blame to a decision-maker for no or inadequate tasking, the intelligence community also faces another key challenge in getting the 'tasking right' and that is the lack of knowledge about how to assess both bio-risks and threats. Better tasking and coordination of bio-threats and risks also rely on how risk and threat methodologies are being applied to the biosecurity context and whether these are sufficient in guiding tasking and coordination.

Risk and Threat Assessment

It is not possible in the space available to provide a full discussion of all risk and threat methodologies used across all the 'Five Eyes' countries. The potential threat/risks space across the one health continuum is so vast and diverse several volumes would be required to do justice to describing the various methodologies used to assess them. Additionally, I am restricted in how I can discuss specific threat and risk models used by intelligence agencies as they are generally classified. However, it is possible to discuss the broader foundational principles upon which many classified methodologies have been built. Hence, this section will discuss key factors that have been used in many risk and threat methodologies that are publicly available. The discussion will highlight how difficult applying such methodologies are, particularly because the available data for previous bio-risks and threats is generally low or non-existent, and fundamental and unresolved debates remain about the intention and capabilities of potential threat actors (threat assessment) and the consequences of bio-attacks (risks). The absence of consistently rigorous threat and risk assessment across intelligence communities does as we shall see in Chapters 4 and 5 impact on the kind of collection and analysis intelligence is able to provide on bio-risks/threats to decision-makers.

Before summarizing some key trends in bio-risk and threat methodologies, it is important to define how the terms 'risk' and 'threat' assessment will be used in this chapter. In Chapter 1, a definition for both bio-threat and risk was included, however what follows here is a more detailed discussion of the variables that constitute bio-threat and risk in order to reduce confusion about how these terms are used in different threat and risks contexts. As Burnette suggests in his discussion of basic principles of threat assessment, confusion occurs when 'biosecurity is discussed in a bio-safety or scientific setting'. Further in his words: 'it is important to distinguish biosecurity risk from biosafety risk' (Burnette 2013: 91).

Defining Bio-risk

In broad terms, risk is 'the likelihood that an adverse event involving a specific hazard or threat will occur and the consequences of that occurrence' (Caskey and Sevilla-Reyes 2015: 45). In very simple terms, Kaplan and Garrick argue 'that assessing a risk involves answering the following questions: what can go wrong? How likely is it and how likely are we to see it coming? What are the consequences?' (Kaplan and Garrick 1981 cited in Caskey and Sevilla-Reyes 2015: 45). More narrowly, in the biosecurity and biosafety context, Burnette defines *biosecurity risks* as being 'determined by measures of vulnerability to and consequences of deliberate acts, as well as the dynamic threats that impact the system or its assets'…whereas *biosafety risks* deal with probabilities and consequences of accidents where no nefarious cause exists' (ibid.: 91). The key difference between biosecurity and biosafety risks is that while both underlie vulnerabilities and have consequences, the former is the result of deliberate acts. It is the former (biosecurity risks), which naturally full under the mandate of intelligence and law enforcement agencies and is our focus.

Assessing the risks in the biosecurity context is easier in some cases than others. For example, in a lab setting the likelihood and consequences that an employee may steal a piece of support equipment such as a lap top for their own personal use at home is maybe more 'quantifiable' than whether that same person will steal sensitive intellectual property from the lab. There is likely to be more data on the incidences of the former (i.e. common theft) and its impact—enabling the institution to improve anti-theft mitigation policies and procedures.

In contrast, the risk posed by an employee stealing sensitive intellectual property may be more difficult to calculate using conventional methods of risk assessment given there is less 'reliable knowledge about likelihood, scale, nature and vectors of harm' (Helm 2015: 103). More recently, however, Gryphon Scientific, a small consulting business made up of life scientists and health researchers, who consult on global health and homeland security issues have provided advice to the National Institute of Health on the risks posed by malicious actors and acts targeting labs in which gain of function (GOF) viruses are studies or stored, and the risks posed by the independent replication of published GOF research by malicious actors (Gryphon Scientific 2016). Their report provides a comprehensive risk assessment methodology. The methodology is a mixture of quantitative and qualitative measures based on a detailed collection of data from historical cases, hypothetical scenarios, legislation, biosafety regulations and interviewing scientists, general counsel, FBI WMD Coordinators and other law enforcement personnel. They then methodically identify potential malicious actors and the attack vectors and consequences for each. For example, in terms of the risk posed to labs undertaking GOF research by malicious actors and acts, malicious actors identified were (lone outsider, lone insider, organized criminals, domestic terrorists and extremists, transnational terrorists including state like terrorist groups and foreign intelligence entities). Attack vectors identified were multiple including for example (armed assault, bomb or arson, theft of pathogens, subversion of employee and cyber covert entry) (Gryphon Scientific 2016: 847). In-depth research and interviews of a range of experts across both the health, scientific and security sectors resulted in a threat matrix of malicious actors, which provides a useful global way of understanding the likelihood and consequences for each act depending on the actor and vector of attack. The Gryphon study concluded that the 'most likely malicious act to be carried out in or on a containment lab include theft of virus stocks, experimental samples, equipment or research animals, deliberate contamination of personal protective equipment of lab equipment of co-workers, and mixing of infected with uninfected samples or animals outside proper containment' (ibid.: 4–5). Though they also assessed given 'the regulatory and security environment, the most *plausible* malicious acts taking place at high containment research labs would involve malicious insiders, who have authorized access to the labs and viruses contained in them' (ibid.). Gryphon Scientific concluded that 'insiders may work alone or in coordination with an outside group. Their motivations range from emotional disturbances to ideological radicalization by domestic and transnational terrorists organisations' (ibid.). The Gryphon study represents progress in developing more reliable risk methodologies that assemble empirically relevant scientific data and intelligence assessments on the intent, capability and consequences of a range of malicious attack scenarios in secure labs working on GOF influenza, MERS-Cov and SARS-Cov research.

As useful as the Gryphon study is it is limited to biosafety and biosecurity risks posed by GOF research, further up the risk scale, some of the even more complex, low probability high impact bio-risks such as a bio-terrorist attack in a major metro subway cannot necessarily be 'measured' using the same risk assessment tools we would use to assess the likelihood and consequences of someone stealing some sensitive information from a secure lab environment. Generally much more is known about the lab physical security environment, security measures and employees compared to the myriad of threat actors, vectors and consequences that could arise from such a bio-terrorism attack in an open environment such as a subway. Systems thinking from engineering could provide some assistance in understanding risk assessment in a number of complex bio-risk incidents. We will come back to the role of other disciplines, including engineering in understanding risk and improving intelligence capability in Chapter 7. Basic risk management methods are also not sufficient to assessing many complex and potential bio-risks, particularly those posed by dual-use biotechnology as they have for the most part not occurred or are still very infrequent thereby lacking the historical data normally required to assess risk.

In brief though systems approaches from engineering may be usefully applied against emerging risks as they allow for uncertainty and complexity and accept that one cannot manage away all potential bio-risk and threats. Additionally, as Helm argues many complex risks cannot be analysed with standard data methods in part because they do not follow normal cause and effect behavior (Helm 2015: 106). For example, no one could foresee all public health, political, social and economic consequences of the 2014 Ebola epidemic in West Africa. With complex risks such as a pandemic (caused intentionally or not) there is likely to be a degree of failure in mitigating some risks. A more comprehensive systems approach that assesses: *risk, resilience* and *adaptation* in an integrated way will likely result in a holistic treatment and mitigation of many complex and potentially emerging bio-risks. Resilience or the ability to plan, absorb and recover and adapt from adverse events is important in understanding complex bio-risks as there is a need to understand the vulnerabilities to a range of sectors in a locality, region, nation or globally. The intelligence community needs to understand what are specific vulnerabilities in particular sectors such as transport, city buildings, food and water supply or airports? While managing complex risks is partly about mitigating the risks to different sectors in the economy before an event occurs, a systems approach to risk management and building effective resilience also requires an understanding of how the public and private sector can respond once an event has occurred.

Mitigating against all potential future bio-risks are impossible and policy-makers are left with tough choices about the cost-benefit analysis of mitigating against exotic high impact-low probability risks, which may not occur– or ones where attempting to mitigate against such risk in the future by for example 24 hour health screening of every passenger coming into a country would not be feasible longer term and may have an impact on the economic status of a country. Adaptation the last step in a systems approach to risk management is linked to measures to increase resilience, but seeks to extend the analysis of risk by 'incorporating various mixes of proactive and reactive measures in order to manage the uncertainty' (Helm 2015: 116).

Defining Bio-threat

In contrast to bio-risks which include vulnerabilities to both accidents and deliberate acts, bio-threats involve humans in all cases and quantifying them is arguably more difficult. As discussed in Chapter 2, policy makers, bureaucrats and the intelligence communities' perspectives of threat assessments on both offensive state bio programs and bio-terrorism have varied significantly since 9/11, which calls into question the kind of threat assessment methodologies relied upon to make such diverging statements on the nature of the threat. For example, the October 2002 US National Intelligence Estimate on Iraq's weapons of mass destruction expressed a high confidence that Iraq had an offensive bio-weapons program deemed a direct threat to the US (NIC 2002). From a non-state actor perspective, the lessons learnt from the analytical failures of Iraq's bio-weapons program, which led to a US led coalition invasion of the country seemed to have not been completely absorbed by the intelligence community if one examines subsequent public announcements on threats posed by bio-terrorists and state sponsored bio-weapons programs. For example, in an address to the Senate Select Committee on Intelligence regarding the ODNI's Annual Threat Assessment, DNI Michael McConnell said: Al Qaeda and other terrorist groups are attempting to acquire chemical, biological, radiological and nuclear weapons (CBRN) (McConnell 2008: 6).

In the same year, the WMD Commission Report established by Congress in 2008 to assess the US programs to prevent WMDs gave a time line for a biological attack stating that:

> Unless the world community acts decisively and with great urgency, it is more likely than not that a weapon of mass destruction will be used in a terrorist attack somewhere in the world by the end of 2013. The Commission further believes that terrorists are more likely to be able to obtain and use a biological weapon than a nuclear weapon. (Graham and Talent 2008: xv)

DNI McConnell's successor, Admiral Blair while agreeing in his 2009 Annual Threat Assessment with much of the assessment made by his predecessor on the growing threat that terrorists will use bio-weapons, also suggested that such weapons may be acquired by states that do not have such programs (Blair 2009: 19).

While it is difficult to extrapolate a full understanding of threat assessment methodologies from open sources, the variations between different decision-maker statements and where the emphasis is placed on different threat scenarios (e.g. state based bio-weapons vs bio-terrorism) shows that different factors are being considered in the threat formulation process whilst others are being left out. The impact of incomplete threat and risk assessments is something we will turn to in the final section of this chapter. Suffice it to say though, improving threat assessments matter as they can as Stern (2002: 94) suggest cause decision-makers to 'choose policies whose cost exceed their benefits' as we saw in the 2002 National Intelligence Estimate provided to the Bush Administration on Iraq's WMD capabilities.

Threats can emanate from an individual or group. Threats can be: internal, external, indirect and clandestine or overt (Burnette 2013: 95). Internal threats as noted earlier are particularly worrying as they involve employees and visitors, who have authorized access to research or a secure lab environment. Dr. Bruce Ivins the number one suspect in the *Amerithrax* incident is a classic example of the 'insider threat'. While intelligence and even psychiatric analysis helped FBI investigators assess the threat posed by him, investigators are not always going to have such information particularly before a bio-incident occurs. While threat assessment methodologies try to extrapolate from previous cases to predict future threatening behaviors, in the case of biosecurity and biosafety there is still relatively few cases to extrapolate from to make current threat assessment methodologies reliable.

Burnette is correct to argue that many threat cases in the past have involved individuals with a profile of violence due to a feeling of being wronged by co-workers, an estranged spouse or some kind of animal extremism (e.g. animal rights, government policy disagreement), yet the context and scenario of each case is different (Burnette 2013: 92). In addition, then to a person's intention to commit an act of violence, how this act evolves is also context driven. In other words, the context of each threat scenario presents different possibilities for an act of violence to evolve as does the varying capabilities of different individuals in different scenarios. It is the differences between cases as much as the similarities therefore that are crucial in refining threat assessment methodologies.

Burnette defines 'indirect threats' as being at the 'wrong place at wrong time' and could be direct threats against employees or someone the attacker has a personal connection with. He cites the 2009 case of Amy Bishop, who as an assistant professor of biology at the University of Alabama, Huntsville killed three colleagues as retribution for being denied tenure (Burnette 2013: 93). Finally Burnette describes 'external threats' as involving threats to an institution or individual from an outsider. Examples include direct threats against employees that are personally or terrorist motivated or some kind of direct attack against the lab, research institute or other related institution (ibid.: 96). We must also remember that not all external threats will involve violence against persons. They could involve stolen property (particularly intellectual property, misuse or destruction of property). Of course external attacks can also involve non research or lab institutions. The list of other potential external attacks is almost endless and could involve, amongst others: office buildings, airports, water supply, food supply and as we saw in the *Amerithrax* case the mail system.

Burnette also describes—the targeted violence process as a useful way to conceptualise how threats evolve from perhaps initially a simple grievance to the implementation of an act of violence. Understanding the targeted violence process, he argues, helps security personnel identify ways to intervene earlier before the violent attack is implemented. The key developmental phases a threat will evolve through are: *intent, ability and opportunity*. Though for each three categories there are a series of sub-categories in the targeted violence process including: *grievance, ideation, planning, preparation and implementation*. Grievance is where intent is first formed. For example, someone working in a laboratory may have a complaint about the way they have been treated or a perceived wrong. Ideation, the next phase, is where the individual identifies a course of action to remedy that wrong. This of course may not be a rational choice of action.

It is at the intent category of threat development, where hopefully pre-emptive security measures inside the lab may detect an individual's behavior or words, which suggest something is not right. For example a co-worker could observe the individual making threatening statement against their employer or another individual. Other pre-emptive measures to prevent the development of *intent* is through the appropriate security vetting and character suitability processes that employees must undergo prior to commencing and at periodic intervals in secure laboratories and other research institutions in most western countries. Such checks are not fool proof, but over time they may pick up in some cases a grievance, which can be dealt with prior to the individual further developing towards an act of violence or some other kind of threat such as theft. The next phase *ability* represents the threat actor's effort to develop a definite pathway to action. It has two sub-categories (*plan and preparation*). Planning 'involves the development of the action to be carried out and preparation is the gathering and staging of the tools and plans to carry out the action' (Burnette 2013: 98). Reflecting on our lab worker scenario, it is possible that the facilities security office may be able to pick up on some early planning and put in place mitigation measures to remove the threat or reduce the risk. Though in other situations the threat assessment process will not be able to pick up early such planning and preparation prior to the threat actor carrying out the planned action.

The final phase (opportunity), as Burnette, indicates, 'is the phase in which the actor has met all needed criteria to carry out an action' (ibid.). Opportunity consist of only one sub-category—*implementation* which is self-explanatory. Again in our lab worker scenario, opportunity represents the point where the threat actor's planned violence is carried out facilitated by vulnerabilities in the environment. It is the actor's threat process described above and the existing vulnerabilities in the environment, which provide an overall risk assessment to their actual or planned actions.

Actual acts of violence that were unable to be prevented by intelligence or law enforcement intervention underscore both the difficulty and validity of threat assessment processes in the biosecurity and bio-terrorism context. In order for threat assessments to improve their ability to assess potential bio-threats in the early phases of intent or early planning it is clear that governments, intelligence, law enforce-ment agencies, universities, research institutions and bio-tech compa-nies all need to consistently and proactively collect better information and intelligence on potential threat scenarios in order to develop coun-ter measures or the early identification of threat actors. In the narrow context of laboratory bio-risk management, having a more strategic and proactive approach to intelligence and information collection about threats is a whole of agency response not something that can just be left to the security department. It requires that employees working in a range of both public and private agencies dealing with biological select agents and toxins (BSATs) are able identify individuals engaged in behavior that may indicate a planned act of violence or theft. Developing better threat assessments that can result in more proactive rather than reactive risk mitigation strategies also rests on the extent that the executive leadership of the relevant agency can set appropri-ate collection requirements in place. Good information collection that brings information sources together more quickly will improve both the validity and outcomes of threat and risk assessment methodologies.

Conclusion

It is clear from the discussion above that there remain challenges for both the 'Five Eyes' intelligence community and their decision-makers on how to more effectively task and coordinate efforts against bios-ecurity threat and risk issues. In some respects, such challenges are no different from other threat types and risk scenarios in cyber and the constantly evolving terrorist threat. In both areas (cyber and ter-rorism), technology is clearly enabling threats and risks and intelli-gence communities struggle to understand the nature of them given the rapidly changing trajectory of technology. As noted in Chapter 2, understanding how the rapid changes in bio-technology—much of it potentially dual-use will evolve confounds biologists/scientists involved in it let alone political decision-makers. Additionally, the cur-rent levels of uncertainty, and the relatively few cases of biosecurity and bio-terrorism incidents compared to conventional terrorism attacks or even cyber-attacks does impact on how 'the Five Eyes' intelligence communities are tasked on biosecurity and bioterrorism issues.

Other than the biological weapons aspect of WMD and a general periodic concern that terrorist *may* make or acquire a bio-weapon, it seems that tasking against a broader potential array of bio-risks and threats is adhoc and inconsistent. This inconsistency of decision-maker's interest in biosecurity and bioterrorism issues in the policy context was discussed earlier. It can be difficult to get a decision-maker's attention on an area that produces a number of potential threat and risk scenarios, which are low probability despite them being of high impact when there are far more 'here and now' issues to occupy their minds. It remains unclear, for example how the Trump Administration 'rates' biosecurity and bioterrorism issues. Nonetheless, the 'Five Eyes' intelligence communities do have a role in making sure that biosecurity and bioterrorism issues do not fall completely off the radar.

Part of the job of any intelligence community is to manage upwards—not just accepting formal tasking from the political leadership. It is also clear from this chapter that intelligence communities (including both national security and law enforcement agencies) themselves need a better understanding of how potential bio-threats and risks may manifest themselves at the tactical, operational and strategic level. Secondary and primary sources also suggest that even formal national tasking of biosecurity threats may not be being clearly articulated and communicated to sub-national security personnel (state and local police, first responders and even the private sector), which results in further lost opportunities to create better understanding of potentially nationally significant biosecurity threats if tasking and coordination processes from the national to local levels are not working well.

Improved tasking and coordination of bio-threats and risks whether that is top down (from decision makers) or bottom up (from the intelligence community) also requires as we saw an improvement in the understanding of risk and threat, including improving risk and threat methodologies.

Conflicting and accuracy issues around multiple risk and threat methodologies applied to biosecurity threats and risks provides the political leadership with different assessments on the probabilities of various threats and their likely impacts. The inexactitudes and sometimes lack of consistency of measuring both likelihood and consequences (e.g. do we use a mathematical approach, a quantitative, semi-quantitative or qualitative approach) to provide an overall risk assessment level of high, medium or low (Caskey and Sevilla-Reyes 2015: 51)—combined with limited resources, and workforce training issues on risk and threat means tasking and coordination of biosecurity threats is not optimal.

In other words, there would likely be more informed tasking from decision-makers if threat and risk modelling in the intelligence community was improved. There also needs to be a more common understanding between governments, labs, private sector on how acceptable vs unacceptable risks are determined and agreed upon. These decisions need to be well documented. Communicating risk decisions with all stakeholders is important and obviously important stakeholders should be informed on key risk assessment and mitigation decisions (Caskey and Sevilla-Reyes 2015: 59).

Finally the 'Five Eyes' intelligence communities as suggested need to expand their understanding of risk and threat to more comprehensive or systems approaches to avoid over-simplified, biased and linear assumptions of risk, which can result in poor decision-making by decision-makers. This is easier said than done, but many future bio-threats and risks whether enabled by bio-technology or not have unpredictable consequences and are difficult to completely mitigate against. Risk management will only by the first step and the intelligence community working with other stakeholders need to play a greater role in identifying what consequences might occur in a range of scenarios, and how they can help society also improve resilience and adaptability to actual bio-attacks as much as potential ones.

In order improve to improve risk and threat methodologies in the biosecurity and bioterrorism context an evidenced based approach to knowledge collection is critical. Arguably, most knowledge may well be outside the intelligence community and residing with the scientific community or the private sector. This is a point that will be discussed in detail in Chapter 7. As we shall see in an area such as biosecurity and bioterrorism gaining this knowledge requires also that the 'Five

Eyes' intelligence communities reflect on current collection strategies to examine whether they are fit for purpose. In Chapter 4, we will look at some of the key collection methodologies and how they are being applied to biosecurity threats and risks. The chapter will also highlight what are some of the key challenges in collecting against complex biosecurity threats and risks.

References

Blair, D. (2009). *Annual Threat Assessment of DNI for the Senate Select Committee on Intelligence*. Washington, DC: ODNI.

Burnette, R. (Ed.). (2013). *Biosecurity Understanding, Assessing, and Preventing the Threat*. Hoboken, NJ: Wiley.

Caskey, S., & Sevilla-Reyes, E. (2015). Risk Assessment. In R. Salerno & J. Gaudioso (Eds.), *Laboratory Biorisk Management* (pp. 45–63). Boca Raton, FL: CRC Press.

Clapper, J. (2016, February 9). Statement for the Record. *Worldwide Threat Assessment of the US Intelligence Community. Armed Services Committee*. Washington, DC: ODNI.

Graham, B., & Talent, J. (2008). *World at Risk: The Report of the Commission on the Prevention of WMD Proliferation and Terrorism*. New York: Vintage Books.

Gryphon Scientific. (2016). *Risk and Benefit Analysis of Gain of Function Research Final Report*. Takoma Park, MD: Gryphon Scientific, LLC.

Helm, P. (2015). Risk, Resilience: Strategies for Security. *Civil Engineering and Environmental Systems, 32*(1–2), 100–117.

Koblentz, G. (2009). *Living Weapons*. New York: Cornell University Press.

Koblentz, G. (2012). From Biodefence to Biosecurity: The Obama Administration's Strategy for Countering Biological Threats. *International Affairs, 88*(1), 131–148.

McConnell, J. (2008). *Annual Threat Assessment of DNI for the Senate Select Committee on Intelligence*. Washington, DC: ODNI.

NIC. (2002). *Iraq's Continuing Programs for Weapons of Mass Destruction: Key Judgments*. Washington, DC. From http://nsarchive.gwu.edu/NSAEBB/NSAEBB129/nie.pdf. Accessed March 15, 2017.

Obama, B. (2010). *National Security Strategy*. Washington, DC: The White House.

Silberman, L., & Robb, C. (2005). *Commission on the Intelligence Capabilities of the US Regarding Weapons of Mass Destruction. Report to the President of the United States* (pp. 1–501). Washington, DC.

Stern, J. (2002). Dreaded Risks and Control of Biological Weapons. *International Security, 27*(3), 89–123.

Vogel, K. (2013). *Phantom Menace or Looming Danger?* Baltimore, MD: The Johns Hopkins University Press.

Walsh, P. F. (2015). Building Better Intelligence Frameworks Through Effective Governance. *International Journal of Intelligence and Counterintelligence, 28*(1), 123–142. https://doi.org/10.1080/08850607.2014.924816.

4

Collection

Chapter 3 showed the importance of effective tasking and coordination processes for steering our intelligence communities towards priority biosecurity threats and risks—or at the very least those that decision-makers are most interested in. Chapter 3 also highlighted that tasking and coordination processes against any threat and risk—regardless of whether they are biosecurity or those emanating from organised crime, terrorism or WMD proliferation are complex and multi-layered.

For example, we have seen since 9/11 in particular, many trans-national threats, such as terrorism often have global, regional, national and local manifestations. The ability for the law enforcement and intelligence communities to respond effectively to such diverse aspects of transnational threats, makes it difficult for them to be aware in all cases who are the decision-makers and what their specific interests are. The complexity of both transnational and even domestic security threats means therefore, that it is not just the political leadership or cabinet of a 'Five Eyes' country doing the 'tasking'. In reality, there are a number of other international, regional, national and local actors, who may be either directly or indirectly tasking national intelligence communities. Beyond the central political leadership, for example, a chief of police

© The Author(s) 2018
P. F. Walsh, *Intelligence, Biosecurity and Bioterrorism*,
https://doi.org/10.1057/978-1-137-51700-5_4

of a major metropolitan law enforcement agency has their own particular tasking requirements, particularly if they are supplying operational resources to a complex multi-agency investigation of the kind we see in terrorism. The chief may not want to read a high level strategic assessment of the changing dynamics of global terrorism, but they would be keen to know how many terrorists plots are unfolding in their jurisdiction and what their potential targets might be. Similarly, the local water company may be interested in knowing from the metropolitan police whether they assess any vulnerabilities, risks and threats to their operation from terrorists. Given decision-makers have different tasking interests at strategic, operational and tactical levels, collection strategies and preferences will differ depending on what is being tasked. Collection strategies against a rogue transnational terrorist group determined to weaponise anthrax will likely be different to an unhinged individual seeking to purchase ricin online to poison their next door neighbour. The former *may* involve SIGINT and imagery, while the later could involve interception of telecommunications/email and physical surveillance. I say *may* in the case of trying to collect SIGINT and imagery against a terrorist group because unless additional sources (e.g. HUMINT) have found premises or people involved in weaponising anthrax, it may be near impossible to locate their communications or physical location. Unlike, the Cold War era where state based bio-weapons programs were conducted in large facilities, terrorists groups may not require large physical infrastructure to mass produce anthrax. A scaled down approach in a small building or even covertly being produced in a legitimate government laboratory within a fragile state makes the application of technical collection platforms such as SIGINT and imagery more difficult and costly compared to using these assets against state based concerns such as Russia, China and North Korea.

So with more complex threats/risks a combination of different collection methods used at the same time will likely bring better results than just relying on one collection method. Adding to the above complexity is of course that budgets and competing collection requirements limit how expensive national assets such as SIGINT and imagery are tasked.

In summary, the complexity of threats/risks and the diversity of inter-ested decision-makers makes it next to impossible for the national intelli-gence community to author a one size fits all collection list for all manner of actual or potential bio-threats and risks. So while officially collection priorities may be articulated by a national government, the granularity of what various decision-makers require at both different threats/risks and level of decision-making (tactical, operational and strategic) will be largely context driven. From one perspective, you could argue that this reality may promote efficiency as decision-makers only get the collec-tion effort they need to mitigate against risks and threats at *their level* rather than needing information directly derived from expensive collec-tion assets such as SIGINT or HUMINT. Though the reality is less clear cut and decision-makers at a local level in some circumstances may still need or benefit from national intelligence collection assets to support decisions being made. Articulating collection priorities against different threats/risks and at varying levels of decision-making (tactical, opera-tional or strategic) is therefore a messy business. Effective intelligence col-lection, therefore, is always a work in progress and relies on many factors including strong leadership amongst relevant stakeholders and decision-makers—particularly high levels of intelligence governance.

With intelligence collection, there are not only technical and organ-isational issues related to each collection platform, but also broader governance issues impact on how efficiently collection occurs within and across agencies in an intelligence community. Additionally, there are also questions about how integrated collection is and the extent to which intelligence collected is shared across an entire community. Such collection issues also relate to how effective intelligence governance is across intelligence agencies and communities. This concept, 'intelligence governance' will be discussed in more detail in Chapter 6, but I define it as a 'set of attributes such as strong sustainable leadership, doctrine design, evaluation, effective coordination, cooperation and integration of intelligence processes' (Walsh 2011: 149).

Accordingly, this chapter focuses on the complexities and difficulties surrounding effective intelligence collection in specific collection plat-forms that might be allocated to bio-threats and risks. In particular, the chapter has three objectives. First it will discuss how the traditional collection methods (e.g. SIGINT, HUMINT and GEOINT) may be applied to bio-threats and risks by national security and law enforcement agencies. This discussion will include a brief evaluation of the strengths and weaknesses of each method.

Second, the chapter will focus on 'non-national security' collection methodologies such as those employed by the scientific, medical and research communities, which are primarily used by health authorities to both treat, track and even 'predict' epidemiologically epidemics and pandemics. There are a growing number of health and bio-surveillance collection platforms, which are also useful sources of intelligence for national security and law enforcement agencies. These platforms like 'traditional collection platforms' also have their challenges and limitations for our understanding of various bio-threats and risks.

Thirdly and finally, the chapter will summarise common collection challenges across both traditional collection methods and scientific, medical and research community methods. Discussion will also identify some factors analysts need to keep in mind in order to improve collection outcomes particularly across the 'Five Eyes' countries.

Traditional Collection Methods

Signals Intelligence (SIGINT)

Signals intelligence (SIGINT) is over a one hundred year old technological development. Early developments occurred with the arrival of radio and the ability of countries (initially the UK and US) to intercept signals from the air. Further technological developments in World War II enabled the UK to intercept and decrypt German naval codes at Bletchley Park allowing allies to more quickly locate German U Boats in the Atlantic. Today SIGINT can be collected using a wide variety of platforms (e.g. planes, ships, satellites and ground stations). The largest SIGINT collector is the US National Security Agency (NSA), and its collection efforts are shared with other 'Five Eyes' partners: Australia, Canada, New Zealand and the UK. In return these partners share their own SIGINT through their respective agencies: Australian Signals Directorate (ASD), Communications Security Establishment (CSE), Government Communications Headquarters (GCHQ) and Government Communications Security Bureau (GCSB).

SIGINT is a broader term for a number of different types of intercepts. Communications interception (COMINT) between at least two people is what most people commonly think of as SIGINT. However, there is also telemetry intelligence (TELINT) and electronic intelligence (ELINT). TELINT relates to the interception of data produced by weapons systems and ELINT refers to picking up electronic emissions made from weapons and tracking systems. The latter is useful in 'assessing the range and frequencies on which such systems operate' (Lowenthal 2012: 96). A clear advantage of SIGINT, particularly COMINT, is the ability to gain direct insight on what an adversary is saying, which obviously provides potentially an idea of their intentions. Such knowledge is critical in monitoring military communications, but it is not just what is said but the way it is said. Modern SIGINT is increasingly about understanding the different codes used in conversation particularly those used by terrorist groups that may indicate operational planning. An important part of SIGINT is also geo-locating the communications in order to target the sender and receiver of the communications.

COMINT like all other collection platforms has disadvantages. Satellite or ground interception of telecommunications relies on open systems, though increasingly since the 1990s with the digital revolution there has been an increased ability by both state and non-state actors to encrypt their communications. For example, the US intelligence community became aware after a leak via the Washington Post of how the NSA was intercepting Bin Laden's satellite phone the Al Qaeda leader stopped using it and relied on less visible subordinates to communicate his orders (9/11 Commission Report 2004: 127).

After 9/11, the sheer volume of telecommunications data (phone, email and increasingly social media) and the fluidity of global terrorism threats required a new kind of SIGINT. A new generation of SIGINT was needed to capture communications between terrorist plotters, who may be communicating between each other overseas, communicating offshore but to a citizen of a 'Five Eyes' country—or the ability to intercept foreign communications traversing for example the US as they were being carried by a US based telecommunications company. Terrorist groups were simply no longer using one form of communication that applying for a warrant to intercept would allow the NSA to intercept. As a result, the early years of the Bush Administration with its desire to prevent a similar attack to 9/11 on American soil again resulted in a greater focus on proactive intelligence collection, including shortly after 9/11 the launch of the NSA metadata program (Stellarwind). Stellarwind was initially a warrantless surveillance and bulk data collection program designed to capture the communications of suspected Al Qaeda and other terrorists from overseas, transiting the US or with those communications by US citizens to suspected terrorists. A separate program called PRISM went operational in 2007 and is discussed below.

Metadata is data that is disassociated from the identities of its subjects but nonetheless contains sufficient basic information (e.g. telephone numbers, time of call, location of call and duration of call) that can help national security and law enforcement intelligence agencies infer links between persons of concern in criminal or terrorist activities. The developments in data mining and analytics techniques and technologies post 9/11 have resulted in the more efficient, speedier interception of telephones and other types of communications and the ability to link or associate various methods of electronic communications for the purpose of intelligence surveillance. This increased focus on data mining and analytics technologies to 'discover knowledge' from disparate data sources was going on across the 'Five Eyes' intelligence communities at the same time non-state threat actors such as terrorists were using multiple and more secure ways to communicate than telephone (Walsh and Miller 2016: 353–354). Initially Stellarwind was initiated every 42 days under direct presidential authorization rather than law and was based on threat assessments prepared by the US intelligence community that demonstrated 'a reasonable basis to conclude that one party to the communication is a member of Al Qaeda, affiliated with Al Qaeda or a member of an organisation affiliated with Al Qaeda' (Inspectors General of DOD et al. 2009: 6). In 2005, the existence of Stellarwind was leaked by the *New York Times* and this put some pressure on the Bush Administration and Congress to put the program on more firm legal footing (Risen and Lichtblau 2005). The program was 'legalised' in 2007 by its inclusion in the following acts: Protect America Act (2007), the FISA Amendments Act (2008) and some of its aspects were also included in Section 215 of the Patriot Act.

NSA's Prism program allowed the agency to access the contents of a large amount of digital information including emails, Facebook and instant messaging. The inner workings of both the metadata and PRISM programs were exposed by NSA contractor Edward Snowden in 2013. His leaking to the media of the ways both programs worked in detail arguably remains the most significant exposure of sensitive intelligence collection methodologies in the post-Cold War era. Snowden and his supporters believed that their exposure to the public was warranted on legal and constitutional grounds as they were an affront to US (and other citizens) rights to privacy. In return senior officials in the US and other 'Five Eyes' intelligence communities argued that these programs were necessary and had prevented terrorist attacks. Many in the US government also believed their exposure only provided further knowledge of sensitive collection platforms enabling terrorists to find even more encrypted telecommunications to plan their operations thereby making it harder for national security and law enforcement intelligence agencies to detect, prevent or disrupt their plans. The impact of the Snowden leaks are in many ways still being felt across the intelligence agencies of western liberal democracies. Former Director of the NSA and CIA, Michael Hayden characterised the leaks as 'the greatest haemorrhaging of legitimate American secrets in history of the republic' (Hayden 2016: 421). While it is difficult to truly gauge their impact on the operational activities of intelligence agencies working against terrorists and other threat actors, the leaks have undeniably made some actors much harder targets, particularly with their increased use of more sophisticated encrypted devices.

There remains an ongoing concern now of threat actor's communications 'going dark' either through exploiting encrypted devices or using the 'dark web', which is a smaller part of the internet that is hard to access without the use of special browsers like the Onion Router—Tor and passwords (Chertoff 2017). Both measures obviously make it harder for law enforcement and intelligence agencies to intercept their communications. This is not helped by major global telecommunications, internet and social media companies (Google, Facebook, Microsoft and Yahoo) taking a less cooperative stance since Snowden to national security and law enforcement agencies in designing or enabling their systems in ways that will allow these agencies to exploit communications from suspected terrorist's phones and computers. Though there are now real concerns about the ability to intercept new telecommunications devices, the Snowden leaks, however unfortunate, did force a debate about the role of surveillance/secrecy vs. privacy/transparency in liberal democracies. These debates while interesting are beyond the scope of this chapter. For further discussion on the legal, ethical and constitutional issues surrounding modern SIGINT collection (see for example Walsh and Miller 2016, Johnson et al. 2014.) We will also come back to debates about intelligence, privacy, transparency and accountability in Chapter 8.

Putting aside the above debate, another problem with SIGINT has always been as technology has improved a lot more information has become available than can be processed and exploited. As Lowenthal (2012: 75) suggests a processing and exploitation imbalance has developed between what is collected and what can be processed and exploited. This imbalance became more challenging after 9/11 with the increased focus on actively targeting counter-terrorism communications and the tactical and operational demands of the US led invasion of Iraq. Given there is more information collected that can be processed, additional investment by SIGINT agencies was made in larger computers that could filter for key words or phrases that might indicate the potential value of one intercept over another.

Another ongoing problem with processing SIGINT particularly post 9/11, was not having enough language translators that could translate the large volume of foreign communications in Arabic, Urdu or Pashto coming into the NSA and other 'Five Eyes' SIGINT agencies. SIGINT translation is not just a matter of merely translating from a foreign language to English and having an immediate understanding of the communication between two or more individuals. Translators need to also understand the culture, context of the communications and whether individuals are using code words—all of which are challenges when there are large volumes of unprocessed information being collected in real time.

The final challenge with SIGINT collection relates to counterintelligence. Counterintelligence literally means countering the intelligence efforts of (normally) adversarial foreign state powers, non-state actors (terrorists, organised crime groups) and other issue motivated individuals. Fuller discussions on counterintelligence can be found in Redmond (2015: 305–316), Van Cleave (2007), and Sims and Gerber (2009). The kinds of intelligence operations adversaries can launch against one or more of the 'Five Eyes' intelligence partners can be to collect political, military and economic information to put them at an advantage over that targeted country. Counterintelligence is normally thought of in two dimensions: defensive and offensive. Defensive counterintelligence are activities that a state deploys to protect their information systems against penetration. Offensive counterintelligence in contrast, involves the state conducting proactive intelligence operations of its own against a foreign power or non-state actor to prevent, disrupt or degrade their ability to collect intelligence from the state by going on the offensive. With the later, a key objective is both denial and deception of any interference in a foreign power's intelligence or broader national activities. Counterintelligence historically has involved 'catching spies' through various espionage activities against a hostile intelligence service or by law enforcement investigations. So it clearly has a human intelligence HUMINT element to it which will be discussed shortly.

The rise of digital technology and cyber since the Cold War increasingly shows how modern SIGINT collection has also facilitated and yet also become challenged by counterintelligence activities of intelligence services of hostile countries (e.g. Russia and China), non-state actors (terrorists and organised criminals) and leaker groups or individuals like Wikileaks and Snowden. The relative anonymity and rapid movement of communication signals and data around the world makes the cyber space a difficult new frontier in which to consistently and accurately attribute or defend against counterintelligence operations by hostile powers. A more aggressive, offensive counterintelligence role by some states is on the rise and became clear during the 2016 US Presidential election with Russian hacking into the server of the US Democratic Party's National Convention communications and the probable sharing of this material with Wikileaks. Members of the US intelligence community have reported that the Putin Government was motivated to sway the election away from Democratic candidate Hillary Clinton and is but one of many examples of Russian denial and deception efforts against the US (Lee 2017).

Human Intelligence (HUMINT)

As the name suggest HUMINT is intelligence collected by humans. Some intelligence scholars are fond of saying that HUMINT is the world's second oldest profession and others no doubt would say the oldest profession (prostitution) has more morals. HUMINT is conducted by an intelligence agency using a variety of methods: diplomatic liaison (declared vs. undeclared), covert action, espionage and counterintelligence. There are several good introductory sources on HUMINT for the uninitiated. Mark Lowenthal's *Intelligence From Secrets to Policy* provides a short yet comprehensive treatment of the subject (Lowenthal 2012: 102–110). Other useful sources are (Hitz in Johnson and Wirtz 2015; Gill and Phythian 2012: 81–91). For an interesting personal reflection on working in the CIA's National Clandestine Service (the HUMINT section of the US Intelligence Community) see, Henry A. Crumpton's *The Art of Intelligence: Lessons from a Life in the CIA's Clandestine Service* (Crumpton 2012).

The general public often focus on the foreign intelligence collection aspects of HUMINT—no doubt in part because of the influence of popular culture and its healthy genre of espionage movies, including the James Bond character and series. It is true that HUMINT can be dominated by the foreign intelligence collection space when one thinks of large foreign intelligence collection (HUMINT) enterprises run in 'Five Eyes' countries such as: the CIA (US), MI6 (UK) or the Australian Secret Intelligence Service (ASIS) in Australia. However, HUMINT is also a major function of domestic security intelligence agencies (e.g. UK's MI5, Australia's ASIO or Canada's CSIS). It is also an important function of national and specialised agencies that have more of a law enforcement function, for example, the Australian Federal Police (AFP) or the FBI.

The brief discussion here of HUMINT activities and methods therefore seeks to consider how this collection 'INT' is used across both the foreign and domestic contexts. The most common HUMINT activity is recruiting an individual close to a target, group or organisation, who can then pass on information about that target, group or organisation's intentions. In other words, the HUMINT officer (sometimes referred to as a case officer) recruits an individual, who can carry out espionage to obtain privileged information not normally available or being concealed by the source. The HUMINT case officer during the recruitment process makes an assessment on the susceptibility of the potential recruit to provide reliable sensitive information on the target, group or organisation's intentions and activities. This assessment naturally includes a determination of what motivation is driving the recruit's preparedness to spy for the foreign intelligence service. Common motivations include money, ego, ideology or that the recruit has some kind of vendetta (e.g. revenge) against the target. Obviously, recruiting someone close to a terrorist or organised crime group that has first-hand knowledge of their activities can provide indispensable knowledge not always available using SIGINT or GEOINT alone. For example, employing a senior ministerial advisor, who has very close access to cabinet level documents and meetings as an agent may provide detailed knowledge of how the political leadership intends to act that is not always available in SIGINT or GEOINT. In other circumstances, recruiting an agent can help confirm or deny the reliability and validity of information collected via SIGINT or GEOINT.

If we look at HUMINT case officers—the kind that the CIA would deploy globally they are usually declared or non-declared officers. Declared CIA officers are usually attached to the US Embassy and depending on the country they are deployed in, may be openly known by the host country's intelligence community as a CIA station officer such as would be the case in other 'Five Eyes' countries. Alternatively, an undeclared officer may or may not be officially have diplomatic status in the deployed country. They may have the cover of a diplomatic title such as 'First Secretary', or they can operate completely isolated from their country's embassy and therefore from diplomatic protection as under-cover agents. In the US, this later HUMINT collection officer is referred to as non-official cover though in other countries the term 'assumed identity' is used. In the non-official cover/assumed identity case, the officer involved is provided with a cover (including new name, passport/identity papers, employment) that allows them to carry out counterintelligence, surveillance, liaison and target exploitation without the target, group, organisation or state being aware that they are a foreign intelligence officer. A variation on non-official/assumed identity roles are sleeper agents.

Another important HUMINT role is covert action. HUMINT focused agencies such as the CIA and the UK's MI6 have long used personnel to influence the political, economic or military conditions in other states. For example, during the Cold War a primary driver for covert action was to counter the spread of communism in developing nations. Nations targeted by the CIA included Iran (1953), Guatemala (1954), Angola (1975), and Chile (1964–1972) (Johnson 2017: 85). An important facet of covert action during the Cold War—right up to the present post 9/11 period is paramilitary covert action, where CIA covert operatives work either secretly alongside US military forces or on their own in targeted military operations. Such paramilitary operations have had their mix of success if you think back to the failed Bay of Pigs (Cuba) episode in 1961, which was a CIA plan to train secretly Cuban exiles to land on Cuba to overthrow the Castro regime. The CIA sponsored Cuban plan was adopted by President Kennedy though 'put into practice half-heartedly in an indefensible location at the Bay of Pigs—abruptly ending a run of success by the CIA in covert action at this time' (Hitz in Johnson and Wirtz 2015: 109). But more recently, paramilitary covert action combining the efforts of intelligence operatives and military personnel have been used aggressively by the Bush and Obama Administrations to track down high value terrorist targets in Afghanistan, Pakistan, Iraq, Libya and Yemen. The 2011 killing of Osama Bin Laden in Pakistan by US Navy SEALS is obviously a recent and historic example of paramilitary covert action that involved special military forces and intelligence operatives and analysts from the CIA. Of course covert action can occur in the domestic intelligence context as well—albeit on a less grand scale than political assassination or trying to overturn the government of a foreign power. Domestic law enforcement and security services such as the AFP and ASIO in Australia or the Metropolitan Police and MI5 in the UK are also involved in covert HUMINT collection. This could take the form of physical or technical surveillance and could also involve covert entry into a target's (suspected terrorist or organised crime figure) location to search for information (digital or hard copy), or the installation of listening devices and cameras.

The gains from HUMINT can be potentially great, particularly when the target is less penetrable to other collection methods such as SIGINT or GEOINT. As noted earlier in the SIGINT discussion, non-state actor targets such as terrorists and organised crime groups are increasingly using encrypted communications making it more difficult for intelligence and law enforcement agencies to gain insights into their activities. The successful cultivation of a HUMINT source within a terrorist cell or a drug dealing syndicate can help fill intelligence gaps about the target's intentions and activities. Similarly covert action involves many HUMINT collection activities that can provide great decision-making advantage to its government in revealing privileged information not accessible any other way—or the manipulation of threat actors environment on the ground in a way that is advantageous to the security interest of the government. In particular, a common principle operating in all HUMINT collection, particularly non-official cover and covert action is plausible deniability. This means that the government sponsoring the HUMINT collection using third parties, assumed identities or covert military action can deny they are directly responsible for or have knowledge of such activities. Naturally plausible deniability is not applicable in all HUMINT collection and in others a foreign power or target may eventually find out that a clandestine intelligence service is involved in their country or organisation.

There are of course disadvantages in using HUMINT collection. One relates to operational tempo. Whereas SIGINT and GEOINT collection platforms can be relatively quickly applied against a new or evolving threat, HUMINT is less flexible due to the time it normally takes to recruit a source or the extensive planning involved in covert action. Think about how long it might take for an under-cover source to be trusted/accepted into a terrorist cell if at all. Given the longer time frame involved in validating and recruiting a source they are also likely to be able to report on a smaller number of intelligence requirements (albeit in greater depth) than technical collection platforms (SIGINT and GEOINT) that can be applied against a broader range of intelligence requirements.

HUMINT collection is also a high risk endeavour where the 'spy' you have recruited, the non-declared clandestine officer or covert force can be detected by the target individual, organisation or state. This could result in the clandestine officer at best being made 'persona non grata' and being removed from the host country, or at worse imprisonment or loss of life for paramilitary covert action personnel. Another challenge, not easily overcome is the validation of HUMINT sources. As will be discussed in Chapter 5, validation of collection sources impacts on the kind of analytical judgments analysts are able to make. HUMINT recruiters are often dealing with potential sources, who have complex motivations with their own hidden agendas. In many cases, recruited sources operating on the periphery of an organised crime or terrorist group will not themselves be the bastion of human goodness.

They can be highly deceptive themselves and deliver false information to their case officer or may be working as a double agent for a foreign intelligence service or target. On the former point, much has been written on the role of 'Curveball' (Rafid Ahmed Alwan al-Janabi) an Iraqi citizen, who arrived in Germany in 1999 seeking asylum. Alwan claimed to the German intelligence agency Bundesnachrichtendienst (BND) that he had worked in the design and running of Saddam Hussein's mobile bioweapons laboratories. The BND later forwarded interrogation reports on Alwan to the DIA, who sent them to the CIA. Alwan was given the code name 'Curveball' and became a primary HUMINT source for the CIA's assessments on Iraq's bioweapons program including the well-known 2002 NIE (National Intelligence Estimate) assessment that Baghdad had transportable facilities (Vogel 2013: 132–147). Curveball's information later proved to be false. Similarly, on the latter example a (double agent), Jordanian Humam Khalil Mohammed originally recruited by the Jordanian intelligence agency (General Intelligence Directorate) blew himself up at a meeting at the CIA's forward operating Base Chapman in Khost (Afghanistan) killing 7 CIA intelligence officers (Oppel et al. 2010). Humam had both the CIA and Jordanians fooled and was actually working for Al Qaeda.

Finally, there are a number of ethical issues involved in HUMINT collection. After all, it involves both deception and stealing information from a source without their knowledge. Recruiting agents, who may themselves be involved in criminal activity clearly presents ethical and legal issues. Additionally since 9/11, HUMINT collection agencies in 'Five Eyes' countries, particularly the CIA and under the Bush Administration has relied on ethically and legally problematic extreme HUMINT collection methods such as coercive interrogation (or torture) to extract information from captured terrorists. It was shown too through a US Senate Select Committee on Intelligence inquiry that coercive interrogation was increasingly out-sourced to contracted third party US companies (SSCI 2014). Additionally, captured terrorists were renditioned to black site locations in Egypt, Syria and Afghanistan, where interrogation sessions were carried out by the local intelligence services—with little or no oversight from the US (Walsh 2011: 195–204). Since the excesses of some of these coercive interrogation became more publicly known 'Five Eyes' intelligence agencies have placed a greater emphasis on knowing the provenance of the intelligence i.e. where and how it was collected (Walsh 2011).

Geospatial Intelligence (GEOINT)

Imagery or IMINT or more recently as it has been referred to as Geospatial intelligence (GEOINT) is the taking of photos by a range of methods include reconnaissance airplanes like the classic U-2 plane that famously took photos of Russian missiles in Cuba during the Cuban Missile Crisis of 1962. GEOINT also includes photos taken by satellites revolving around the Earth, which are sent digitally to ground stations that can then feed them to decision-makers. Increasingly too GEOINT also includes unmanned aerial vehicles (UAVs) or drones such as the Global Hawk, the Predator and the Reaper that have become critical in post 9/11 counter-terrorism operations in Afghanistan, Iraq, Syria and Yemen. The improved resolution of GEOINT sources such as satellites and drones can provide decision-makers compelling and in some cases irrefutable evidence of impending threats. Drones became increasingly used by the Bush and Obama Administrations in providing surveillance intelligence and reconnaissance for counter-terrorism operations in hostile terrains in Iraq, Yemen, Afghanistan and Syria. Drones can get in closer to targets instead of satellites making high altitude orbits. Additionally, drones have been used increasingly in covert para-military operations to destroy high value terrorist targets (Walsh 2017: 411–440; Johnson 2017). The benefits of GEOINT are many. First it can provide a decision-maker with an almost immediate understanding of a potential threat or risk. Pictures are more easily interpreted by decision-makers over intelligence assessments where words can be open for multiple interpretations. GEOINT is also useful as many threat actors operate routinely out in the open where satellites and drones can detect easily their activity. For example, military exercises where large numbers of troops, tanks and naval vessels are highly visible can easily be detected by GEOINT. By extension, GEOINT has also been useful historically in providing clear unambiguous information to the international community about dangerous WMD proliferation. As mentioned, during the Cuban Missile crisis the US Ambassador to the UN, Adlai Stevenson was able to get onside other Western powers by 'laying on the table clear U-2 photos of Russian missiles in Cuba' (Johnson and Wirtz 2015: 77). But there are some clear limitations of GEOINT, particularly satellite imagery when the target is smaller (i.e. a group of terrorists), who do not necessarily have extensive physical infrastructures that can be captured in the same way as a large military installation. Deception too is another challenge when collecting satellite imagery. Many state based threats and established terrorists groups such as Al Qaeda are aware of satellites orbiting above and take measures to either camouflage or even create fake sites to prevent timely and accurate GEOINT collection. In April 2017, a good example of a state's awareness of regular satellite

GEOINT collection and efforts at deception (perhaps even some mischief) was evident from imagery of the command centre of North Korea's nuclear test site located at Punggye-ri, where workers were seen playing volley ball (McGurry 2017) in the midst of expectations by the west that another nuclear test was imminent from Kim Jong Un regime. Another disadvantage of satellite imagery is that it represents one picture in time and does not reveal over time how a threat is evolving or indeed how rapidly.

Some of the disadvantages of satellite (GEOINT) have been overcome by the increased capability and use of the use of pilotless drones (UAVs). In contrast to satellites, as noted earlier, UAVs are able to fly close over the target and stay for longer periods than an orbiting satellite. Second given they are unmanned and operated remotely they remove the danger of exposing a piloted plane extracting imagery over a hostile site. Third, UAVs provide real time streaming (high definition video images) that can be exploited immediately for intelligence collection and many carry missiles (e.g. hell fire) that have increasingly been used in counter-terrorism operations in Libya, Syria, Afghanistan and Yemen.

Open Source, Scientific, Medical and Research Collection Platforms

Open Source Intelligence

In this next section, we shift discussion away from 'covert' or 'closed' collection methods to open source intelligence, before concluding with an assessment on the challenges of applying collection platforms against the 'bio-threat' space. Open source intelligence (OSINT) is clearly information that is openly available. The list of sources are diverse and almost endless. OSINT can be retrieved from the media (newspapers, radio, TV), government reports, academics/researchers and social media. OSINT is not a new 'invention' and has been an important intelligence source for all the 'Five Eyes' countries during World

War II, the Cold War through to present post 9/11 period (Bean 2007: 240–257). Although there has been lingering bias in many intelligence agencies that covert or secret sources are superior to OSINT, it's clear that the latter has in many circumstances provided much needed knowledge and context about threats and risks in addition to providing contestability of the validity and reliability of information provided from closed (classified) sources. For example, Mercado argues that OSINT 'constituted a major part of all intelligence gathered on the Soviet Union, China and other adversaries' (Mercado 2014: 121). He gives the example of the Foreign Broadcast Information Service, which monitored radio services of foreign powers along with the Foreign Document Division. Both were led by the CIA as being instrumental in detecting signs of the Sino-Soviet split from reading propaganda material from both country during the 1950s. This was in contrast to some analysts working with classified sources, who mistakenly believed the OSINT was disinformation for several years (ibid.).

The development of the internet, the digital revolution and now the developments in social media have particularly since the 1990s resulted an even larger and diverse volume of information—much of it available in real time for everyone including our intelligence agencies to use in their analysis of a multitude of threats. As information communication platforms and sources became more available in the public domain, once sensitive collection methods such as GEOINT and aspects of HUMINT and SIGINT, have also become more widely used by the private sector and the community for non-military or intelligence purposes. For example, companies can use commercially available satellites for agriculture and weather.

Leaving aside the potential utility of other OSINT sources such as research reports, over the last decade, it is the escalation in the development and use of social media particularly in western countries that has captured the interest of many intelligence agencies. As the use of fixed line telephone communication by the international community reduces, other social media platforms have become increasingly exploited by people for both legitimate and more nefarious purposes. Estimates suggest for example, that in Facebook 250 million photos are added per day as are 200 million tweets on Twitter (Omand et al. 2012: 802). It is clear then that both law enforcement and national security agencies are now increasingly relying on communications from a multitude of social media platforms for increased situational awareness of current events and covert intervention of platforms, where criminal intent is suspect and the goal is to collect social media communications to prevent, disrupt or prosecute offenders.

Omand et al. (2012: 806) provides a useful summary of some of the obvious uses and advantages of social media for intelligence collectors. First, the constant tweeting, messaging, photos generated by the public via various social media platforms provides contextual and situational awareness of events generated by the crowd. Accordingly, social media has been very useful for intelligence agencies in recording natural disasters, conflict, pandemics and the activities and propaganda of global terrorists groups such Al Qaeda and Islamic State. In some respects, the masses using their social media to record and communicate about events has made them either 'freelance journalists' or 'citizen intelligence collectors' benefiting intelligence agencies, that may not have their own collection assets on the ground or in the air. Second, Omand et al. refer to the benefit social media provides for not just capturing a single event, but for more in-depth understanding of a complex phenomenon such as radicalisation (ibid.: 805). Thirdly, social media is a very useful intelligence source as it can provide 'real time situational awareness' (ibid.). For example, the political upheaval in North Africa and Middle East in 2011–2012 was facilitated in part by protestors using Twitter and Facebook. Although in this case, the US intelligence community was struggling to make sense of the increasing volume of social media feeds (Rovner 2013), most 'Five Eyes' intelligence communities have developed more sophisticated monitoring platforms, which can monitor and cluster several social media feeds as well as geo-locate these to various indicators such as violence or unrest. Such systems are not yet at the stage, where they can necessarily 'predict' the next Arab Spring, rather they can track crowd sentiment to various locations that *may suggest* an adverse event might occur. Sentiment analysis in this context frequently relies on an algorithm that looks for certain words or properties in a text that can be considered to correlated statistically with an emotion or 'sentiment'.

The data analytics technology that allows the generation of sentiment analysis was originally developed in the private sector by advertising or large companies looking for a competitive edge over other companies. They relied on a general understanding of consumer preferences and attitudes rather than a deeper knowledge of their motivations and behaviours and the risk these posed—the later kind of information being more important in the intelligence context. While improvements are being made in 'Five Eyes' intelligence communities' ability to develop more sophisticated sentiment analysis, the information still needs validating against other collection sources. While disinformation and deception has historically always been part of modern intelligence practice (Hulnick 2002), we have seen more recently in global politics—particularly in the US with the rise of the Trump presidency in 2016—a rise of non-factual social media by both the Administration, but also in the community. This development raises challenges for intelligence analysts seeking to validate such information. Additionally, while there is likely to be further development in social media analytics such technology only represents part of the solution for both improved collection and analysis of evolving threats and risks. Relying solely on the results generated from algorithms for texts or 'behaviours' that may be of interest to intelligence requires a broader understanding of the socio-cultural context of the social media communications and how that influences what is considered meaningful or perhaps even deceptive. From a methodological perspective therefore, there remains both technological and organisational barriers in most 'Five Eyes' intelligence communities to fully exploiting the increasing volumes of social media in ways that can consistently reveal patterns of risk in real time (Walsh 2011; Bean 2007). There is also still a lack of understanding of how various threat groups even those we know more about such as Islamic State use social media platforms, tactically, operationally and strategically.

Finally, social media collection is an important source where law enforcement and intelligence agencies require interception of its related communications, which are not publicly available or may have been encrypted yet where there is reasonable cause to suggest such communication are being used for criminal intent. Interception of social media communications in this context is for preventative, disruptive or prosecution purposes and usually requires a warrant for access. While a great deal of social media can be considered to be in the 'public space', its use by law enforcement and intelligence agencies does provide some ethical dilemmas around privacy. Given the public nature of social media its users cannot expect the high levels of privacy afforded by email or phone data. Nonetheless social media users have not explicitly or implicitly consented to interception/collection by persons 'outside the social group in question and for security purposes' (Walsh and Miller 2016: 355–356). Individuals may be more guarded if they knew their communications were being accessed for law enforcement or intelligence collection purposes. This issue of social media and expectations of privacy obviously differs in other circumstances such as when there is 'reasonable suspicion of unlawful and immoral activity of a serious nature' (ibid.).

Scientific, Medical and Research Collection

The last section provided an overview of how OSINT methodologies have been applied in the law enforcement and national security intelligence contexts. In this last section, I briefly introduce how disciplines from the scientific, medical and research communities can also provide a wealth of OSINT relevant to understanding both current and emerging bio-threats and risks. It is impossible to provide a detailed description of all scientific sources of OSINT that may be of interest to law enforcement and the national security and intelligence communities. Instead, this section will first discuss in a broad sense the kind of role the scientific community can play in being a source of a range of OSINT. Second and thirdly, it will discuss two disciplines (epidemiology and forensics) and their role in providing law enforcement and intelligence agencies with relevant OSINT. Two caveats are needed prior to further discussion. First as mentioned earlier, this section will provide a brief overview of a select few OSINT sources that may be derived from the scientific community. Further sources and examples will be discussed in Chapter 7 in the context of areas of expertise different types of scientific stakeholders can bring to each 'Five Eyes' intelligence community. Second, while a lot of information generated by the scientific community may be openly available via peer reviewed sources or attending conferences, not all scientifically derived information is OSINT. Clearly, a great deal of scientific research underway may have restricted access due to funding, ethical, legislative or intellectual property reasons. Information from public health authorities and the ability to share it beyond clinicians may also have privacy, legal and ethical restrictions in place thereby not making it OSINT in the narrowest definition of the term.

The Scientific Community

In private and public sector research laboratories, companies and universities the scientific community is working on a range of biological agents for medical, health, defence and broader biotechnological applications. Such activity, as noted in Chapter 2 includes work in high containment labs and on dual use research such as gain of function (GOF) research, where for example, the development of a highly contagious virulent strains of influenza in recent years has raised controversy given the concerns that while such research may present options for the development of more robust vaccinations they also post significant biosecurity risks. So it is clear that law enforcement agencies and intelligence agencies need to engage with this very broad scientific community for their expertise (e.g. molecular biology, virology, microbiology, public or animal health) on the who, what, where and how of bio-threats and risks.

The scientific community will have expert knowledge on biological agents that may provide potentially more risk in certain contexts. They will have useful and evidenced based insights that law enforcement and intelligence agencies can collect about analysing the risks for example, of accidental (biosafety) incidents vs. those related to biosecurity, where there may be intentional misuse of information from research by threat actors (criminals, terrorists). For example, since 9/11 many scientists have been working on improving bio-sensors that use a variety of techniques to detect dangerous pathogens in cities such as cultures, polymerase chain reaction and immunoassays (Kim et al. 2015). Scientists working closely with colleagues in particularly sensitive work environments such as high containment labs, will also have intimate knowledge in some circumstances of potential threat actors working amongst them. Co-workers are likely to have some knowledge of colleagues, who appear emotionally disturbed, have become recently overly religious (radicalised), politicised, or might be spending unexpected amounts of time with select biological agents or reviewing associated IP files. Such behaviours may indicate an 'insider' threat actor's intention to steal biological material or related IP. This kind of insider information would not be immediately available to law enforcement or intelligence agencies and the ability for a concerned scientist to report it clearly becomes an important collection source. Of course this is not to suggest that law enforcement or intelligence agencies would be looking to turn scientists working in high containment labs into spies. It is understandably unlikely that most scientists would ever desire such a role in its formal sense, nor except in some exceptional cases would security authorities seek a recruitment of a scientist to conduct surveillance of a colleague in the same lab. Though one would think that most scientists with a well ingrained biosafety ethos would likely report irregular activities or safety non-compliance by other colleagues particularly if these jeopardised safety or the professional reputation of the institution.

Additionally, the scientific community generates vast quantities of biological knowledge, on as noted above, reproducing dual use strains of agents using synthetic biology, vaccines, weaponisation, pathogenicity and transmissibility of agents and the public health response to biosecurity incidents (intentional or unintentional). Hence their knowledge as represented in peer review journals or via direct contact with law enforcement and intelligence agencies is another potential source of collection. Scientists regularly attending their professional conferences will also have good knowledge on what peers are working on and whether any dual use areas seem concerning or not easily explained.

Epidemiology

As discussed above, the diversity of disciplines in the scientific community represents potentially a wealth of specialist and technical information for law enforcement and national security intelligence agencies, who are interested in how malevolent (intentional) bio-threat actors might behave and the risks they pose locally and globally. Epidemiology is one critical scientific discipline, where the security community requires information in order to understand how and why disease is distributed across populations of interest, particularly if there are suspicions arising from other intelligence sources that such distributions may be the result of an intentional criminal act. Epidemiological studies have long been of interest to both military and civilian decision-makers seeking to assess the impact of disease on populations as a result of bio-warfare and bio-terrorism (Bombardt 2000). In this book, I adopt the broad definition of epidemiology of Last: 'as the study of the distribution and determinants of health-related states or events in specified populations and the application of this study to control of health problems' (Last cited in Gordis 2009: 3). Gordis lists five objectives of epidemiology, which together are critical for understanding, preventing, treating and evaluation of public health measures related to disease (ibid.). First, epidemiology seeks to identify the etiology (cause) of disease and the associated risk factors. In other words, how is the disease transmitted (person to person, animal to person) and who are most at risk of becoming sick or dying from the disease?

Second, it helps determine the extent of disease in a community, which is obviously critical for planning the kind of health interventions required to manage the disease. Third, epidemiology studies can provide baseline data about the prognosis of the disease and how this might change again with public health interventions. Fourth, it can assist decision-makers in evaluating whether current or emerging prevention and therapeutic measures are having an impact on health outcomes, particularly survival for highly pathogenic diseases. Finally, epidemiological studies are useful for developing 'public policy relating to environmental problems, genetic issues, and other considerations regarding disease prevention and health promotion' (Gordis 2009: 3). Environmental factors are clearly important to understanding bio-crime or bio-terrorism incidents as variations in climate, seasons, and physical (man-made) spaces will all contribute or inhibit the spread of disease in different ways. A more detailed discussion on the importance of epidemiology, particularly the role of national bio-surveillance programs to the prevention, disruption and treatment of biosecurity threats will be developed in Chapter 7.

Forensics

Similarly to other criminal investigations collecting traditional forensic material (e.g. finger prints, documents, photos, DNA, cyber, ballistics/explosive residue) from a crime scene or part of a warranted entry into a suspect's location will be useful in a bio-terrorist or bio-criminal investigation. Increasingly however, since microbial forensics was applied to the 2001 case concerning anthrax contaminated letters sent through the US postal system, members of Congress and some media companies (*Amerithrax*), microbial forensics (sometimes also referred to bio-forensics or forensic microbiology) has also become increasingly used by relevant intelligence agencies and investigators (Murch 2003; Shea 2006; Tucker and Koblentz 2009; Koblentz and Tucker 2010; Inglis et al. 2011) In the US intelligence community, the FBI and DHS play a role in investigating actual and potential bio-terrorism and bio-crime incidents. In the case of *Amerithrax* it took nine years to attribute the anthrax as originating from the US Army Medical Research Institute of Infectious Diseases military laboratory (USAMARID) and the alleged offender Dr. Bruce Ivins (DOJ 2010).

The FBI has the lead role in any investigation of actual criminal acts with the Department of Justice prosecuting offenders, while the DHS manages the National Bio-Forensic Analysis Center (NBFAC). The NBFAC is a bio forensic lab, which is responsible for analysing evidentiary samples in a bio-forensic investigation. A US Government Accountability Office (GAO) review of the NBFAC in 2017 demonstrated that since *Amerithrax*, there has been dramatic improvement in the NBFAC's capabilities in particular methods based approaches (e.g. whole genome sequencing, analytical chemistry). They can now detect and sequence not only the well-known select agents (e.g. anthrax) 'but a number of other biological agents in a fraction of time' (GAO 2017: 19). The FBI, who were interviewed by GAO said that 'improvements in techniques and technologies have led to potential increases in obtainable information and significant reductions in analysis times supporting bio-terrorism investigations' (ibid.). However, the GAO review report also concluded that NBFAC has several capability gaps, which are too detailed to discuss here, but are related to three broad areas (science, technology and methods, bioinformatics and data) (ibid.: 18). The report also recommended that DHS needed to conduct a formal capability analysis to 'identify scientific and technical gaps and needs in bio-forensic capabilities to help guide current and future bio-forensics investments and update its analysis periodically' (ibid.: 19).

Collection Challenges

It's clear from our discussion of both 'traditional intelligence collection sources (SIGINT, GEOINT, HUMINT and OSINT) and specialised sources available from a diverse scientific community, that multiple challenges exist to developing and applying the best collection strategy against specific and evolving bio-threats and risks. By way of concluding this chapter, the challenges (e.g. technical, organisational barriers, integration of collection assets) discussed above need to be managed so that intelligence analysts and investigators are able to increase their understanding of actual and potential bio-threats and risks. There are five factors the analysts needs to keep in mind when approaching any intelligence collection planning, and they apply just as equally to the biosecurity context than any other threat and risk types. First, as discussed earlier, *what* and *how* intelligence is collected is first and foremost defined by the level of decision-making support required. For example, let's for illustrative purposes only suggest that one 'Five Eyes' country has been investigating a terrorists groups' acquisition of anthrax in order to weaponise it. At a tactical level the kind of information required to arrest the individuals involved might be relatively superficial (i.e. physical address and checking police data bases to see if those involved possess weapons or have a history of violence). At an operational level, with the investigation still ongoing the law enforcement and security agencies involved would likely depend on a broader range of collection sources (e.g. consultations with microbial forensic specialists about the likely nature and source of the anthrax involved, SIGINT and HUMINT might also be involved). At the strategic level, the focus may be less on specific SIGINT reports or GEOINT, but rather a higher level synthesis of all available case information to look for broader drivers of how this group got involved in anthrax manufacture and weaponisation and an assessment if similar groups are likely to weaponise anthrax).

Second, what collection choices are made will also be dependent on the nature of the threat and risk. A local threat actor, for example an angry ex-employee, who sends Ricin to his ex-boss, while serious, will likely only involve a smaller selection of collection assets discussed above. It might involve surveillance of the ex-employee, forensics and telephone interception, but given its local dimensions it is less likely to involve SIGINT, GEOINT or HUMINT that would normally be reserved for threats that have national or international links. Third, collection choices will also be made with acknowledgements by intelligence and law enforcement agencies of the various limitations of different collection platforms (e.g. technical, legal/ethical, level of coverage, reliability, validity). As discussed earlier, all collection platforms have their limitations. SIGINT and GEOINT may not provide initially good coverage of communications or location of a small group of terrorists attempting to make anthrax in a non-descript warehouse in an industrial park outside a major city. Though HUMINT by the way of tips from a concerned security officer seeing people coming and going at odd hours during the night from the warehouse, additional physical surveillance and covert entry to retrieve a sample for microbial forensics combined provides a more complete assessment of the threat. In summary, in this later potentially more dangerous threat scenario, multiple sources of collection would be required at different times not only to more accurately assess the threat, but to achieve a sufficient burden of evidence that would be admissible in court. Given then the limitations of most collection platforms discussed earlier, it is the triangulation of various approaches that provide a more valid and reliable understanding of threat and risk rather than relying on one source.

The fourth factor that the analyst needs to keep in mind when trying to overcome the many challenges in accessing and assessing multiple collection sources; is the need to be flexible with what can be accessed in the timeframes available to produce the intelligence product. The desire to interrogate more expensive national intelligence assets such as SIGINT given other priorities of government may not be possible in which case other sources need to be quickly identified for collecting the information if possible.

Finally, and perhaps a more obvious point, analysts need more knowledge about what collection sources are available in specialised areas of biosecurity and bioterrorism. This is particularly important if analysts do not have training in biological sciences, medicine, public health and animal health to name only a few disciplines. In the absence of specialised scientific knowledge, analysts will need to know how to tap into such expert knowledge in order to provide richer and more valid assessments on bio-threats and risks for decision-makers. In Chapter 5 we shift the focus away from the many challenges in collecting biosecurity and bio-terrorism related intelligence to the equal number of difficulties in assessing that information. The analytical challenges are many and include, but are not limited to: organisational leadership issues, intelligence failure, workforce planning and ongoing insufficient understanding of the relative threat and risk posed by those working in the biological sciences, bio-criminals and bio-terrorists. While the challenges are many, Chapter 5 also provides a survey of areas where improvements in analytical tradecraft could make a difference to the quality of assessments made on bio-threats and risks.

References

9/11 Commission. (2004). *The 9/11 Commission Report: Final Report of the National Commission on Terrorist Attacks Upon the United States.* Washington, DC: 9/11 Commission.

Bean, H. (2007). The DNI's Open Source Center: An Organizational Communication Perspective. *International Journal of Intelligence and Counterintelligence, 20*(2), 240–257.

Bombardt, J. (2000). *Contagious Disease Dynamics for Biological Warfare and Bioterrorism Casualty Assessments.* Alexandria, VA: U.S. Department of Defense.

Chertoff, M. (2017). A Public Policy Perspective of the Dark Web. *Journal of Cyber Policy, 2*(1), 26–38. https://doi.org/10.1080/23738871.2017.1298643.

Crumpton, H. (2012). *The Art of Intelligence: Lessons from a Life in the CIA's Clandestine Service.* New York: Penguin Publishing Group.

DOJ. (2010). *The United States Department of Justice. Amerithrax Investigative Summary.* Washington, DC.

GAO. (2017). *Bio Forensics DHS Needs to Conduct a Formal Capability Gap Analysis to Better Identify and Address Gaps.* Washington, DC: GAO.

Gill, P., & Phythian, M. (2012). *Intelligence in an Insecure World.* Cambridge: Polity Press.

Gordis, L. (2009). *Epidemiology* (4th ed.). Philadelphia, PA: Saunders Elsevier.

Hayden, M. (2016). *Playing to the Edge.* New York: Penguin Press.

Hulnick, A. (2002). The Downside of Open Source Intelligence. *International Journal of Intelligence and Counterintelligence, 15*(4), 565–579.

Inglis, T., et al. (2011). Forensic Investigation of Biological Weapons Use. In J. Gall & J. Payne-James (Eds.), *Current Practices in Forensic Medicine* (pp. 17–42). Chichester, UK: Wiley.

Johnson, L. (2017). *National Security Intelligence.* Cambridge, MA: Polity Press.

Johnson, L., & Wirtz, J. (Eds.). (2015). *Intelligence: The Secret World of Spies.* New York: Oxford University Press.

Johnson, L., et al. (2014). An INS Special Forum: Implications of the Snowden Leaks. *Intelligence and National Security, 29*(6), 793–810.

Kim, J., et al. (2015). Advances in Anthrax Detection: Overview of Bioprobes and Biosensors. *Applied Biochemistry and Biotechnology, 176*(4), 957–977.

Koblentz, G., & Tucker, J. (2010). Tracing an Attack: The Promise and Pitfalls of Microbial Forensics. *Survival, 52*(1), 159–186. https://doi.org/10.1080/00396331003612521.

Lee, M. (2017, January 5). Julian Assange's Claim That There Was No Russian Involvement in Wikileaks Emails. *The Washington Post*. From https://www.washingtonpost.com/news/fact-checker/wp/2017/01/05/julian-assanges-claim-that-there-was-no-russian-involvement-in-wikileaks-emails/?utm_term=.bee14c837aef. Accessed March 15, 2017.

Lowenthal, M. (2012). *Intelligence from Secrets to Policy*. Thousand Oaks, CA: CQ Press.

McGurry, J. (2017). Volleyball Games Appear to Take Place at North Korean Nuclear Test Site. *The Guardian*. From https://www.theguardian.com/world/2017/apr/20/north-korea-volleyball-nuclear-test-site-punggye-ri. Accessed March 15, 2017.

Mercado, S. (2014). Open Source Intelligence. In L. Johnson & J. Wirtz (Eds.), *Intelligence: The Secret World of Spies* (4th ed., pp. 120–129). New York: Oxford University Press.

Murch, R. (2003). Microbial Forensics: Building a National Capacity to Investigate Bioterrorism. *Biosecurity and Bioterrorism: Biodefense Strategy, Practice, and Science, 1*(2), 1–5.

Office of Inspectors General DOD, CIA, NSA, ODNI, & DOJ. (2009). *Report on the President's Surveillance Program Volume 1*. Washington, DC.

Omand, D., et al. (2012). Introducing Social Media (SOCMINT) Intelligence. *Intelligence and National Security, 27*(6), 801–823.

Oppel, R., et al. (2010, January 4). Attacker in Afghanistan Was a Double Agent. *The New York Times*. From http://www.nytimes.com/2010/01/05/world/asia/05cia.html. Accessed March 15, 2017.

Redmond, P. (2015). The Challenges of Counterintelligence. In L. Johnson & J. Wirtz (Eds.), *Intelligence the Secret World of Spies* (4 ed., pp. 305–316). New York: Oxford University Press.

Risen, J., & Lichtblau, E. (2005). Bush Lets US Spy on Callers Without Courts. *The New York Times*. From http://www.nytimes.com/2005/12/16/politics/bush-lets-us-spy-on-callers-without-courts.html. Accessed March 15, 2018.

Rovner, J. (2013). Intelligence in the Twitter Age. *International Journal of Intelligence and Counterintelligence, 26*(2), 260–271.

Shea, D. (2006). The National Biodefense Analysis and Countermeasure Center: Issues for Congress *CRS Report* (Vol. RL32891). Washington, DC: Congressional Research Service, The Library of Congress.

Sims, J., & Gerber, B. (2009). *Vaults Mirrors and Masks Rediscovering US Counterintelligence*. Washington, DC: Georgetown University Press.

Tucker, J., & Koblentz, G. (2009). The Four Faces of Microbial Forensics. *Biosecurity and Bioterrorism: Biodefense Strategy, Practice, and Science, 7*(4), 389–397. https://doi.org/10.1089/bsp.2009.0043.

Van Cleave, M. (2007). *Counter Intelligence and National Security*. Washington, DC: National Defense University.

Vogel, K. (2013). *Phantom Menace or Looming Danger?*. Baltimore, MD: The Johns Hopkins University Press.

Walsh, P. F. (2011). *Intelligence and Intelligence Analysis*. Abingdon, UK: Routledge.

Walsh, P. F. (2017). Drone Paramilitary Operations Against Suspected Global Terrorists: US and Australian Perspectives. *Intelligence and National Security, 32*(4), 429–433.

Walsh, P. F., & Miller, S. (2016). Rethinking 'Five Eyes' Security Intelligence Collection Policies and Practice Post Snowden. *Intelligence and National Security, 31*(3), 345–368.

5

Analysis

Chapters 3 and 4 discussed a range of factors relevant to the production of biosecurity and bioterrorism intelligence. Both chapters showed how critical it is that intelligence is both tasked and collected appropriately so timely decision-making support can occur. It is also clear that several barriers can arise in the tasking and collection of intelligence. Such barriers have consequential effects on the kind of intelligence analysis and analytical products that can be produced for senior decision-makers. As noted earlier, the tasking and coordination and collection issues related to the faulty analysis of Iraq's WMD capability (prior to the US led invasion in 2003), illustrates the high stakes when intelligence agencies get it wrong.

Failure of whatever magnitude in the earlier stages of the core intelligence processes (tasking and coordination and collection), therefore has a cumulative impact on the kind of analysis 'Five Eye' countries are able to produce on a range of bio-threats and risks. For example, a misunderstanding by the political leadership on the potential bio-threat scenarios or risk posed by the malicious use of a

© The Author(s) 2018
P. F. Walsh, *Intelligence, Biosecurity and Bioterrorism*,
https://doi.org/10.1057/978-1-137-51700-5_5

type of biotechnology such as CRISPR, and an insufficient or mis-guided collection will waste resources—resulting in a poor under-standing of an emerging threat. In other words, failure in tasking or collection can clearly limit the validity and value of any analyt-ical product drafted on a bio-threat or risk issue. It is also not possi-ble to ameliorate against all potential failure points in tasking and collection. Decision-makers sometimes do task intelligence agencies inappropriately to produce intelligence on threats/risks, where there is no or insufficient information available—particularly in emerging, technologically enabled areas such as cyber or biotechnology. Additionally as discussed in Chapter 3, decision-makers can also task their intelligence communities based on political rather than evidenced based policy considerations. In collection, assets may not be accessible for tasking, or not easily retrievable due to information, communica-tions and technology organisational factors. In a sense, then all analy-sis regardless of the nature of the threat or risk under consideration is limited by the quality of tasking and collection that is available at that time. To minimise tasking and collection failures to the extent that this is possible, relies on the application of an effective skilled analytical workforce using robust analytical methodologies—as well as selecting the right kind of product format that will best engage a decision-maker.

This chapter will explore the role of the intelligence analyst work-ing in the bio-threats and risks context across the 'Five Eyes' intelli-gence communities since 9/11. This broad aim will be explored by examining three objectives. The first concerns defining the role of an intelligence analyst. Is the analyst's role different in the biosecu-rity and bio-terrorism threat-scape compared to colleagues working on non-bio-terrorism or organised crime topics? A second focus is what methods and techniques would be most useful in helping analysts assess complex threats that result in quicker and better decision-mak-ing support? The final objective is a reflection on the earlier two (e.g. role of analysts and techniques), and examines whether analysts across the 'Five Eyes' countries are fit for purpose to work on current and evolving bio-threats and risks.

Intelligence Analysts in the Bio-Threat and Risk Sectors

Before exploring the role of intelligence analysts in the bio-threat and risk sectors, it is important to first define in a general sense what analysts do? For seasoned analysts reading this book, feel free to jump to the next section, but for those new to the discipline it is important to define the analyst's role. Analysis is at the heart of the intelligence enterprise. Intelligence analysis is not merely synthesising information (classified and unclassified), but its real mission is to answer the 'so what' question? What does this information mean for a decision-maker? Additionally, and increasingly given the vast information sources now available to decision-makers other than intelligence, good intelligence analysis must provide *distinctive value*. How one describes 'value' is not an objective assessment necessarily. Decision-makers often have different perspectives than the analysts on where the value lies in their intelligence products. Generally, though 'value' is ascribed to an analytical product that is promptly delivered and tells the decision-maker something that they did not know. The latter being a challenge in and of itself in today's competitive knowledge and information environment.

Intelligence analysis can also be thought of as *the person* (analyst) doing the professional analytical role in one of the agencies across the 'Five Eyes' intelligence countries. Intelligence analysis also clearly results in *products*. Both of these dimensions of analysis (personal/professional and product) help us understand important aspects of intelligence analysis. Another dimension to understanding the role intelligence analysts, is to define 'contemporary analysis in terms of some of the key *methodological* and *cognitive* approaches that have underpinned it' (Walsh 2011: 235). Both approaches will also be discussed below.

The discussion thus far provides some parameters for how we might conceptualise the role of intelligence analysts. There is now a growing body of literature from the intelligence studies field reflecting on this broader question of how one defines what the role of an intelligence analyst is (Walsh 2011: 235–254; Marrin 2012; Lowenthal 2012;

George and Bruce 2014; Gill and Phythian 2012). All these sources and many others, examine different aspects of analysis, and are helpful in understanding the analytical role, but what is also clear from the literature is there are no straightforward ways to describe the role of intelligence analysts. 'Analysis like intelligence itself is context-driven, based on where it is practised, and also what levels of decision-making it supports' (Walsh 2011: 236). For example, what the role of intelligence analysis might mean in a local police department examining a recent spate of house burglaries results in different decision-making outcomes from the analysis of nuclear proliferation in North Korea (ibid.). Given how context shapes meaning, there seems little point trying to define a one size fits all role for analysts that work in such diverse areas (e.g. national security, law enforcement, and private sector, military). 'The more relevant point is to state what is commonly meant by analysis regardless of the context or the type of information used' (ibid.). 'In my view then, analysis is both a cognitive and methodological approach to processing and evaluating information – some of which is privileged – in order to produce an assessment for a decision-maker about the security environment' (ibid.).

The role of an analyst assessing bio-risk and threats in different contexts (e.g. bio-terrorism, bio-crime, private sector/scientific community), therefore, will all use similar cognitive and methodological approaches. Many of these approaches are also used by analysts working in other contexts (e.g. non-bio-terrorism, money laundering, strategic and military threats or anti-corruption work).

So where across the 'Five Eyes' intelligence communities are analysts working on bio-threat and risks issues? Interviews and secondary research conducted for this book did not provide a complete picture of exactly how many analysts were working on these issues nor where they were working. There are sensitivities for some agencies going on record with their 'analytical headcount' or the profile of their analysts as it's a question of capability. One thing, however that was clear from interviews and secondary research was that historically there had always been dedicated analytical assets in each country's defence department working on 'bio-issues'—given the central role the military has played in both strategic and battlefield WMD counter-proliferation. The military always needed a few analysts assessing WMD (including bio-weapons) to ensure that they were able to prepare the battle space and protect soldiers from such attacks—whether they were emanating from state or non-state actors.

In addition to defence, interviews suggested there were small numbers of analysts working in all-source assessment agencies such as the CIA in the US and the Joint Intelligence Committee (JIC) in the UK. The number of bio-weapons analysts in all source assessment agencies in Australia, Canada and New Zealand have traditionally been very small and often have carried the accounts for nuclear and chemical weapons as well. Again, as discussed in previous chapters, much has been written in recent post 9/11 history about the role of analysts in both the CIA (US), the JIC (UK) and the Office of National Assessments (ONA) (Australia) in providing faulty assessments on Iraq's bio-weapons program (Vogel 2013a; Koblentz 2009: 176–199; Flood 2004; Walsh 2011: 153).[1] Hence it is difficult to assess how many analysts have moved on from those early days of the 2000s after the multiple reports and investigations were completed in most 'Five Eyes' capitals detailing the failures in assessments about Iraq's bio-weapons programs.

Additionally, no doubt the post 9/11 bureaucratic restructuring that has occurred in all 'Five Eyes' countries—though most acutely in the US with the creation of the ODNI and DHS has also impacted on the number and skillsets of analysts working on bio-threats and risks. The establishment of the ODNI in 2004 meant the transfer of the National Intelligence Council (NIC), which previously was under the control of the CIA over to the ODNI. The NIC is made up of National Intelligence Officers (NIOs), who are responsible for producing longer term National Intelligence Estimates (NIE)—or strategic assessments for those not working in the US intelligence community. The NIOs in the Council are organised broadly along geographical lines, although there are also NIOs for thematic areas like transnational threats and economics, WMD and science and technology. It was, for instance, the

---

[1]Note: In 2017, the ONA—following an Australian Government sponsored independent review of the Australian intelligence community was renamed the Office of National Intelligence (ONI).

WMD and science and technology NIOs that produced an assessment in 2016 that 'genome editing probably increases the risk of the creation of potentially harmful biological agents or products' (Clapper 2016: 9).

It is less clear whether other institutions and fusion centres across the 'Five Eyes' intelligence communities have analysts, who have subject matter expertise on bio-threat and risk issues. In particular it is not known (publicly) whether the multiple counter-terrorism fusion centres across the 'Five Eyes' (e.g. Australia's National Terrorism Threat Assessment Centre, US National Counter Terrorism Threat Center or the UK's Joint Terrorism Analysis Center), have specialist analysts working on bio-threat and risk issues. I suspect not given these centres are 24 hour analytical operations, where analysts must triage enormous amounts of terrorism operational related information close to real time. In such environments, a generalist is probably more suited—one who can sort the 'wheat from the chaff' and alert the broader intelligence enterprise of indicators for potentially new evolving terrorists operations.

Given the negligible number of bio-weapon attacks since 9/11 and the low probability and high impact descriptor often ascribed to such threats and risks, I suspect also that analysts working in CT fusion centres aren't looking for future bio-terrorists either. The current trends in terrorism attack are low tech (vehicles, weapons, improvised explosives) mass casualty methods—not the use of biological agents as weapons (Walsh 2016). From the national law enforcement perspective, again research suggest that there does not seem to be many analysts specifically working on bio-threats and risks. There are exceptions to this rule though in some agencies. For example, over the last decade the FBI has had a very active counter bio-weapons program as part of its WMD Directorate that has done a lot of outreach to universities and the scientific communities. Further discussion of the FBI program and others across the 'Five Eyes' countries can be found in Chapters 6 and 7.

Foreign ministries have also since 9/11 had a small number of intelligence analysts working on bio-threats and risks, particularly in monitoring country's adherence to the BWC and terrorists groups' utilisation of bio-weapons. For example, the US State Department's own intelligence arm—the Bureau of Intelligence and Research (INR) historically developed specialised analytical expertise in bio-weapon analysis since 9/11, though the numbers of people are thought to now be only a few. It's also unclear what effect the ongoing budgetary pressures on the State Department under the Trump Administration will have on staffing in specialised areas such as this.

Given the diversity of the bio-threat environment, there are a number of other intelligence contexts, where one may find analysts working on bio-threat and risk issues. For example, in agriculture and other primary industries, animal health and border protection departments intelligence analysts can be found. In all 'Five Eyes' countries, biosecurity protection against animal and plant disease being imported and the protection of agricultural exports is critical—particularly in primary industries dominated economies such as Australia and New Zealand. In Australia, the approach to biosecurity for animal and plant health has seen a growing awareness over the last decade by the government for the development of more robust biosecurity surveillance and intelligence capabilities. The Australian Government has recently invested further resources to develop an advanced analytics capability for biosecurity and is employing more data analysts to operate this system within the Department of Agriculture and Water Resources. Data analysts are of course not the same thing as intelligence analysts. It's not clear if these data analysts will also take on a broader intelligence analyst's role longer term that will enable them to interrogate other intelligence collection sources within their department and across the broader Australian intelligence enterprise (e.g. HUMINT, SIGINT or GEOINT). A fusion of data and intelligence analytical skills would more likely help them develop targets (biosecurity offenders) for further prevention, investigation or prosecution.

In summary, it is difficult to get an accurate picture of how many analysts are working on bio-threats and risk across each 'Five Eyes' intelligence community. The information I was able to glean from interviews as noted earlier, suggest in the civilian intelligence agencies across the 'Five Eyes' the number of analysts working specifically on such issues are very small. There are pockets of expertise (subject matter expertise) in some agencies—more so in the US intelligence community—though elsewhere the trend appears to be that analysts may work additionally on other related WMD categories of nuclear and chemical—or rotate through such proliferation areas rather than being specialists. Regardless of what the exact analytical head count might be across the 'Five Eyes' intelligence communities, there are a number of methods and techniques available to them and this is where our discussion now turns.

Analytical Methods and Techniques

There are several analytical methods and techniques that intelligence analysts might bring to working on bio-threats and risks. Some of these work on cognitive issues that analysts may face in carrying out their work. Other methods help improve analytical depth, probability, reliability and validity of judgements. In Chapter 2's discussion on defining the biosecurity environment, it was seen how analytical perspectives have been framed partially by international relations theories—particularly realism and social constructivism. This section will discuss, however, examples of other methods and techniques that work on both the cognitive and analytical process aspects of being an intelligence analyst; and how they impact on interpreting bio-threats and risks. The discussion will be divided into two sub-headings: *interpretivist* vs *empirical* methodologies.

Interpretivist and empirical are broad methodological frameworks that are useful in understanding how scholars think about the generation of knowledge and theorising in the intelligence studies field (Walsh 2011: 284–287). Broadly, the terminology comes from the social sciences and describe the main methodological approaches social scientists use to understand the social world. Interpretivist or post-positivist social scientists argue that the complexity of human behaviour and social interactions do not allow such behaviour to be reduced down to hypotheses that can be tested empirically through the similar kinds of experiments we might see in the physical sciences. Interpretivists whether they are doing research in criminology, psychology or economics argue that rather than trying to explain complex human behaviour, the best we can do is to understand it in the context in which it occurs. This approach therefore does not rely on generating hypotheses, but rather deploying social science methods that will allow for a deeper understanding of the social world rather than developing grand theories that can explain human behaviour (ibid.). Empirical approaches in contrast are underscored by a 'belief that all knowledge is scientific and can be gained using scientific methods, which include developing theories based on observations' (O' Leary 2007: 10). The inter-disciplinary nature of intelligence analysis, which historically has been an amalgamation of several social science related disciplines (e.g. political science, criminology, international relations, economics, history and sociology) shows that both broad methodological frameworks have influenced the development of the analytical and intelligence studies fields (Walsh 2011; Marrin 2012). Therefore, gaining an understanding how various analytical methodologies and techniques might be used in the bio-threat and risk context can usefully be reached by considering what is the purpose of the particular technique? Does the technique seek to *interpret* or *explain* threat and risk behaviour?

The usefulness of classifying various analytical methodologies and techniques as 'interpretivist or empirical' is naturally limited. Such bi-polar classification implies that in both the intelligence studies field and the broader social sciences both terms sit on the opposite ends of the theoretical spectrum. In reality, and as shown below, both scholars and analysts often employ aspects of both interpretivist and empirical approaches to their research and analytical practice. The trick is knowing which methodological approaches will be most useful in assessing a particular threat or risk. For example, in a hypothetical tactical or operational situation, where a known terrorist group has displayed intent and capability to develop a bio-weapon, analysts may more likely use analytical techniques and methodologies that help them explain unfolding events that are already partially knowable. Though those same techniques and methodologies may be less useful to an analyst trying to assess whether a terrorist group is likely to show interest in or develop capability to exploit or develop a synthetic biological agent in the future. In this situation, analytical methodologies that help the analysts understand (rather than explain) potential social and technical drivers needed to exploit the synthetic biology would arguably be more useful to the analyst. However, providing warning to decision-makers of developing bio-threats and risks requires analysts being able to explain events and patterns seen in the current intelligence space as well as understand how they are evolving in the strategic intelligence space. In providing warning assessments therefore, a combination of interpretivist and empirical methodologies would be useful.

A final precaution in using interpretivist vs empirical terminology to describe techniques and methodologies that may be useful to analysts working on bio-threats and risks is to keep in mind that not all techniques used by analysts will come obviously from the social sciences. As discussed below and more fully in Chapter 7, many will also need to come from the physical sciences (e.g. microbiology, molecular engineering, forensic sciences, chemistry and epidemiology). So it is important to also consider how methodologies adopted from the physical sciences either help explain or interpret bio-threats and risks.

Interpretivist vs Empirical Methodologies

Interpretivist Methodologies

Space and security constrictions do not allow an exhaustive discussion of all interpretivist methodologies that might be used by analysts working on bio-threats and risks. Potentially there are many methodologies that can be useful in helping analysts understand current and emerging bio-threats and risks. For a more detailed discussion of analytical methodologies (see Walsh 2011: 241–246). A brief discussion of some of them will follow, but given the closed secure environments most intelligence agencies operate in, it is difficult to know the full range of interpretivist methodologies being used across the 'Five Eyes' intelligence communities. What follows then is a brief discussion of the types of social science methodological perspectives that we know have influenced the analysis of bio-risk and threats, as well as some we don't know much about yet their adoption might be useful in the analytical process.

Political science has long been an influence on intelligence studies including: politicisation of intelligence, intelligence failure, bureaucratic politics and decision-making (Betts 1978; Zegart 2007; Allison 1971). These theoretical perspectives may be useful in some circumstances in helping analysts understand issues such as a state's interest in a bio-weapons program. Though there are limitations to applicability. For example, rational actor explanations that in part underscored Allison's work on bureaucratic politics has its limitations in understanding how a foreign power makes decisions. Other political science perspectives that may be useful are the role of political institutions in failing states and their capability to prevent and respond to pandemics.

Pandemics could be the result of natural or intentional actions and knowledge of the strength of political institutions to respond to a health security incident may help analysts understand the level of risk posed by that country or region (Hirschfield 2017). Political science perspectives can also be useful for an analysts trying to understand the impact of arms control (WMD counter-proliferation) measures such as the Biological Weapons Convention (BWC) have on state based or non-state actor exploitation of bio-weapons. Additionally, the politics of global health security initiatives such as the Global Health Security Agenda launched under the Obama Administration in 2014, debates around disease surveillance; or the impacts on securitising health rather than seeing it solely as a medical/humanitarian priority—are also useful for analysts to understand as they guide the political, security and economic agendas of donor and recipient states response to disease (Davies and Youde 2015; Horton 2017; Lakoff 2015).

Similarly economics might bring useful insights for analysts assessing the risks posed by bio-threat actors by helping decision-makers frame risk management choices that consider cost-benefit analysis of various policy interventions for disease prevention and preparedness (Millet and Snyder-Beattie 2017). There are also a number of social science approaches that have in recent years influenced how intelligence analysts view the role of technology in assessing current and emerging bio-threats and risks. Two models that were introduced briefly in Chapter 2 are: (1) the biotechnology revolution and (2) the biotechnology evolution approach. The biotechnology revolution model argues that advancements in biological knowledge and biotechnology are growing exponentially and are on a linear trajectory. Adherents see this rapid growth in technology as the primary driver determining whether states or terrorists weaponise biological agents (Carlson 2003; NRC 2006). They further argue that bio-threat actors are more likely to take advantage of biotechnology advances given technological advancements have lowered many of the costs and barriers to accessing biotechnology. In contrast, other scholars—including sociologists such as Paul Martin have argued for a 'biotechnology evolution' model to understanding current and emerging bio-threats and risks (Nightingale and Martin 2004; Ouargrham-Gormley 2012; Vogel 2008, 2013a, b).

The biotechnology evolution approach does not privilege the role of material technology as the key determinant shaping biotechnology innovations and whether a bio-threat actor will use them to develop a bio-weapon. Adherents to the evolutionary approach do not argue that technology is not an important aspect in understanding how and if bio-threat actors will weaponise biotechnology. However, they see that both the trajectory and use of biotechnology also needs to be understood by how other drivers: social, economic, political and cultural determine its development and exploitation by malevolent actors. For Ouargrahm-Gormley in particular, other non-technical factors also need to be considered such as organisational factors (structure of the organisation and project management, knowledge transfer) and 'tacit knowledge'—or the know how scientists learn on the job based on experience over time rather than just the technical (theoretical) knowledge they bring to the laboratory (Ouargrahm-Gormley 2012).

In addition to social science disciplinary knowledge that has shaped analytical frameworks about the role technology plays in understanding the intentions and capabilities of bio-threat actors, other qualitative analytical tools have developed over several decades influencing how analysts assess bio-threats and risks. Some of the analytical tools have been imported into the intelligence world from the business and management sector and include environmental tools such as PESTELOM—or political, economic, social, technological, environmental, legislation, organisation and media and SWOT analysis-or strength, weakness, opportunities and threats. Both PESTELOM and SWOT are considered very basic analytical tools, but they are useful particularly in the strategic intelligence context in helping analysts order their thinking on the multiple drivers that may be impacting on the development of an emerging bio-threat or risk.

Other more complex analytical tools such as force field analysis, competing hypothesis have originated partly or wholly from the business and engineering disciplines. Collectively over time all these analytical tools have become known as Structured Analytical Techniques (SATs). Heuer and Pherson (2010) provide a comprehensive coverage of SATs for readers not familiar with the full range of tools available. I have taught many strategic analysis courses in Australia and in other 'Five Eyes' countries that have included SATs. SATs are designed to help the analyst challenge the inevitable cognitive biases that arise when an individual absorbs and then assesses the significance of different information sources. Richards Heuer's classic book, *Psychology of Intelligence Analysis* provided a significant amount of the intellectual foundation for the development of SATs in the US intelligence community in the 1990s. Heuer's work drew on psychological research, which demonstrated how people use 'mental short cuts' to reduce the burden of processing information when making judgments and decisions (Heuer 1999: 111). But these short cuts can often lead the analyst to faulty judgments or cognitive biases (ibid.). Cognitive biases have historically influenced how analysts have viewed various major historic events such as the Cuban Missile Crisis in 1962. Additionally, as discussed in earlier chapters, cognitive biases have also influenced bio-threat and risk related assessments in recent years, particularly assessments on whether Saddam Hussein's Iraq possessed offensive bio-weapons. Hence the deployment of structured analytical techniques can help analysts make some of these biases more explicit in their analysis—thereby hopefully improving the validity and reliability of their assessments.

While many intelligence agencies across the 'Five Eyes' intelligence communities have trained their analysts to use SATs, their adoption and effectiveness in the analytical practice remains uneven and unclear in many agencies (Coulthart 2016). SATs take time to do properly and analysts are often operating on tight timeframes to get mainly current rather than strategic intelligence products out the door (Walsh 2011). Vogel has shown that a combination of factors: a risk adverse US intelligence community in making analytical judgments on bio-weapons, time and resource constraints (given bioweapons threats attract relatively little resourcing within intelligence) also impact on how SATs are being used by analysts working on bio-threat and risk issues (Vogel and Knight 2014: 14–15). In summary, SATs are likely to be a useful aid in some bio-threat and risk assessment analytical tasks, but they are no substitute for detailed subject matter knowledge analysts need to produce more accurate analytical judgments. Other related qualitative methodological tools such as scenario generation, indicators and early warning, which originated in the military context several decades ago are also now being applied by analysts in other national security and even law enforcement contexts (Grabo 2004; Walsh 2011). Scenario generation allow the analysts to try put some boundaries on the uncertainty surrounding emerging threats by assessing how various drivers may interact over time to produce different 'future states'. This then allows the analyst to collect intelligence against various scenarios to monitor if one or more of these may be emerging so a warning report can be dispatched to decision-makers in sufficient time that the emerging threat/risk can be prevented, disrupted or mitigated against. Naturally developing good scenario generation, indications and early warning systems is contingent on many factors. Time frames, type of threat/risk, ability to collect sufficient intelligence and the development of clear indicators that one scenario may be evolving over another are all challenges for providing effective strategic warning of emerging threats and risks.

A final technique we will discuss which is potentially useful to analysts working on some bio-threats is Social Network Analysis (SNA). The pioneers of SNA came from sociology and social psychology, but it has it has been applied in a range of other fields including counter-terrorism, organised crime, biology, epidemiology and computer science (Walsh 2011: 243). In the policing and national security contexts, SNA enables the generation of a holistic understanding of the relationships between threat actors operating in a group or network. In SNA it is the relationship between different individuals and their role in a network that are most important. For example, in a counter-terrorism network understanding what roles each actor plays (e.g. financier, transport/logistics, bomb maker and so on) is critically important to intelligence and investigators—as is knowing which nodes in the network are most vulnerable for disruption and prosecution to prevent a terrorist attack (Leuprecht et al. 2017). Providing tactical or operational understanding to a decision-maker about either a bio-criminal or bio-terrorist group's exploitation of a bio-agent could be improved by analysts using SNA. SNA does have its challenges however, which include that even when an analyst uses automated analytical software it can take time to develop a comprehensive understanding of a threat actor network. SNA can quickly also become historic and less useful in real time operations if there are insufficient intelligence collection efforts to fill gaps in the network. Effective SNA also relies on collection efforts that not only provide information about the role of each actor in the network, but such information also needs to allow the analyst to assess the relative risk posed by each actor in the node.

Leaving aside some of these challenges, SNA techniques also provide a useful bridge for analysts in bringing together an understanding of both the security aspects of a bio-threat network (e.g. intent and capability) and the epidemiological risks (disease dynamics and impact) associated with their actions. For several decades now epidemiologists have been examining the effect of social networks and the spread of disease (Klovdahl 1985). More recently too studies have started to look more on the impact of changes in disease networks to identify high risk individuals for the prevention of disease (Stattner et al. 2011: 559–573; Christley et al. 2005: 1024–1031). Such social network epidemiological approaches are likely to be useful to analysts because in most planned or actual bio-terrorism events, they will need to make judgements about the overall threat and risk using both security intelligence collected on the intent and capability of a threat actor(s) and epidemiological intelligence about the public health risks.

The discussion here of SNA also provides a good example of how in reality analysts working on bio-threats and risks will likely draw on a combination of qualitative and interpretivist techniques and more quantitative and empirical techniques such as forensics and epidemiology that were discussed in detail in Chapter 4. Further discussion of both methodologies will also be included in Chapter 7, so there is no need to repeat their role in improving the analysis of bio-threats and risks here. Instead the focus will now turn to a broader review of recent empirical methodological frameworks that can help analysts explain bio-threats and risks to decision-makers.

Empirical

Increasingly since 9/11, scientists have participated in many workshops on understanding threat and risks scenarios posed by the misuse of biotechnology and synthetic biology (Center for Biosecurity UPMC 2011; NAS 2016, 2017a, b; Gryphon Scientific 2016). Some of these have resulted in general observations about potential threat and risk trajectories of biotechnology and synthetic biology, and concluded that threat actors would exploit 'simple paths' such as naturally produced bio-agents than weaponising synthetic biology technologies and applications (Center for Biosecurity UPMC 2011). Other scientific reports have gone further by attempting to develop more detailed analytical frameworks that may provide better assessments about the security concerns related to specific synthetic biology technologies and applications.

For example, Jonathan Tucker developed a decision framework that he argues 'policy makers can use to assess the risk that individual emerging technologies will be misused for hostile purposes, and to develop tailored governance structures' to help mitigate against them (2012: 67). Tucker's framework consists of two main dimensions that require further assessing: *risk of misuse* and the *governability* of emerging dual-use technology (ibid.: 68). Both dimensions are examined using a number of parameters. For example, risk of misuse is evaluated by considering four parameters (accessibility, ease of misuse, magnitude of potential harm, imminence of potential misuse), while governability is evaluated using five parameters (embodiment, maturity, convergence, rate of advance, international diffusion) (ibid.: 69). Each of the four parameters for risk of misuse are ranked (high, medium or low) with an average take of all scores to provide what Tucker describes as 'a rough estimate of risk associated with a given technology' (ibid.: 70). So an average score of high suggests 'that the technology has both an imminent risk of misuse and a significant potential for large scale harm, whereas a low score means that risk posed by the technology is far into the future or is not significant in terms of potential for large scale harm' (ibid.). In Tucker's framework, a low risk of misuse would default to a continuation in monitoring the technology for the time being, whereas medium or high risks would require an assessment of the other dimension—governability to determine what governance measures including: policy, compliance, codes of conduct, training, regulation, legal and presumably enforcement actions might be required to manage the risk (ibid.).

What kind of governance intervention measure is required would depend on the kind of target of concern (e.g. state, institution, individual, product or knowledge) (ibid.: 77). A final aspect to Tucker's model after identifying appropriate governance measures is to subject these to a further cost benefit analysis (ibid.: 78). Different governance measures are likely to have varied costs and benefits. More stringent legislation or export control may increase security yet impact unfavourably on other sectors that could benefit from using dual use technology such as the biotechnology industry, economy or public health authorities. So there are likely trade-offs in the kind of governance measures that can be adopted given the often divergent views of important stakeholders, who have an interest in dual use technology such as biotechnology companies, researchers, government to name a few. Getting the governance and 'regulation' right is a subject we will come back to in Chapter 8.

Tucker's applied decision framework was developed in his seminal edited work: *Innovation, Dual Use and Security* (Tucker 2012). In the same volume the framework was applied to 14 emerging dual use technologies to assess risk of misuse and governability. There were several interesting results, for example DNA Shuffling and Directed Evolution and Synthesis of Viral Genomes were rated high whereas Personal Genomics and gene therapy were rated low (ibid.: 306–310). Tucker's analytical framework provides a useful way to order a risk rating for mis-use of various emerging dual use technology, which includes many of the factors intelligence analysts need to consider in making assessments about the relative risk of misuse by bio-threat actors. Its assessment of risk of misuse and governability is a particularly useful approach to stra-tegic analysts, who also have to identify intervention opportunities for decision-makers. Tucker's approach may be useful in some 'Five Eyes' countries, where strategic analysts are expected to not just estimate the evolving threat (misuse of dual use technology), but also help deci-sion-makers identify areas for effective policy interventions.

There have been other robust methodological approaches to assessing bio-threats and risk posed by the malicious use of synthetic biology. As noted in Chapter 3, US based consulting company Gryphon Scientific released a report on the risks and benefits of Gain of Function (GOF) research. The report examined three factors in order to provide an assessment of the risks and benefits of GOF research. These included: a risk analysis of accidents and natural disasters, a biosecurity risk assess-ment and a benefit assessment (2016: 12). The methodology used in the report is a sophisticated mix-method approach that included, amongst other things, advanced quantitative probabilistic risk assessments of the kind used to risk assess natural disasters and epidemiology. The method-ology also included qualitative historical analysis of incidents involving life sciences laboratories and hospitals to understand the motivations and capabilities of a variety of malicious actors and the probability and risk posed by any future event that may occur in such environments. This resulted in the development of a matrix of malicious actors, acts and their consequences, which was also reviewed by intelligence and law enforcement officials (Gryphon Scientific 2016: 13–15).

More recently, in 2017, the National Academy of Sciences was com-missioned by the US Department of Defense to develop a framework to guide the assessment of security concerns related to advances in synthetic biology. The NAS established the *Committee on Strategies for Identifying and Addressing Biodefense Vulnerabilities Posed by Synthetic Biology* to draft a framework for identifying potential vulnerabilities posed by syn-thetic biology (NAS 2017a). The Committee's framework, although still a work in progress has been well conceptualised. It first lists a series of synthetic biology technologies and applications (e.g. automated biological design, metabolic engineering, phenotype engineering, horizontal transfer and transmissibility, editing of genes or genomes and directed evolution) (NAS 2017a: 7). It then introduces several additional factors to assess capability for the malicious use of particular synthetic biology capabilities. These factors include: *use of technology, use as a weapon attributes, attributes of actors* (ibid.). Each of these is further drilled down to a discussion of additional questions that would be relevant in determining further characteristics of a malicious actor and whether they would use a particular synthetic biology technology or application.

These questions are comprehensive and include: whether the technology is rapidly developing compared to those considered by experts to be far off into the future; and whether the technology is expected to survive for a long time or be displaced by the next generational innovation. Other factors involve what aspects of the technology are improving? (E.g. processing time, costs, lab space). Also relevant to the pace in the uptake of technology is does the technology have multiple different markets that would spur further technological development and innovation; or is the technology narrowly focused on one specific market? (ibid.). This is not an exhaustive list, but the questions posed require deeper thinking about the nature of the technology itself. For example, technology that is common place is likely to be more accessible than technology that is being phased out. More accessible technology that can be used for a number of different applications and phases (design, build or test) in synthetic biology would be more attractive to a malicious actor than a platform that has only one narrow application.

The second factor listed in the Committee's framework to assess capability for malicious use is *use as a weapon*. Here the framework lists several considerations to keep in mind when making an assessment on whether an individual or group of threat actors would use synthetic biology or more broadly biotechnology as a weapon. There is insufficient space to provide detailed discussion of them all, though the framework raises some important questions that need to be addressed about whether a particular synthetic biology technology or application would be weaponised. In Chapter 2 for example, it was shown how reliably producing pathogens like anthrax that could be delivered as a weapon was difficult for both state (e.g. Iraq's bio-weapons program under Saddam Hussein) and non-state actors (e.g. Aum Shinrikyo or Al Qaeda). The key question is whether synthetic biology 'could lower the barriers to bio-agent production, stabilization, testing and delivery' of classical bio-agents such as anthrax (NAS 2017a: 26). Additionally, do some synthetic biology techniques overcome barriers to weaponisation by enhancing existing pathogens, creating new ones or removing the need for the use of a pathogen all together by deploying a genetic construct, toxin or other entity (ibid.)?

The final factor used to determine whether various synthetic biology technologies and applications are capable of being used maliciously is an exploration of the *attributes of actors*. The Committee's framework list several issues that were important to know about the actor(s), including: *access to expertise, access to resources* and *organisational footprint requirements* (ibid.: 30–31). Access to expertise should consider whether specialist knowledge is required to exploit particular synthetic biology techniques or if knowledge in a related field would be transferable to the task. Other considerations include would exploitation of biotechnology be enhanced by engagement with the legitimate scientific community or could the activity be performed autonomously? (ibid.: 29). Access to resources is always part of assessing the overall capability of a threat actor in any context not just in the bio-threat and risk contexts. Money, time, equipment, personnel and expertise are all relevant resourcing issues.

The Committee's framework discusses briefly issues that may impact on access to resources. For example, for simpler applications of biotechnology a 'do it yourself' approach might be doable, though the exploitation of more complex techniques and applications could require theft of resources or blackmail of scientists, who have access to resources. Alternative pathways for access might be enrolling in a graduate program or biotechnology company where access to technology becomes possible (ibid.). The final key issue in assessing attributes of actors is organisational footprint requirements. Is the exploitation of biotechnology something that can be done by an individual using basic techniques and commonly available equipment even in a home environment, or does the attack require a larger, well equipped laboratory with several people involved? Can threat actors lever off existing (dual use) environments or would the work require a secret facility to ensure it remains undiscovered? (ibid.: 31).

The second step in the Committee's framework for determining the overall level of concern posed by bio-threat actors potentially using synthetic biology technologies and applications, is an exploration of 'factors to assess capability for mitigation' (ibid.: 7). Again the framework lists four factors (*deterrence and prevention capabilities, capability to recognize attack, attribution capabilities* and *consequence management capabilities*) that provide metrics to determine whether relevant national security, intelligence, law enforcement and other public health authorities have the capacity to mitigate against the use and effects of various synthetic biology technology and applications (ibid.). These factors will be explored in greater detail in Chapters 6 and 7.

Fit for Purpose

Given the discussions above about the role of analysts working in the bio-threat and risks context and the methodologies available to them, can we say that the current cadre across all 'Five Eyes' countries are fit for purpose in assessing the increasingly complex potential bio-threats of the future? Without further research on where exact gaps in capability lay across relevant intelligence agencies it is a difficult question to answer with precision. However, from the research gathered to this point on the capability status of analysts working on bio-threat and risk issues, at the very least it would be fair to say that capability is not optimal. It is also important to keep in mind, though, that just like other technologically enabled threats such as cyber, no amount of increased investment in analytical capability can produce analysts that will be able to anticipate all possible trajectories of such a complex evolving threat environment as biotechnology. So while the goal of any intelligence enterprise should be to continually improve the validity and reliability of the assessments, there will always be threats and risks that analysts will not have a complete understanding of and this could result in intelligence failure.

Managing current capability gaps across the 'Five Eyes' countries are complicated by a number of factors. For one, decision-makers are now less focused on bio threat issues compared to chemical and nuclear weapons or terrorism in general. Less attention eventually leads to less investment and this seems to have been the case particularly after the series of inquiries in the UK, US and Australia about the faulty assessments on Iraq's bio-weapons capability (Blue Ribbon Study Panel Report 2015). Another challenge to improving analytical capability is the tension between generalists vs Subject Matter Experts (SMEs) in our intelligence agencies; as well as the pressure to produce tactical/operational rather than strategic intelligence. Such pressures do not uniformly affect every agency in the same way, but looking across the entire intelligence enterprises of each 'Five Eyes' country, they do impact on whether intelligence communities have the right mixture of generalist and specialist analytical knowledge to work on bio-threats and risks in ways that will result in rigorous intelligence assessments for decision-makers.

It becomes a difficult if not an impossible question to know exactly the skill set analysts will require working on bio-threat and risks in Australia, the US, UK, Canada or NZ. Surely it will depend to some extent on the function of the intelligence agencies (e.g. civilian vs military; security vs law enforcement; public health vs animal health), and on the unique architectural arrangements of each country's intelligence community. Different countries have and will continue to place greater emphasis on managing bio-threats and risks. Further, the brief discussion above on analytical methodologies, both interpretivist and empirical perspectives show that a number of techniques, tools and knowledge are available to assist analysts working on these issues, yet research suggests these are not widely understood or used by analysts in many agencies. This too impacts on the overall capability of analysts.

There are no silver bullet solutions to address analytical capability issues raised in this chapter, and in many ways they are reflections of broader more fundamental and structural issues across 'Five Eyes' countries about whether our intelligence enterprises are 'fit for purpose'— not just against bio-threats and risks but a broader range of emerging threats and risks.

Conclusion

This chapter outlined the role of intelligence analysts working on bio-threats and risks since 9/11 as well as surveying the major interpretivist and analytical methodologies available to them. It's also clear from the discussion that challenges remain in making analysts 'fit for purpose' to work on complex emerging bio-threats and risks. However, managing such challenges is bigger than just focusing on the professional development of analysts. Making the current and future cadre of analysts professionally equipped to deal with bio-threats and risks also requires that the agencies and communities in which they work function more effectively.

Function is partly a product of managing effectively various aspects of the intelligence process already discussed in Chapters 3–5. But intelligence is not merely a set of segmented or sequential processes. Intelligence in the 'Five Eyes' intelligence communities is enabled by a number of structural factors that must be working well together in order to support each process step responsible for the production of intelligence. It is these structural factors and particularly the critical importance of intelligence governance that is the subject of the next chapter. If the many challenges to enhancing the effectiveness of intelligence support on bio-threat and risk issues identified in Chapters 3–5 are to be addressed then the 'Five Eyes' intelligence communities need to focus on improving intelligence governance and other organisational and community wide structural enabling activities as well.

References

Allison, G. (1971). *Essence of Decision: Explaining the Cuban Missile Crisis.* Boston: Little, Brown and Co.

Betts, R. (1978). Analysis, War and Decision: Why Intelligence Failures Are Inevitable? *World Politics, 31*(1), 61–89.

Blue Ribbon Study Panel. (2015). *Blue Ribbon Study Panel on Biodefense. A National Blueprint for Biodefense: Leadership and Major Reform Needed to Optimise Efforts.* Washington, DC: Hudson Institute for Policy Studies.

Carlson, R. (2003). The Pace and Proliferation of Biological Technologies. *Biosecurity and Bioterrorism: Biodefense Strategy, Practice, and Science, 1*(3), 203–214. https://doi.org/10.1089/153871303769201851.

Center for Biosecurity of UPMC. (2011). *US Government Judgments on the Threat of Biological Weapons: Official Assessments, 2004–2011* (pp. 1–26). Baltimore, MD: Center for Biosecurity of UPMC.

Christley, R., et al. (2005). Infection in Social Networks: Using Network Analysis to Identify High Risk Individuals. *American Journal of Epidemiology, 162*(10), 1024–1031.

Clapper, J. (2016). Statement for the Record. Worldwide Threat Assessment of the US Intelligence Community. Armed Services Committee.

Coulthart, S. (2016). Why Do Analysts Use Structured Analytic Techniques? An In-Depth Study of an American Intelligence Agency. *Intelligence and National Security, 31*(7), 933–948. https://doi.org/10.1080/02684527.2016.1140327.

Davies, S., & Youde, J. (Eds.). (2015). *The Politics of Surveillance and Response to Disease Outbreaks*. Surrey, UK: Ashgate Publishing Ltd.

Flood, P. (2004). *Report of the Inquiry into Australian Intelligence Agencies*. Canberra: Australian Government Printing Office.

George, R., & Bruce, J. (Eds.). (2014). *Analyzing Intelligence National Security Practitioner's Perspectives*. Washington, DC: Georgetown University Press.

Gill, P., & Phythian, M. (2012). *Intelligence in an Insecure World*. Cambridge: Polity Press.

Grabo, C. (2004). *Anticipating Surprise Analysis for Strategic Warning*. Lanham, MD: University Press of America.

Gryphon Scientific. (2016). *Risk and Benefit Analysis of Gain of Function Research Final Report*. Takoma Park, MD: Gryphon Scientific LLC.

Heuer, R. (1999). *Psychology of Intelligence Analysis*. Washington, DC: Center for the Study of Intelligence.

Heuer, R., & Pherson, R. (2010). *Structured Analytical Techniques for Intelligence Analysis*. Washington, DC: CQ Press.

Hirschfeld, K. (2017). Failing States as Epidemiologic Risk Zones. *Health Security, 15*(3), 288–295.

Horton, R. (2017). Offline: Global Health Security—Smart Strategy or Naive Tactics. *The Lancet, 389,* 892.

Klovdahl, A. (1985). Social Networks and the Spread of Infectious Diseases: The AIDS Example. *Social Science and Medicine, 21*(11), 1203–1216.

Koblentz, G. (2009). *Living Weapons*. New York: Cornell University Press.

Lakoff, A. (2015). Real Time Bio politics: The Actuary and the Sentinel in Global Public Health. *Economy and Society, 44*(1), 40–59.

Leuprecht, C., et al. (2017). Hezbollah's Global Tentacles: A Relational Approach to Convergence with Transnational Organised Crime. *Terrorism and Political Violence, 29*(5), 902–921.

Lowenthal, M. (2012). *Intelligence from Secrets to Policy*. Thousand Oaks, CA: CQ Press.

Marrin, S. (2012). *Improving Intelligence Analysis: Bridging the Gap Between Scholarship and Practice*. Abingdon, UK: Routledge.

Millet, P., & Snyder-Beattie, A. (2017). Existential Risk and Cost Effective Biosecurity. *Health Security, 15*(4), 373–383.

NAS. (2016). *Gain of Function Research. Summary of the Second Symposium*. Washington, DC: National Academy of Sciences.

NAS. (2017a). *A Proposed Framework for Identifying Potential Biodefense Vulnerabilities Posed by Synthetic Biology Interim Report*. Washington, DC: National Academy of Sciences.

NAS. (2017b). *Human Genome Editing. Science Ethics and Governance*. Washington, DC: The National Academies Press.

Nightingale, C., & Martin, P. (2004). Biosecurity, Bioterrorism and the Governance of Science. *Research Policy, 36*, 1635–1654.

NRC. (2006). *Globalization, Biosecurity and the Future of the Life Sciences*. Washington, DC: Institute of Medicine and National Research Council.

O'Leary, Z. (2007). *The Essential Guide to Doing Your Research*. London: Sage Publications.

Ouagrham-Gormley, S. (2012). Barriers to Bioweapons: Intangible Obstacles to Proliferation. *International Security, 36*(4), 80–114. https://doi.org/10.1162/ISEC_a_00077.

Stattner, E., et al. (2011). Diffusion in Dynamic Social Networks: Application in Epidemiology. In A. Hameurlain, et al. (Eds.), *Database and Expert Systems Applications* (pp. 559–573). Heidelberg: Springer-Verlag GMBH.

Tucker, J. (Ed.). (2012). *Innovation, Dual Use and Security*. Cambridge, MA: The MIT Press.

Vogel, K. (2008). Biodefense. In A. Lakoff & S. Collier (Eds.), *Biosecurity Interventions* (pp. 227–255). New York: Columbia University Press.

Vogel, K. (2013a). Intelligent Assessment: Putting Emerging Biotechnology Threats in Context. *Bulletin of the Atomic Scientists, 35*(1), 45–54.

Vogel, K. (2013b). Necessary Interventions. Expertise and Experiments in Bioweapons Intelligence Assessments. *Science, Technology and Innovation Studies, 9*(2), 61–88.

Vogel, K. & Knight, C. (2014). Analytic Outreach for Intelligence: Insights from a Workshop on Emerging Biotechnology Threats. *Intelligence and National Security*, 1–18. https://doi.org/10.1080/02684527.2014.887633.

Walsh, P. F. (2011). *Intelligence and Intelligence Analysis*. Abingdon, UK: Routledge.

Walsh, P. F. (2016). Australian National Security Intelligence Collection Since 9/11: Policy and Legislative Challenges. In K. Warby (Ed.), *National Security, Surveillance and Terror* (pp. 51–74). Cham, Switzerland: Springer International Publishing.

Zegart, A. (2007). *Spying Blind*. Princeton, NJ: Princeton University Press.

6

Intelligence Governance

Its clear improvements have been made by the US and other 'Five Eyes' in managing bio-threat and risks, particularly since the harsh findings on the capabilities of the US intelligence community contained in Silberman and Robb's *Commission on the Intelligence Capabilities of the US Regarding WMD* (2005). Nonetheless, discussion on core intelligence processes in Chapters 3–5 highlight several capability challenges remain, which in turn reduce the ability of 'Five Eyes' intelligence communities ability to provide effective decision-maker support.

While issues relating to key aspects of the intelligence production process, such as improving collection and analysis need addressing in situ, they cannot be solely dealt with in isolation. Given the interconnectedness and dynamic nature of each stage of intelligence production, tasking, collection and analytical issues also need to be addressed at the organisational and community wide level. Building sustained and adaptable organisational and community level improvements in bio-threat and risk intelligence capabilities for the future will rely, therefore, on making improvements to intelligence governance and other key structural enabling factors.

© The Author(s) 2018
P. F. Walsh, *Intelligence, Biosecurity and Bioterrorism*,
https://doi.org/10.1057/978-1-137-51700-5_6

This chapter is organised into three sections. First, it will introduce 'intelligence governance'—a concept I have developed in previous research (Walsh 2011, 2015). Second, it will explain why this concept and the broader effective intelligence framework it is part of is relevant to improving the function of intelligence processes applied to bio-threats and risks. Thirdly, it will briefly go through each key component of the effective intelligence framework (governance, ICT, Human Resources, and Research) to illustrate how improvements in these may over time advance intelligence capability support to decision-makers concerned about emerging bio-threats and risks. Legislation is also a key enabling activity, but is linked to accountability and oversight and will be discussed in Chapter 8.

Intelligence Governance

Before explaining intelligence governance, it is first necessary to provide a foundational understanding of the theory and practice of governance. The use of the term 'governance' and associated theorising has been in existence for over two decades in the scholarly literature. When one thinks of 'governance' often the ethical and effective running of companies comes to mind (Aras and Crowther 2010), but from a theoretical and practical perspective, governance is a concept explored across multiple sectors: politics, economics, developmental studies, international politics and socio-legal studies (Chhotray and Stoker 2008: 1). Perhaps because of this diversity in theory making on governance across different disciplines, the concept remains loosely defined. It is not relevant to our broader discussions here to engage in a deep analysis of different theoretical debates about what 'governance' means; or how it has been applied in different sectors. Readers interested in such debates can access Chhotray and Stoker's (2008) edited volume, which provides an excellent starting point of the cross disciplinary theoretical and practical approaches to governance. These authors define governance as being 'about the rules of collective decision-making in settings, where there are plurality of actors or organisations and where no formal control systems can dictate the terms of the relationship between these actors and organisations' (2008: 3). I agree with this definition to a point. Governance does seem at least in part to be about both the formal and informal rules over how decisions are made by actors or organisations. However, I disagree that the term is especially defined by the absence of formal control systems that are able to dictate the terms of relationships between actors and organisations. Globalisation and the growth of liberal democracies may well mean a more diffuse and collective focus of power between actors and organisations, yet in the context of bureaucratic politics or public administration there remain powerful actors (e.g. the political leadership), who still exert (or try to) formal control over the terms of relationships between actors and organisations. A less explicit yet more useful definition of governance is provided by Chhotray and Stoker earlier than the one above when they state: 'governance seeks to understand the way we construct collective decision-making' (2008: 2). This definition fits more accurately with governance in the bureaucratic political context of intelligence communities post 9/11.

With that theoretical background on governance in place, we now turn to how I have developed the concept 'intelligence governance' before explaining why it is important to improving bio-threat/risk prevention, disruption and treatment by our intelligence communities in the years ahead. From 2009–2010, as part of an investigation on how to improve intelligence capabilities in the post 9/11 era, I interviewed 61 intelligence analysts, managers and leaders from across the 'Five Eyes' countries. These were semi-structured interviews, where participants were asked a series of thematic questions about how they saw improvements could be made in the structure and processes of the 'Five Eyes' intelligence communities. A detailed discussion of the methodological approach to this study can be found in my book *Intelligence and Intelligence Analysis* (Walsh 2011: 89–131) and an abridged version of the study is also available in a later article (Walsh 2015). In summary, though, a thematic analysis of the interviews provided key components for the development of a theoretical model called 'the effective intelligence framework'. The framework attempts to strip back the

functions and the structure of intelligence agencies and their communities to activities that can be either classified as *core intelligence processes*
(e.g. tasking and coordination, collection, analysis, and production and
evaluation), *or key enabling activities* (e.g. governance, ICT, Human
Resources, Legislation and Research).

The core intelligence processes are as the name implies the key steps
in the 'manufacturing of intelligence' on the 'factory floor'. However,
intelligence is not produced in a vacuum, the processes are embedded
in and facilitated by key enabling activities such as governance, ICT,
Human Resources, Legislation and Research. As depicted in Fig. 6.1,
it is the optimal interaction between each of the key enabling activities
and the influence of these on individual and collective core intelligence
processes that will either result in effective, sustainable intelligence

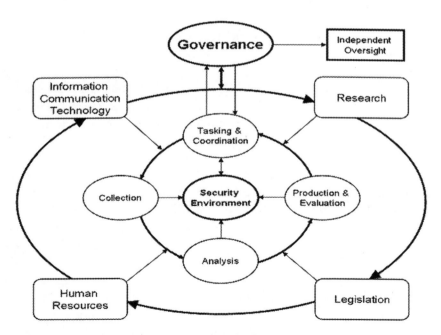

Fig. 6.1 Effective intelligence framework (*Source* Walsh, *Intelligence and Intelligence Analysis*, p. 148)

organisations and communities or ones that are mal-adaptive or fail. In the development of the effective intelligence framework, I argue that while all aspects of the model are important, the role of intelligence governance is most critical to the development of effective intelligence capability.

I define *intelligence governance*, as 'a set of attributes and rules pertaining to strong sustainable leadership, doctrine design, evaluation and effective coordination, cooperation and integration of intelligence processes' (Walsh 2015: 135). Ultimately, effective intelligence governance—relies on sound organizational (and community) leadership that can marshal both an organisation's core intelligence processes and key enabling activities in ways that make organizations and communities responsive, effective, adaptive and sustainable as the security environment changes (ibid.).

Why Intelligence Governance?

It should now be pretty clear that intelligence governance is critical to understanding how both governments and leaders of intelligence communities/agencies enter into collective decision-making about how to improve both core intelligence processes and key enabling activities. Intelligence governance will only become more critical in the future to the success or otherwise of intelligence supported decision-making as several factors increasingly impact on the longer term sustainability and effectiveness of intelligence frameworks across 'Five Eyes' countries. For example, the increasingly complex and uncertainty of the security environment, technology, changing workforce, the politicisation of intelligence and tensions between secrecy and privacy in liberal democratic states all impact on how decision are made *in* intelligence agencies and *across* communities. The ability, or lack thereof, of external intelligence governance (political leadership) and internal governance (intelligence agency and community leadership) to manage all these factors will determine greatly how effectively 'Five Eye's communities are structured, led and adapt to an increasingly complex and dynamic security environment.

Intelligence Governance: Bio-Threats and Risks

What then does effective intelligence governance look like in the bio-threat and risk context? There are several issues that could contribute to better intelligence governance across the 'Five Eyes' intelligence communities as far as managing bio-threats and risks are concerned. Some of these issues were identified during interviews conducted with staff working in a selection of intelligence agencies across the 'Five Eyes'. Others are covered in the secondary literature, particularly sources discussing governance in the US biodefense community.

Rather than drill down to the specific intelligence governance issues across each 'Five Eyes' country, a synthesis is provided here that identifies common areas that need addressing across all five countries. As the framework depicted in Fig. 6.1 shows, intelligence governance is the most important key enabling activity. This is because at its essence intelligence governance is about how decisions are made by both external (governments) and internal (intelligence agencies and communities). Put more simply, intelligence governance is about the kind of leadership that exists and how it makes decisions on prioritising the prevention, disruption and treatment of bio-threats and risks. Earlier chapters showed that much has been done, to improve (particularly in the US) since 9/11 the capability of the intelligence community to address bio-threats and risks since 9/11 and the damming Silberman and Robb report on the intelligence capabilities of the US regarding WMD in 2005 (Silberman and Robb 2005). However, the large expenditure, particularly during the Bush Administration on bio-defense upon which the US intelligence community benefited is one thing, it still takes effective intelligence governance or leadership to utilise these funds effectively and provide a coherent effective intelligence framework to manage bio-threat and risks.

In this section, we will drill down into how leadership has failed to fully optimise key enabling activities (intelligence governance, ICT, Human Resources, Research) and what measures both strategic and operational might be useful to improve them. In 2014, a Blue Ribbon Study Panel on Biodefense was established to identify gaps and provide recommendations to improve US biodefense (Blue Ribbon Study Panel

2015). In 2015, the Panel published a *National Blueprint for Biodefense: Leadership and Major Reform Needed to Optimise Efforts* (ibid.). This report and subsequent ones released by the Panel in 2016 (*Biodefense Indicators*) and 2017 (*Defense of Animal Agriculture*) have provided a useful 'report card' on the state of US biodefense, which includes commentary on intelligence capability.

In the preamble of the 2015 Blue Ribbon Study Report, the two Chairs (Senator Joe Lieberman and Secretary Thomas Ridge) make it clear that there remains (still 17 years after 9/11) a 'lack of strong centralised leadership at the highest level of government' (2015: iv) in biodefense. They go on to say: 'ten years after the Report on the Commission on the intelligence capabilities of the US regarding WMD, the insufficiency of our myriad and fragmented biodefense activities persist because biodefense lacks focused leadership' (ibid.). The 2015 report aligns closely with key points made by interviewees and other secondary sources assembled for this book about the current leadership and coordination issues both in the US intelligence community, but also in the wider though fragmented biodefense enterprise (GAO 2017: 32). Indeed Chapter 1, Section 1 (of the Blue Ribbon Study Panel Report) is titled 'the imperative for cogent governance', and lists several intelligence governance issues, including: the lack of prioritisation and therefore the resources for the collection and analysis of bio-threat and risk issues; and a lack of effective coordination of different intelligence agencies' roles in managing these issues (2015: 11). These are all points made earlier (Chapters 3 and 4).

While further evidence is required to make a definitive assessment, interviews and secondary sources about the state of intelligence governance in other 'Five Eyes' countries (Australia, Canada, NZ and the UK) indicate similar issues in these countries regarding a lack of priority shown to bio-threat and risk issues as well as insufficient coordination and leadership over these issues. Since 9/11, while transformation of the US intelligence community has been the most dramatic, with the creation of the ODNI and DHS amongst other major initiatives, Australia, Canada, the UK and NZ have also in their own ways implemented significant reform to their intelligence enterprises. All have introduced tranches of legislation, (particularly Australia) that has allowed a more proactive collection of intelligence—lowering in many cases the ability to seek warrants for communications interception, covert entry and preventative detention measures (Walsh 2011, 2016).

More recently following a 2017 independent review of Australia' intelligence community, the conservative government led by Prime Minister Malcolm Turnbull announced arguably the largest restructure of the Australian intelligence community since World War II (Baxendale 2017). There are several changes planned for the community, but the most noteworthy has been the creation of a super ministry—the Department of Home Affairs similar to the one operating in the UK. The other major change in 2018 is to the remit of the current Office of National Assessments (the government's all source intelligence assessment agency) to become the Office of National Intelligence. There is some speculation that the new Office of National Intelligence (ONI) may have a broader oversight remit of the national security intelligence agencies (e.g. ONA, ASD, ASIS, ASIO, AGO, DIO) though its actual functions are still evolving at the time of writing.

The new Department of Home Affairs will include the following existing agencies: the AFP, ASIO, ACIC, AUSTRAC, Immigration and Border Protection and the Office of Transport Security. These agencies will still exist as separate entities, but they will report to the one minister rather than four. In my own testimony to the Independent Intelligence Review, I argued for greater coordination across the community, but through the establishment of an assistant minister for intelligence and security rather than the creation of a new ministry (Walsh 2016). There is no evidence that the Australian intelligence community had been struck by catastrophic intelligence failure warranting such a centralised approach; and in private officials working in these departments questioned the need for such a major revamp of the community (Baxendale 2017).

The profound changes planned for the broader Australian intelligence enterprise over the next few years (2017–2019)—both its national security and law enforcement agencies like all reform present both opportunities and threats to improving effective intelligence governance. What remains clear enough, is political, and intelligence community leadership driving the major changes described above will influence directly whether intelligence capability remains effective and relevant to decision makers or not. Under the new arrangements now evolving in the Australian intelligence community, the lack of prioritisation, coordination and collection against bio-threats and risks may well continue into the future regardless of improvements made in managing a host of other threats and risks. However, the rapid development of other technologically enabled threats such as cyber, which arguably today still has 'Five Eyes' intelligence communities in 'catch up mode' demonstrate how what were seen by many as emerging over the horizon threats can become clear and present dangers in a relatively short time frame.

This is not to suggest that bio-threats and risks, which remain largely low probability high impact threats demand absolute front of centre attention by policy makers instead of more present dangers such as WMD proliferation in North Korea, Russia, global terrorism and cyber. Nonetheless, a lack of prioritisation, effective collection and coordination around bio-threats and risks makes 'Five Eyes' intelligence communities and countries vulnerable potentially to strategic and even operational surprise in these areas. There are no quick-fixes to improving intelligence governance issues as they relate to managing bio-threats and risks. At the political level, for the foreseeable future, however, it seems doubtful that 'Five Eyes' governments will place a greater prioritisation on bio-threats and risks in what is already a crowded menu of more pressing threats and risks. Sometimes as history as shown the political leadership will either over or under-sell the level of priority associated with various threats and risks. This can make it difficult for the intelligence community to get traction on emerging or 'exotic threats' with decision-makers who are 'tuned out' or have their own world view. While the extent to which the political leadership will become engaged in understanding future bio-threats and risks is unknown, leadership is not just external to the intelligence community it is occurs across and within its agencies. Heads of intelligence communities and agencies can play a critical role in influencing the political leadership over threats and risks that can in turn improve the overall governance and response to such threats.

Leadership

The likelihood that a change in political attitude relating to bio-threats and risks occurs, may be more likely if there is more effective leadership displayed on the issue within and across 'Five Eyes' countries. Heads of agencies need to see first the need for, and then act to bring about greater prioritisation, collection and coordination on bio-threats and risks before persuading the political leadership of the merits on focusing on them. This will increasingly rely on having in place future leaders of our intelligence community and agencies, who are adept at integrating both the relevant organisational structural change and improvements where necessary in workforce skill sets to place sufficient focus on bio-threats and risks (Walsh 2017: 441–459). What effective leadership looks like in any intelligence context remains an open question and 'intelligence leadership' as a concept is currently under theorised in intelligence studies literature (Walsh 2017).

The Blue Ribbon Panel Report (2015) discussed earlier identified a number of initiatives that might improve the leadership over managing bio-threats and risks in the future. At the US political leadership level, the Report suggested the establishment of a Biodefense Coordination Council at the White House led by the Vice President with Deputy Secretary participation from all agencies with a biodefense portfolio interest (2015: 6). Having White House buy in at the Vice President level should bring about greater political prioritisation, coordination and collection against bio-threats and risks, however at the time of writing there remains no evidence that such a Council will be established (Blue Ribbon Study Panel 2016). Across the other 'Five Eyes' countries, a similar national (executive level) biodefense coordination council could also be established, though in the case of Australia, Canada, the UK and NZ, it is likely that a senior minister would be most appropriate for chairing the council. In Australia, the Deputy Prime Minister or the new Minister for Home Affairs could be a good fit for the role. In Canada, the Minister of Public Safety and Emergency Preparedness seems the ideal chair, whilst in the UK and NZ the Home Secretary and National Security and Intelligence Minister respectively would provide high level coordination and prioritisation of bio-threats and risks.

While the Panel's recommendation for the establishment of a cabinet level coordination council is a good idea, its suggested name '*biodefense*' coordination council is not. As discussed in earlier chapters the role intelligence plays in managing malicious bio-threat and risk actors should not (at least initially) be separated from those threats/risks that are the result of accidents or natural infectious disease events. A fuller contextual understanding of what specific threats/risks may be malicious compared to naturally occurring disease events can only be understood by viewing all threats along the one health continuum (plant, animal and human). It may seem pedantic, but better intelligence governance results would likely arise for the 'Five Eyes' intelligence communities if a coordination council was called the: *Health Security Coordination Council*—rather than siloing 'health security' away from 'biodefense' which arguably has been one of the key barriers to improving the prioritisation, coordination and collection of bio-threats and risks. Finally, while 'biodefense' is a major part of what the intelligence community and its stakeholders are involved in, using the term 'health security' implies not only defense, but also 'offense', which increasingly since 9/11 have underscored a range of intelligence collection and operational activity.

A key task for a Health Security Coordination Council would be as the Panel Report suggests, develop a common biodefense strategy (Blue Ribbon Panel 2015: v). Again in terms of branding and to ensure the strategy adopted a multi-disciplinary and one health strategic approach, referring to 'the strategy' as a *national health security strategy* for each country would be more appropriate. Establishing a national strategy is essential for all 'Five Eyes' countries to better coordinate intelligence activities with those working in animal, environmental and human health to prevent, disrupt and manage bio-threats and risks. If there was a broader number of stakeholders, who had membership of the Coordination Council, the executive members of intelligence agencies would have ongoing close collaboration with health experts that can only enrich the reliability and validity of any downstream intelligence collection and analysis.

Again the Blue Ribbon study sees multiple functions for a national strategy, including 'better integration and clearer prioritization, aligning funding and importantly the implementation of national bio surveil-lance capability' (2015: vii). Clearly also, one key output of any high level national strategy must be the development of more evidence based bio-threat and risk frameworks that can better inform political deci-sion-makers and drive the identification of collection and assessment priorities. Chapter 5 showed how there are many different perspectives to help analysts frame their understandings of risk and threat, particu-larly the misuse of biotechnology and synthetic biology. However, a strategic plan should include as one of its objectives the development of more holistic, multi-disciplinary approaches to framing risk and threat that is informed by the broadest array of evidence and insights gathered by members of the Health Security Coordination Council.

Operationalising a National Health Security Strategy

Achieving 'buy in' by the political leadership to prioritise bio-threat and risk issues, set collection and assessment expectations and to harness the disparate skills and responsibilities of intelligence agencies, scientific, health workers and other stakeholders will be a major feat in itself. It remains unclear if such a refocus is possible in the medium term (i.e. by 2023). If renewed political interest was achieved, including the establishment of an executive policy forum such as a Health Security Coordination Council in each 'Five Eyes' country, then it would be pos-sible for each country to also develop a national health security strategy. The Trump Administration has announced plans to produce a National Biodefense Strategy sometime in 2018 (Riley 2018), though ideally its implementation should wait until a Health Security Coordination Council was established to better inform such a strategy. Even if a Council and Strategy were possible by 2023, any externally driven improvements to intelligence governance by the political leadership can-not be fully realised if the high level national health security strategy is not operationalised effectively by both heads of intelligence agencies and the leadership of other stakeholders who play a vital role in manag-ing bio-threats and risks.

This is where the role of *internal* intelligence governance becomes relevant, particularly whether heads of agencies and their senior management teams can demonstrate effective leadership that delivers improvements in specific aspects of each key enabling activity (see discussion below). But providing a lower level operational plan that identifies activities, responsibility and other deliverables agencies are tasked with both individually and collectively by the health security coordination council will remain challenging. As discussed above, if 'Five Eyes' governments increasingly express concern about potentially emerging bio-threats and risks, this would allow heads of intelligence communities and agencies to provide sufficient resources for a more focused and prioritised investment in the collection and analysis of bio-threats and risks. Without that vital political focus operationalising any high level strategic plan will likely result in ineffective intelligence governance, particularly in the coordination of collection, analysis and distribution of intelligence efforts.

While intelligence governance and leadership over bio-threats and risks remains sub-optimal and much depends on whether the political leadership is willing to invest in improving governance issues, there are still measures that each 'Five Eyes' intelligence community can do to improve its overall capability to manage such threats and risks. For example, the Blue Ribbon Panel Report suggested in the US that the ODNI could improve the management and coordination of bio-threats and risks by creating a national intelligence manager for biological threats (2015: 19). Currently as noted earlier, health security issues seemed to be dealt with either/or by the NIM WMD and NIM for science and technology. The Panel Report suggested that 'the DNI should make the NIM the executive agent for distributing certain funds for biological intelligence activities, transferring responsibility from the CIA' (2015: 19). A centralised focus point in each 'Five Eyes' intelligence community for coordinating and funding bio-threat and risk collection and analysis makes sense. In particular, the vast US intelligence community has virtually double the number of agencies of other 'Five Eyes' countries so any initiative to better coordinate and integrate collection efforts is logical. Though we know that the ability of ODNI to play this central coordination and integration role across other threat types has met with mixed success since its establishment in 2004 (Walsh 2017; Johnson 2015; Gentry 2015), and so it is likely that one or two of the 16 US intelligence agencies such as the CIA or DIA might resist the reallocation of authority over bio-threat and risk resources to the ODNI.

In other 'Five Eyes' countries a centralised management of the collection and analysis of bio-threat and risks also makes sense though in part for different reasons than the US. The communities in Australia, UK, Canada and certainly NZ are smaller in headcount and budgets, so wastage/duplication of collection and analytical effort particularly on complex emerging bio-threats and risks is likely to lead more quickly to noticeable intelligence governance challenges. It's not the place of this chapter to provide prescriptive advice on where in their intelligence enterprise Australia, the UK, Canada or NZ should place the centralised portfolio responsibility for managing bio-threat and risk intelligence. However, in Australia this role may well be better placed in the newly forming ONI, which will have a whole of government role for the coordination of intelligence. In Canada and New Zealand, the Intelligence Assessment Secretariat (in the Privy Council) and the National Assessment Bureau (in the Department of the Prime Minister and Cabinet) respectively may be the appropriate bureaucratic venue for a more centralised coordinated approach to managing bio-threats and risks.

In the UK, the Joint Intelligence Organisation, which provides all source intelligence assessments to the Cabinet might be a good fit for this new function. In the non US 'Five Eyes' countries, the agencies mentioned above have been historically relatively smaller, but with nonetheless close proximity to the Prime Minister of each country. The ability to develop a more effective centralised leadership over bio-threat and risk intelligence will have less to do with the overall size of the agency and more with how effective heads of these national intelligence coordinating and assessment agencies are in maintaining the support of their Prime Ministers—and the extent to which they can marshal all members of the intelligence community and its stakeholders to improve intelligence governance.

In addition to the creation of a national institutional focus for improving intelligence capability on bio-threats and risks, further intelligence governance work could be done at the sub-national level in each 'Five Eyes' country. Any fully effective operationalised national health security strategy cannot rely solely on the executive activities of a national intelligence coordination agency like the ODNI. A national health security strategy must include an operational sub-plan that shows how key national intelligence governance initiatives discussed earlier (prioritisation, better collection and analysis) can be actioned at the state, county, provincial and local levels across each 'Five Eyes' country. While national law enforcement and security agencies may generally have the remit to investigate bio-threats and risks, particularly relating to bio-criminal or terrorist activities, all threats and risks have local manifestations.

This means just like any other crime category, state, provincial and local law enforcement, emergency responders and other relevant stakeholders will have information that is relevant to the national intelligence community agencies in each 'Five Eyes' country. However, challenges remain—despite significant efforts since 9/11 to share more information from local to national levels and vice versa. We will discuss these shortly in the ICT section below. Before surveying some of the ICT issues however, a more fundamental intelligence governance issue needs addressing that goes beyond how information flows across the national health security intelligence enterprise. The issues relate to understanding what are the optimal ways to design intelligence architecture at the sub-national level in order to promote better intelligence governance across all levels: international, national and sub-national. Again when it comes to managing bio-threats and risks, there is no template approach to achieving better coordination and integration of intelligence effort across the international, national and sub-national spectrum in 'Five Eyes' countries. The differing political cultures, bureaucratic missions, fiscal realities and potentially the sheer number of stakeholders that may have a role or information relevant to understanding bio-threats and risks means each 'Five Eyes' country must find its own way to improve intelligence governance at the sub-national and international level.

Across each 'Five Eyes' country, multi-agency task forces, fusion centres and secondments between national and sub-national agencies are common place in dealing with a range of other intelligence responses to threats including but not limited to: counter-terrorism, organised crime, financial intelligence, drug trafficking and border protection. Since 9/11 there has been a proliferation of fusion centres in the United States with some estimates suggesting at least 78 such centres have been stood up in major cities, regional hubs and some rural areas (Walsh 2011, 2015). In particular, the Bush Administration gave the new Department of Homeland Security a central role in bringing federal, state and local stakeholders together to promote better sharing of information and intelligence. However, evidence suggest that the effectiveness of some fusion centres has not lived up to expectations. Some have served either as 'post boxes' for information other federal or local agencies have already produced; or the agencies in the one centre are not sufficiently working as an integrated unit in the tasking and coordination of intelligence priorities- whether these are collection, assessment or operational objectives (Walsh 2015). At the time of writing, legislation is being introduced into the US House of Representatives (the DHS Field Engagement Accountability Act) to improve information sharing and engagement among the DHS fusion centres. Part of the expected legislation is to hold field personnel from the DHS Office of Intelligence and Analysis accountable for their performance at fusion centres including their role in supporting state and local law enforcement (Martin 2018). It remains to be seen how this legislation will improve capabilities on the ground given funding of fusion centres is frequently tied to short term DHS grants rather than longer strategic resourcing to improve their performance.

Despite some of the problems with fusion centres, the complexity of many threats and risks and budgetary constraints by local authorities tends to engineer joint approaches by default even though such fused arrangements can be found at times wanting. In the case of the US, with 17 national intelligence agencies and approximately 18,000 law enforcement agencies (leaving aside all other stakeholders such as state and county health authorities), fusion centres still provide the architecture, where improved intelligence governance can occur between the national and sub-national agencies in managing bio-threats and risks. Given that malicious bio-attacks are low probability high impact threats, there is no financial justification for establishing fusion centres just for bio-threats and risk. However, bio-threats and risks could be managed through existing fusion centres. In the US, in particular, a more enhanced bio-threat and risk intelligence capability could be built in existing viable, either metropolitan or rural fusion centre locations. A full time health security intelligence analyst could be employed–either from the FBI, DHS or a major metropolitan law enforcement agency. Their role would be to operationalise the collection and assessment priorities set by the National Intelligence Officer and the National Health Security Coordination Council. Although the FBI have long had in place a WMD coordinator in every field office and a very successful academic outreach program to liaise positively with sectors of potential concern (e.g. universities, biotechnology companies, students and researchers)—a deeper and broader understanding of the potential threat and risk environment, particularly the emerging environment is required at the local level (Hummel 2017).

A health security intelligence analyst can provide that broader environmental scan that the locally engaged busy case driven FBI WMD coordinator may not always be able to do. FBI WMD coordinators like other FBI agents are also rotated regularly from their locations back to headquarters in Washington DC—making it difficult for them to capture a full understanding of the threat and risk environment over time. The analyst can also work as a knowledge broker between all national and local agencies in the fusion centre to help all stakeholders participate in providing a fuller assessment of current and emerging bio-threats and risks. The analyst can provide tactical, operational and strategic intelligence support for intelligence and enforcement activity emanating from the fusion centre agencies combined; or operational outcomes directed by key national or local authorities.

There is insufficient space to provide a full discussion on what sub-national intelligence governance arrangements might be potentially workable in Australia, Canada, NZ and the UK. Clearly NZ a small country with a much smaller intelligence community and only one national police force, fusion centres across the country may not be required. It might be easier to place a health security intelligence analyst in NZ Police's National Intelligence Centre in Wellington and have that person travel regularly to small districts. In Australia, it may be more appropriate to place a health security intelligence analyst in joint terrorist task forces in each state. These task forces already comprise a number of federal and state agencies, who have a counter-terrorism remit. Similarly in the UK, a health security intelligence analyst could be co-located with other multi-disciplinary and jurisdictional intelligence colleagues across the country's eleven regional counter-terrorism units. This discussion is merely illustrative of possible sub-national intelligence governance arrangements. Each country will need to carefully consider how to make this work, but the important point is that moving forward there needs to be a more institutionalised approach to managing bio-threat and risk intelligence at the sub-national level then hitherto is the case.

Briefly too at the international level there is room for further development of intelligence governance arrangements that can help prioritise collection and analysis against some bio-threats and risks as well as improving the prevention, disruption and treatment of them. Since 9/11 at the multi-lateral level, several global health initiatives such as the Global health Security Agenda and Canada's Global Partnership Program have been aimed at achieving good health outcomes yet at the same time supporting bio-safety and counter-terrorism activities in fragile states. The 'Five Eyes' intelligence communities should enhance their engagement with their colleagues in their respective foreign ministries, development institutions along with relevant UN agencies (WHO, BWC, FAO)—and private sector donors such as the Bill and Melinda Gates Foundation—to support their health security capacity efforts—particularly in locations of concern where there are weak public health and biosafety capabilities that could be exploited by terrorists or other criminal actors.

Finally, another important way to improve intelligence governance of bio-threats and risks is for the 'Five Eyes' partners to put these issues on their agendas of their regular meetings. There are regular 'Five Eyes' meetings each year at the ministerial, head of agency and senior officer levels. These meetings take place amongst agencies with a more traditional national security focus, but also those with a greater law enforcement remit. Such meetings always include discussion on emerging threat areas and capability issues so there are opportunities for the agencies concerned to begin raising awareness of bio-threats and risks and to collectively determine how they can better coordinate collection, analysis and dissemination on them. We will turn now to a brief discussion on how some of these strategic and operational issues impact on the other key enabling activities. As mentioned at the opening of this chapter, the only key enabling activity that will not be discussed below (legislation) will be addressed in Chapter 8 because it is related closely to issues of oversight and accountability.

ICT

There are several ICT issues that need attention if 'Five Eyes' countries are able to access, process and assess bio-threat and risk information required for tactical, operational and strategic decision-making. In many respects, the ICT issues preventing better understanding of bio-threat and risk issues are not unlike those that challenge intelligence communities generally. After 9/11 in the US, the establishment of the DHS, ODNI and the promotion of initiatives such as the Information Sharing Environment (ISE) were efforts by the Bush Administration to create platforms and processes for enhanced sharing and integration of information between federal, state and local agencies (Walsh 2011). Indeed more recently during Jim Clapper's tenure as DNI, it was clear that the US intelligence community has made improvements since 9/11 to promote a culture for the integration, collaboration of information held across what Clapper described as 'the confederation of IT enterprises' (Johnson 2015: 10). Further in a 2014 interview, Clapper indicated that the next logical step for the US intelligence community was the development of an IT Enterprise of the Future (ICITE) that would create a single IT enterprise (ibid.). However, despite such efforts, there still remain challenges in developing information architecture and promotion of cross community culture for information sharing in all 'Five Eyes' countries. For example, in a 2017 a report by the Inspector Generals for the US Department of Justice and Homeland Security into sharing of domestic counter terrorism information while noting significant improvements in information sharing, also listed several issues related to challenging work relationships in the field and with information sharing between the FBI and parts of DHS, notably ICE HSI (Inspectors General DOJ and DHS 2017: 10). The Office of Inspectors General report made several recommendations including that the ODNI, DHS and DOJ needed to review inter-agency information sharing MOUs as well as moving away from 'personality based coordination' of information sharing arrangements (ibid.).

In summary, overcoming cultural institutional barriers for sharing and the real time access to information from several data bases remains a significant barrier to effective intelligence collection, analysis and operational response across 'Five Eye's law enforcement agencies (Walsh 2011, 2012; L'Estrange and Merchant 2017; Inspectors General DOJ and DHS 2017). In the US with close to 18,000 law enforcement agencies, cultural issues, out dated legacy IT systems, and conflicting legislative and privacy statutes between federal, state and local levels can conspire against real time sharing of information. In Australia, with only about 15 federal and state core law enforcement agencies, there are less bureaucratic barriers for law enforcement agencies to share, collaborate and integrate information in real time. However, the history of Australian law enforcement IT systems demonstrates the same challenges seen with their US and other 'Five Eyes' counterparts such as Canada and the UK (Walsh 2011, 2012). In Australia, the thirty year old Australian Criminal Intelligence Database (ACID), where Federal and State agencies were encouraged to share intelligence has not been fit for purpose for many years, and a pilot of a new system–the National Criminal Intelligence System (NCIS), which concluded in June 2017 (ACIC 2016) reportedly demonstrated a superior ICT system for federal, state, territory to share in real time information across multiple data sets. Although the NCIS was successfully piloted, appropriate funding and high level ministerial oversight of a more permanent implementation will be required if the benefits of the new system can be realised. As mentioned earlier, at the time of writing, the major federal security and law enforcement agencies in Australia (AFP, ASIO, ACIC, Immigration and Border Force, AUSTRAC, Office of Transport Security) have been amalgamated into a new super ministry called the Department of Home Affairs. It is possible that this amalgamation will provide impetus for the implementation of the NCIS, and this in turn over the next few years should result in improved sharing of intelligence amongst federal and state agencies about a range of risks and threats. However, as the recent (2017) Independent Intelligence Review in Australia's intelligence community showed, improvements still need to be made in improving connectivity between national security intelligence agencies and those of the new Department of Home Affairs (L'Estrange and Merchant 2017: 79).

The 2015 Blue Ribbon Study Panel Report echoed many of the difficulties in the sharing and integrating of data, information and intelligence seen across the 'Five Eyes' countries is also seen in the bio-defense context (Blue Ribbon Study Panel 2015: 29–32). Space does not allow a full discussion of all of these, but the Report notably evaluated the role of the National Biosurveillance Integration System (NBIS) that in 2004 was envisioned ambitiously to provide an 'integrated and comprehensive attack warning system to rapidly recognise and characterise the dispersal of biological agents in human and animal populations, food, water, agriculture and the environment (ibid.: 29). The report concludes that the DHS has been unable largely to make the NBIS the one stop integrated ICT system for managing all relevant bio-threat and risk information because other federal agencies are not mandated to populate it. Additionally, other critical non-intelligence community stakeholders such as the CDC, state and county public health authorities and other animal health and agriculture authorities that would have valuable epidemiological data are not automatically captured by the NBIS (ibid.: 31). DHS continues to try to improve information feeds into the NBIS, but the report argues that this information 'is years behind where Congress and the Administration expected the system to be' (ibid.). There are also questions about how national attribution (forensic) centres information such as that produced by the US

National Bioforensics Analysis Center (NBFAC) is shared, coordinated and integrated with other information generated by the IC and law enforcement agencies.

Improving the ICT architecture and information sharing ecology in 'Five Eyes' intelligence communities will continue to present these countries with significant challenges. Further, the amount of information to be collected, assessed and disseminated continues to grow exponentially as the security environment changes in short time frames. In the future, there will be also real fiscal constraints, even in the US intelligence community, to funding expensive ICT platforms that do not facilitate close to real time collection analysis and dissemination of intelligence. As a result, there will be increasing pressure for intelligence communities to develop common integrated platforms that enable greater collaboration between partners (including stakeholders not in the IC), and also support real time monitoring of threats and risks. It is not impossible for each 'Five Eyes' intelligence community to do this, though it will likely take strong political and community leadership. A senior officer with the appropriate authority from the political leadership, perhaps the new national health intelligence officer discussed earlier could play a central role in the design and implementation of a health security intelligence platform that is linked to an IC integrated platform, but also can receive automatically valuable information from key stakeholders. Alternatively, rather than creating yet another ICT system bio-threat and risk information could be captured by existing information sharing systems. For example, in the US the Homeland Security Information Network (HSIN) which allows federal, state and local agencies to share information across the national network of fusion centres might be an appropriate system to collect, share, assess and disseminate bio-threat and risk information. Regardless of what ICT solution is adopted in each 'Five Eyes' intelligence community, each will have its own security, cultural, legal and privacy issues that will need careful consideration. Such challenges need to be met however, as failure to provide a federated intelligence and information sharing platform for bio-threats and risks will likely result in either in-adequate collection, duplication of collection or analysis, in-effective monitoring or potential intelligence failure.

HR

Chapter 5 provided a detailed exploration of the key analytical workforce challenges for analysts currently working on bio-threat and risk issues across 'Five Eyes' intelligence countries. This section will not revisit this detail. In summary though, Chapter 5 did raise three important broader HR questions that require further investigation by the political and community leadership in each country. These are: first, what is the size of the analytical workforce that is focused full or part-time on assessing bio-threats and risks? A subsidiary question from this one could also be what is the size of the 'intelligence collection workforce' working on such threats as well? Second, what role these analysts play across the biosecurity enterprise (e.g. public health, research, private sector, national security, law enforcement, military, animal health). Third, are these analysts fit for purpose?

In an ideal world, if each country as suggested earlier appointed a national health security intelligence officer, (who had cabinet level oversight and authority over managing bio-threats and risks in each Five Eyes country), this person would be the appropriate officer to implement a workforce capability audit to address the above three questions. This would not be easy an easy task but nonetheless a necessary one. As noted earlier, currently there is a lack of understanding, agreement, planning, coordination and prioritisation of bio-threats and risks and this impacts the IC agency's ability to develop their workforce in order to understand the evolving bio-threat and risk landscape, particularly in synthetic biology. Workforce planning is therefore an important intelligence governance task. Of course it is not possible to anticipate all potential evolving bio-threats and risks and plan a workforce around them, but the results of a workforce capability audit should provide some baseline evidence of how 'Five Eyes' intelligence countries might invest in their workforce so that they can work more effectively within, across the intelligence community and with important stakeholders in more integrated and knowledgeable ways.

Without pre-judging the results of a workforce capability audit, it is likely that planning the bio-threat/risk analytical workforce ideally for the next five to seven years at least would not, as discussed in Chapter 5, attempt to create a 'super analyst', who can work across the full one health spectrum. Such a 'breed' is not necessary and likely different specialised skills and training are required in different contexts (animal, human health, national security, defence, law enforcement). But the health security intelligence leadership in each country can use the audit results to provide better advice to government of whether there are any gaps in specialist bio-threat and risk analytical training areas. Further, the audit can provide evidence for determining what additional training and education might be useful for more generalist analysts, who need to write intelligence assessments on bio-criminal or bio-terrorist issues for senior decision-makers, who do not have technical knowledge on such topics.

Hence, generalist analysts, who may be writing thematic and strategic products as opposed to technical reports on bio-threats and risks will still need a sound knowledge content on the biosecurity, synthetic biology or biotechnological issues they are writing about. So if the audit is comprehensive enough, it can help the IC leadership determine what generalist skill set analysts might be needed in agencies, particularly those with all source assessment roles? An audit might also help frame other training decisions such as: are we looking for an analyst that has advanced training in public health? Or is the IC better served with one that has excellent training in criminology and security studies, but has had some training/experience in epidemiology and/or the biological sciences?

At least some training and technical knowledge in one or more of the biological sciences seems essential—even for generalists to increase the validity and reliability of analytical key judgments. Knowledge from the biological sciences is also essential so that analysts have some research literacy across relevant disciplines (e.g. microbiology, genetics, and synthetic biology). Such literacy is important for analysts in knowing what scientists may need to be accessed, particularly those who understand developments in synthetic biology. At least some formal under-graduate training in one or more of the biological sciences will help analysts understand contextually how developments in synthetic biology may result in the intentional and malicious manipulation of 'biological functions, systems or micro-organisms—resulting in the production of a disease causing agent or toxin' (NAS 2017: 3). It would also seem reasonable to expose generalist analysts, where practical, to short internships and rotations through scientific labs (e.g. research, private sector and forensics) to make connections with stakeholders in the scientific community and to understand how their scientific colleagues assess what they see as the more likely concerning bio-threats and risks. The objective would not be for generalist (non-scientists) to work formally in lab environments rather to visit, discuss threat and risk characterisations with colleagues with scientific training and build a community of experts that they can turn to discuss issues or seek peer review on issues that they have to write about. Generalist analysts would also benefit from understanding first-hand about the environment in which scientists work and the challenges they face in doing research.

Also in an ideal world, the outcomes of a workforce capability audit should inform an intelligence community wide common approach to bio-threat and risk intelligence training for analysts working in these areas or who are expected to do so. Since 9/11 there has been increasing discussion across 'Five Eyes' countries about the nature and structure of analytical training (Walsh 2011: 255–282, 2017; Campbell 2011: 307–337; Rudner 2009: 110–130; Marrin 2009: 131–146). Much of this literature has covered fundamental debates about what skills, knowledge and competencies an analyst needs and whether this is better delivered via internal training or external training/education providers or a combination of both. Since 9/11, to varying levels, improvements have been made in many 'Five Eyes' countries to adopt more holistic approaches to an analyst's career by looking beyond just distinct training programs to constructing continuing professional development pathways that support different phases of their careers. However, for the most part such initiatives remain works in progress and further work is needed to bed down strategic approaches to continual professional development both within IC member agencies as well as across entire communities (Walsh 2011).

While much is yet to be settled about the training, professionalization of analysts and indeed whether courses delivered to analyst are effective to improving workplace outputs (Walsh 2017), there is a need to start addressing as part of this broader debate the workforce planning of the next cadre of analysts working on bio-threats and risks. Since 9/11, similar workforce issues have been raised with the intelligence communities, including in establishing 'the right kind of capability' to deal with cyber threats (GAO 2005, 2011a, b). There is an opportunity for IC leaders and governments preparing for the next generation of potential bio-threats and risks to learn from mistakes and missteps taken in the cyber environment.

Given it is difficult to know when (or if) each 'Five Eyes' country will implement a national health security strategy in the next five years (2018–2023), it also remains unclear what kind of political or policy catalyst may bring about a national capability audit. Sadly, major reviews of capabilities have frequently arose from a parliamentary or independent inquiry after a major security event, where intelligence failure has been linked to that event. In the absence of political leadership and intelligence failure, hopefully, as the bio-threat and risk environment becomes more complex over the next decade, the intelligence leadership could itself take the initiative to conduct an audit. Though progress may at best be piecemeal if there is not a consistent leadership approach to implementing an audit across the entire intelligence community. Although a capability audit is needed, the best intentions of key intelligence leaders across each 'Five Eyes' intelligence community may be bypassed by other higher priority threat issues compared to bio-threats and risks which will likely remain low probability high impact threats.

Research

Research is another critical key enabling activity for intelligence communities' ability to improve its capability to work on bio-threats and risks. Research generates new knowledge that improves theoretical perspectives, but more importantly delivers better practice outcomes for intelligence agencies. My first book (*Intelligence and Intelligence Analysis*) devoted an entire chapter to research and theory building in the intelligence discipline (Walsh 2011: 283–298). Since 9/11, there has been an increased willingness by some agencies across the 'Five Eyes' intelligence communities to look outside their secure environments for solutions to a range of capability issues (e.g. ICT, data analytics, analytical training and technical areas such as surveillance and interception).

In the US intelligence community in particular, there has been for decades significant commissioning of research and consultancy projects and this includes as we shall see in the next chapter in the biodefense context. But what seems to be missing in all 'Five Eyes' countries is a more strategic and whole of government approach to intelligence capability research and this extends to research being done in the bio-threat and risk areas. In all 'Five Eyes' countries it is not that no research is going on which can help address bio-threat and risk capability issues, rather it is the case that research or consultancy projects tend to be commissioned at the agency rather than whole of community level. This raises the question of whether research commissioned by the US DOD, DHS or FBI might have a wider applicability and utility beyond that one agency. In the bio-threat and risk context, it is likely that in many cases a research project that may help improve capability or practice in one agency would likely also have a broader impact on capability across other agencies in the IC.

So while efforts have been made across 'Five Eyes' communities to collaborate on research projects, a more strategic approach will be required in the future as budgetary and political pressures in each country force agencies to identify common priority capability areas for research funding (Walsh 2011: 283–298). We have seen, for example, in the Trump Administration's initial 2018 budget proposal a desire to slash $1.25 billion from the proceeding year's biodefense allocation, which includes overseeing research on dangerous pathogens and the development of a national biodefense strategy (Inglesby and Haas 2017). If budgetary pressures continue in the US and in other 'Five Eyes' countries, then a well-developed research strategic plan could help agencies identify research areas that are more critical than others for improving bio-threat and risk capabilities. Additionally, a 'whole of community' approach to research funding would have the benefit of giving the community some control over funding allocation decisions rather than not collaborating on these and seeing decisions being made in more arbitrary ways by the political leadership.

Research like all the other key enabling activities discussed earlier (e.g. HR and ICT) are linked to effective intelligence governance. This means that ideally the development of a community wide strategic research plan for improving bio-threat and risk capability requires strong leadership at the apex of each intelligence community and across its membership agencies. The logical place to articulate what the key research capability issues are over say the next 5 years would be in the national health security plan implemented by a national health security coordination council. This approach will allow the political leadership to 'have their say' on what they see as the research priorities, but also be advised by the executive leadership across each 'Five Eye's intelligence community. An operational bio-threat and risk research capability plan could then be decided upon based on the strategic priorities identified by the national health security coordination council.

It is unwise to be prescriptive at this time about what issues, questions and topics should be in an operational bio-threat and risk research capability plan. Over the next 5–7 years, this would need to be decided based on what evidence can be assembled on the likely trajectory of bio-threats and risks in each 'Five Eyes' country. Based on the exponential growth in synthetic biology and biotechnology it is also unlikely that each intelligence community will be able to get a strong fix on all potential threats and risks. So decisions will need to be made about where limited resources for research should go based on incomplete information. Nonetheless, a further expansion of a strategic and cross disciplinary approach to research that includes national security, law enforcement, military, the scientific community and the private sector will likely identify areas of common priority and concern for research.

An intelligence research strategy for addressing bio-threat and risk capability gaps also needs to consider holistically where gaps reside. These could be technical or scientific gaps as discussed in the next chapter (Chapter 7) or knowledge or practice deficiencies in the way intelligence is produced. Hence, any strategy needs to consider where capability vulnerabilities lay in both the core intelligence processes (tasking and coordination, collection, analysis) and other key enabling activities.

Conclusion

This chapter summarised the challenges (to a lesser or greater extent) each 'Five Eyes' country faces in developing stronger intelligence governance within their ICs and how this may impact on the management of bio-threats and risks in the future. Intelligence governance is a critical key enabling activity that needs improvement, though significant progress also needs to be made in other enabling activities such as ICT, HR and research. Rather than providing detailed prescriptive remedies to all the challenges, the chapter provided some general options that might improve the bio-threat and risk capabilities of 'Five Eyes' intelligence communities. However, the actual 'solutions' to the many challenges identified will likely be different in each country for budgetary, political and cultural reasons. While the focus of this Chapter was broadly on what 'Five Eyes' intelligence communities can do *internally* to better manage bio-threats and risks, Chapter 7 explores how key stakeholders of the IC (scientific community, private sector, public health community) can also play a critical role in building intelligence capability into the future.

References

ACIC. (2016). *ACIC 2016–17 Annual Report*. Canberra: Commonwealth of Australia.

Aras, G., & Crowther, D. (2010). *A Handbook of Corporate Governance and Social Responsibility*. Farnham, UK: Taylor and Francis.

Baxendale, R. (2017, July 18). Australia to Get Super Home Affairs Ministry. *The Australian*.

Blue Ribbon Study Panel. (2015). *Blue Ribbon Study Panel on Biodefense. A National Blueprint for Biodefense: Leadership and Major Reform Needed to Optimise Efforts*. Washington, DC: Hudson Institute for Policy Studies.

Blue Ribbon Study Panel. (2016). *Biodefense Indicators One Year Later. Events Outpacing Federal Efforts to Defend the Nation*. Arlington, VA: Potomac Institute for Policy Studies.

Campbell, S. H. (2011). A Survey of the U.S. Market for Intelligence Education. *International Journal of Intelligence and Counterintelligence, 24*(2), 307–337. https://doi.org/10.1080/08850607.2011.548207.

Chhotray, V., & Stoker, G. (2008). *Governance Theory and Practice: A Cross-Disciplinary Approach*. London, UK: Palgrave Macmillan.

GAO. (2005). *Critical Infrastructure Protection. DHS Faces Challenges in Fulfilling Cybersecurity Responsibilities*. Washington, DC: GAO.

GAO. (2011a). *Cybersecurity Human Capital Initiatives Need Better Planning and Coordination*. Washington, DC: GAO.

GAO. (2011b). *Defense Department Cyber Efforts: DOD Faces Challenges in Its Cyber Activities*. Washington, DC: GAO.

GAO. (2017). *Biodefense Federal Efforts to Develop Biological Threat Awareness*. Washington, DC: GAO.

Gentry, J. (2015). Has the ODNI Improved US Intelligence Analysis? *International Journal of Intelligence and Counterintelligence, 28,* 637–661.

Hummel, K. (2017). A View from the CT Foxhole: Edward You, FBI WMD Directorate, Biological Countermeasures Unit. *CTC Sentinel, 10*(7), 9–12.

Inglesby, T., & Haas, B. (2017, November 21). Ready for a Global Pandemic? The Trump Administration May Be Woefully Underprepared. *Foreign Affairs*.

Johnson, L. (2015). A Conversation with James R. Clapper Jr. The Director of National Intelligence in the United States. *Intelligence and National Security, 30*(1), 1–25.

L'Estrange, M., & Merchant, S. (2017). *Independent Intelligence Review*. Canberra: Commonwealth of Australia.

Marrin, S. (2009). Training and Educating U.S. Intelligence Analysts. *International Journal of Intelligence and Counterintelligence, 22*(1), 131–146. https://doi.org/10.1080/08850600802486986.

Martin, A. (2018, February 27). Legislation Aims to Boost Accountability, Collaboration of DHS Fusion Centers. *Homeland Preparedness News*.

NAS. (2017). *A Proposed Framework for Identifying Potential Biodefense Vulnerabilities Posed by Synthetic Biology Interim Report*. Washington, DC: National Academy of Sciences.

Office of Inspectors General DOJ & DHS. (2017). *Review of Domestic Sharing of Counter Terrorism Information*. Washington, DC: Office of Inspector General, Department of Homeland Security.

Riley, K. (2018, February 28). Blue Ribbon Study Panel on Biodefense Warns Congress Against Delaying Federal Funds Tied to Comprehensive Strategy. *Homeland Preparedness News*.

Rudner, M. (2009). Intelligence Studies in Higher Education: Capacity-Building to Meet Societal Demand. *International Journal of Intelligence and Counterintelligence, 22*(1), 110–130. https://doi.org/10.1080/0885060080 2486960.

Silberman, L., & Robb, C. (2005). *Commission on the Intelligence Capabilities of the US Regarding Weapons of Mass Destruction. Report to the President of the United States* (pp. 1–501). Washington, DC.

Walsh, P. F. (2011). *Intelligence and Intelligence Analysis.* Abingdon, UK: Routledge.

Walsh, P. F. (2012). *Submission and Testimony to Inquiry into the Use of Criminal Intelligence, by Joint Parliamentary on Law Enforcement* (Final Report). Australian Parliament, Canberra. Retrieved from http://www.aph.gov.au/parliamentary_business/Committees/Senate_Committees?url=le_ctte/criminal_intelligence/submission.htm.

Walsh, P. F. (2015). Building Better Intelligence Frameworks Through Effective Governance. *International Journal of Intelligence and Counterintelligence, 28*(1), 123–142. https://doi.org/10.1080/08850607.20 14.924816.

Walsh, P. F. (2016). Australian National Security Intelligence Collection Since 9/11: Policy and Legislative Challenges. In K. Warby (Ed.), *National Security, Surveillance and Terror* (pp. 51–74). Cham, Switzerland: Springer International Publishing.

Walsh, P. F. (2017). Making Future Leaders in the US Intelligence Community: Challenges and Opportunities. *Intelligence and National Security, 32*(4), 441–459. https://doi.org/10.1080/02684527.2016.1253920.

7

Intelligence and Stakeholders

Chapter 6, explored what more the intelligence communities across 'Five Eyes' countries can do from their broader organisational levels to better identify, prevent, disrupt and treat potential and emerging bio-threats and risks. In this chapter, the aim is to survey how *external* partners and stakeholders of intelligence communities can play a greater role in helping the ICs build bio-threat and risk capability in the future. The role of stakeholders can involve building capability internally or externally to national security and law enforcement agencies.

Chapter 6 demonstrated that building stronger intelligence governance and key enabling activities is crucial to developing adaptable and responsive intelligence enterprises that are better able to interpret emerging bio-threats and risks for decision-makers. However, as discussed in the previous chapter, the 'Five Eyes' countries, cannot alone improve their understanding of complex bio-threats and risks without the input from important partners and stakeholders. As discussed in Chapters 4 and 5, intelligence stakeholders, depending on the specific bio-threat or risk can be a large and diverse number of people and institutions. Subject matter expert scientists (e.g. epidemiologists, microbiologists, forensic analysts, clinicians, public health specialists, molecular biologists,

© The Author(s) 2018
P. F. Walsh, *Intelligence, Biosecurity and Bioterrorism*,
https://doi.org/10.1057/978-1-137-51700-5_7

agricultural scientists and veterinarians) can all be critical stakeholders for intelligence communities. Without them it would be almost impossible to see how the IC alone can fulfil its mission to identify, prevent, disrupt and treat potential and emerging bio-threats and risks.

Indeed as seen in Chapter 4 'the scientific community' brings a lot of expertise to the intelligence community about how to assess bio-threats and risks in a number of different ways and contexts. These include understanding potential risks through GOF experiments, the development of biosensors and knowledge about weaponisation, pathogenicity and transmissibility of various bio-agents. Chapter 4 also surveyed briefly the role of scientists working in epidemiology and forensics as providing central roles in the prevention, disruption and treatment of bio-threats and risks. Additionally, Chapter 5, highlighted the critical role the scientific community plays in helping the intelligence community better frame their understanding of potential threats and risks emerging from the fast paced changing biotechnology and synthetic biology sectors.

This chapter provides a thematic analysis of how important stakeholders can contribute to reducing current and emerging bio-threats and risks. In contrast to Chapter 6, which focused on what *internally* the intelligence community can do to better equip itself to manage bio-threats and risks, this chapter surveys what important *external stakeholders* can bring to the table to improve intelligence capability and to reduce bio-threats and risks themselves. Paraphrasing research impact scholar Mark Reed's definition, I define a stakeholder of the intelligence community as any person, organisation or group that is affected by or can affect a decision, action or issue relevant to preventing, disrupting or treating bio-threats and risks (Reed 2016: 41). Specifically, I am referring to stakeholders in the scientific, research, clinical, policy, first responder and private sectors that can provide capability, expertise to the intelligence community and/or contribute to biosecurity through their own actions.

In particular, the thematic analysis of the role of stakeholders in this chapter is organised around three sub-headings: *prevention, disruption and treatment*. Traversing the literature and interviews with a select number of stakeholders shows there that there is a large and diverse number of individuals and organisations that could potentially play a role in either preventing, disrupting or treating future bio-threats and risks. Hence, it is not possible to explore individual stakeholders in great detail in the space available. While some stakeholders will be mentioned by name for illustrative purposes, the discussion below provides analytical generalisations of scientific innovations, techniques, research, policies and other initiatives that stakeholders can bring to improve the future capability of intelligence communities as well as contributing themselves to prevent, disrupt and treat bio-threats and risks.

Prevention

Improving Bio-Surveillance Capability

Before discussing what knowledge and capabilities various bio-surveillance stakeholders can bring to the intelligence community it is important first to define the term. Unsurprisingly, there are several definitions to choose from. In this section I have selected a comprehensive definition cited in a US GAO report.

> In the biological context, surveillance is the ongoing collection, analysis, and interpretation of data to help monitor for pathogens in plants, animals, and humans; food; and the environment. The general aim of surveillance is to help develop policy, guide mission priorities, and provide assurance of the prevention and control of disease. In recent years, as concerns about consequences of a catastrophic biological attack or emerging infectious diseases grew, the term bio surveillance became more common in relation to an array of threats to our national security. Bio surveillance is concerned with two things: (1) reducing, as much as possible, the time it takes to recognize and characterize biological events with potentially catastrophic consequences and (2) providing situational awareness—that is, information that signals an event might be occurring, information about what those signals mean, and information about how events will likely unfold in the near future (GAO 2011: 9).

This definition highlights how the functions and roles of bio-surveillance has changed from a more narrow concern of mapping disease in the public health sector to represent a diverse array of knowledge and capabilities that are vital in understanding bio-threats in the national security context. The definition also underscores the ongoing multiple challenges in improving bio-surveillance capabilities and their utility in the national security context. Three key challenges in particular remain for improving national bio-surveillance capabilities and they are: methodological, information sharing and integration issues. The information sharing and integration issues have already been discussed in Chapter 6 so this section will focus on the bio-surveillance methodology issues. By methodological issues, I am referring to both the technical methods (biosensors) and the broader different disciplinary approaches to bio-surveillance that now inform debates amongst stakeholders on how to improve bio-surveillance capabilities.

From a technical perspective, there has been a range of bio-sensor research from inside and outside the IC to detect the release of dangerous pathogens into the environment. Perhaps the most well-known of these initiatives—Biowatch was developed by DHS in 2003 with the aim to detect aerolised bio attacks for high risk bioagents in major US cities. The program however, has had mixed success relating to the reliability of results and the delay in the publication of these once samples were collected from the field (GAO 2016, 2017). The DHS tried to speed up the detection times from the first generation manual systems to Gen 3 acquisitions, which promised speedier autonomous systems though testing difficulties remained. Further analysis, however, of alternatives by the DHS as showing any advantages of an autonomous system over the current manual system were insufficient to justify the cost of a fully technology switch (GAO 2016: 7). In the US, research continues to improve the robustness, sensitivity, specificity, timeliness and cost of biosensor equipment. While conventional PCR based methods and immunoassay are still being used other biochemical, microbiological and genetic solutions are being trialled such as the incorporation of antibodies and peptide molecules, which may greatly reduce detection times to minutes instead of several hours (Kim et al. 2015). Leaving aside efforts to improve aerolised biosensors, the expected rapid growth of synthetic biology and biotechnology and the potential (however unknown) that bioengineered material may be used maliciously in a way that threatens public safety or national security may shift the focus into other scientific research that can detect signals of bio-engineering including types of changes, location and possibly in the future where changes were made. In July 2017, IARPA commissioned a new program—Finding Engineering Linked Indicators (FELIX) to meet such objectives. IARPA is seeking interest from a range of scientists (synthetic biologists, micro biologist, immunologist, statisticians and computer scientists) to carry out 3–5 research projects addressing the two main focus points of FELIX (Eaves 2017). If this research can produce reliable results, it will provide another useful collection and analysis point for the IC by allowing the detection of previously undetectable signatures of bio-engineered material in bio-criminal and terrorism cases.

In addition to the various technical innovations in biosensors, a range of other bio-surveillance methods have been deployed. In the late 1990s, the US CDC pioneered syndromic surveillance systems, which were initially aimed at improving the early warning of infectious diseases and bio-terrorism and have now evolved to include situational awareness (Buehler et al. 2004). Similar syndromic surveillance systems have developed in other 'Five Eyes' countries such as the UK's Real-Time Syndromic Surveillance Team (ReSST), which collects four national syndromic surveillance systems from several sources. Additionally and more recently, the Robert Koch Institute is creating an early warning system based on machine learning and natural language processing that will include 'appealing' interactive web applications and be linked to the German electronic reporting and information system DEMIS (Robert Koch Institute 2018). Syndromic surveillance systems are a critical adjunct to traditional public health lab surveillance as they strive to provide real time or near real time collection, analysis and dissemination of health data to enable early identification and management of public health threats as they are not based on lab confirmed diagnoses—and assess a wider set of health related data including: clinical signs, absenteeism, pharmacy sales or animal health production collapse (Buehler 2004). A clear benefit of syndromic surveillance is it can be cheaper, faster and potentially more transparent then a state's public health lab surveillance system. However, as with the use of big volumes of data more broadly in the IC, data quantity, quality and structural variation all impact on the utility, accuracy and timeliness of some rapid epidemic intelligence from internet based surveillance methods (Yan et al. 2017).

Increasingly these syndromic surveillance systems rely on the use of big data, machine learning and analytics. Additionally, web based epidemic detection systems like BioCaster Portal developed by the National Institute of Informatics in Tokyo (Collier 2015) and Canada's Global Public Health Intelligence Network (GPHIN) an event based surveillance system which looks at news feeds globally have also contributed to syndromic surveillance systems (Mawudeku et al. 2015). Several event based internet surveillance systems have grown in number in the last decade. Using PubMed, Scopus and Google Scholar data bases, O'Shea's study found 50 based internet systems all using different technology and data sources to gather data, process and disseminate it to detect infectious disease outbreaks (O'Shea 2017). In line with the broader IC development of exploiting social media analytics discussed in Chapter 4, in 2013 DHS piloted another approach to bio-surveillance. The pilot involved DHS trialling various social media analytics from self-reported information on Facebook and twitter to determine pandemics and acts of terrorism given social media feeds can provide close to real time reporting of symptoms, sickness access to hospital or pharmaceuticals (Insinna 2013).

Additionally, other private companies have entered the bio-surveillance space—providing novel methods for capturing bio-surveillance data. Wilson's discussion of how a private company (Veratect Corporation) assessed signal recognition in global media reports to provide warning on the emergence of the 2009 H1N1 influenza pandemic shows how the IC warning culture methodology can be employed usefully along with what he described as the 'risk adverse forensically oriented response culture favoured by traditional public health practitioners' (Wilson 2017: 1). The Veratect case shows that the private sector has a role in developing better bio-surveillance capability as well.

As can be seen from the brief discussion above about different methodological approaches to bio-surveillance. There are also different views amongst bio-surveillance scholars and practitioners about the merits of each, particularly in their abilities to predict the 'next pandemic'. Can for example, a national bio-surveillance system informed by one or more methods discussed above predict the emergence of the next pandemic or outbreak, particularly novel new viruses? Some scientists argue that the prediction of a micro-evolutionary process of some biological agents such as a virus (i.e. a short term emergence or cross species transition) is incredibly difficult given evolutionary and epidemiological timescales are fundamentally different. Geoghegan and Holmes argue that instead it would be better to build surveillance capability that 'assesses the fault line of disease emergence at the human-animal interface, particularly those shaped by ecological disturbances' (2017: 7).

Others have argued differently. Scientists working on the USAID funded PREDICT and the Global Virome Project examine disease hotspots globally in order to sequence (rather ambitiously) almost all the viruses in birds and mammals that could potentially spill over into humans. In particular, researchers working on the Global Virome Project believe that prediction of which viruses might spill over from animal to human health is possible. Geoghegan and Holmes in response argue focusing on disease hotspots relies on very small amounts of data that can be unreliable given they are rare events. They give the example of Saudi Arabia which has not classically been a hotspot, yet MERS recently jumped into humans from camels there. Sequencing these viruses may provide useful evolutionary information, but Geoghegan and Holmes argue it won't necessarily provide early warning of what is going to affect us (Geoghegan and Holmes 2017).

Other scientists are trying to change the ecology of disease, which presumably in some cases would make the early warning of some pandemics easier. In recent years, the scientific community has increasingly exploited CRISPR gene editing techniques to change the genetic makeup of malaria mosquitoes. Additionally, advances in gene drives have recently been shown to change the ecological parameters of disease. Gene drives are artificial 'selfish' genes that can force itself into 99% of an organism's offspring instead of the usual 50%. Currently there is a global research effort funded by the Gates Foundation to cause female mosquitoes to become sterile within 11 generations or 1 year. The objective would be to release the genetically altered mosquitoes into malarial areas by 2029 (Regalado 2016). There are concerns by the FBI however that gene drives could be misused to create a 'designer plague' (ibid.).

In addition to the 'predictability' challenges presented by various bio-surveillance methods, there are also differences in opinion amongst members of the bio-surveillance community about what an effective bio-surveillance system looks like. On what metrics can an 'effective bio-surveillance' system be evaluated given the multiple methodological approaches and systems that have developed for bio-surveillance? Clinician and public health security specialist Jim Wilson has argued that the development of an effective global surveillance and response system is probably at least a decade or more away (Wilson 2017: 222). In the interim, we are left with multiple approaches of varying validity and reliability. So based on the current fragmented bio-surveillance efforts how do we learn the lessons that need to be learnt that will enable the implementation of the long awaited national bio-surveillance capabilities? How do we know if progress is being made to that goal? Importantly, beyond national efforts, how do we assess the current capability of state, local agencies to contribute to a national bio-surveillance capabilities? Where are the gaps and vulnerabilities in the current sub-national bio-surveillance and detection systems? (GAO 2011). Compounding the current challenge of evaluating bio-surveillance capabilities in order to construct a viable national approach is that different bio-surveillance systems have been created for different end users (e.g. animal and human). The Blue Ribbon Project report into animal health detailed information sharing challenges in animal health bio-surveillance and its integration with other bio-surveillance data including in human health (Blue Ribbon Report 2017: 25). This lack of integration makes it difficult to assess how information collected for animal or agricultural bio-surveillance could improve national approaches to bio-surveillance, particularly in scenarios where the emergence of disease could be an intentional or a malevolent act.

Different approaches to bio-surveillance have been informed by multi-disciplinary perspectives, which can be both a strength and weakness to developing a national perspective. Current efforts across the 'Five Eyes' to develop fully national and integrated bio-surveillance capabilities remain works in progress and the political will to steward them into being seems insufficient. For example, in the US a program designed to provide a national bio-surveillance and integration system was eliminated in the President's Budget Request for FY 2018 (Blue Ribbon Report 2017: 41).

Any evaluation of the effectiveness of various methods and approaches for building a national bio-surveillance capability also needs to consider how national efforts can both enhance and lever off global bio-surveillance capabilities. Gaps and impediments in global bio-surveillance have become increasingly evident to the world in the wake of the largest Ebola epidemic ever—in which these challenges impacted the ability to prevent, detect, and respond. Under the looming threat of MERS-CoV, leishmaniasis, influenza, multidrug-resistant tuberculosis, and plague, the global public health community now realizes the urgent need to address shortcomings in global bio-surveillance and the broader public health security system. Properly preparing for the next major outbreak hinges on our willingness to transform global health surveillance systems and those of countries with fragile health infrastructures (Shaikh et al. 2015: 183–186). In some respects, similar challenges in developing national bio-surveillance capabilities exist in those at the global level including: siloed systems, inadequate training and technical expertise, different information and communication technology (ICT) standards, concerns over data sharing and confidentiality, poor interoperability, and inadequate analytical approaches and tools.

There is likely not one bio-surveillance method, technique or tool that is going to detect in real time disease outbreaks, particularly unusual ones which might imply malicious intent. A fully integrated approach to bio-surveillance may rely on more than one method or capability which together can provide reliable and valid bio-surveillance data and early warning at the national and global level. It may mean investigating ways that older legacy systems can be integrated or at least made interoperable with newer more mobile platforms such as mobile or wireless health technologies particularly in the developing world (Shaikh et al. 2015). It should be clear by now that improving bio-surveillance capabilities is essential to improving the prevention of natural and suspicious outbreaks of disease. It is important for the 'Five Eyes' intelligence and law enforcement communities to understand broadly the theoretical and practical developments in bio-surveillance so that they are able to more effectively lever relevant knowledge on bio-threats and risks.

Improving National, Regional and Global Health Security Capacity

A second cluster of stakeholders that are useful in the prevention of bio-threats and risks (both natural and malicious) are those working in national, regional and global health. The Ebola epidemic (2014–2015) was a recent reminder of the consequences of weak public health capability and infrastructure in failing to prevent, identify and respond quickly to infectious disease. The Ebola epidemic also had a catalytic effect on many public health authorities, practitioners and researcher's views about the capability of the traditional UN response to global health crisis mainly coordinated through the WHO. Many public health watchers are now arguing the need for a broader more effective focus—not just on prevention and response to infectious disease, but one that also included reframing the focus as a human security issue. Adherents to this view make a compelling point when seen through the Ebola case that continues to have significant impact on the economic and social stability of countries impacted (Sparrow 2016; Marston et al. 2017; WHO 2015; MMWR 2016). Beyond West Africa, similar vulnerabilities in capabilities such as diseases surveillance, detection, contract tracing, clinical care, community engagement and communications exist globally as was also seen with the proliferation of Zika in Latin American/Caribbean and MERs in the Middle East. In 2016, the Commission on a Global Health Risk Framework for the Future that met after the Ebola crisis estimated 4.5 billion per year investment would be needed for better detection and response tools. The same Commission report also estimated that the economic cost for global pandemics per year was $60 billion (Schnirring 2016; Dzau and Sands 2016).

Effective national bio-surveillance relies on not only what 'Five Eyes' countries can do to improve the scientific and technical capability of bio-surveillance, but also how they can improve bio-surveillance globally particularly in at risk areas. Beyond effective bio-surveillance, effective prevention of pandemics whether natural, accidental or malicious relies on good global (multilateral), regional and national public health responses.

There are several multilateral instruments, institutions and initiatives that are relevant, but I will focus here on what have become the key ones rather than attempting to traverse in detail all major international health initiatives struck since 9/11. They include WHO International Health Regulations (IHR), UN Security Resolution 1540, the Global Health Security Agenda (GHSA), the Biological Weapons Convention (BWC) and the Australia Group.

WHO IHR

The WHO international health regulations (2005) entered into force in June 2007 to prevent, protect against, control and provide a public health response to the international spread of diseases (detect, assess, notify events has a biosafety and biosecurity function) and includes all 192 members of the UN. The IHR 2005 has improved accountability of countries about progress towards building national core public health capability targets in several areas including, but not limited to: surveillance systems, creating rapid response teams, border management. However, the IHR annual reporting process has been by self-assessment of core capacities to the World Health Assembly (WHA) by all state parties, which has resulted in incomplete or not credible reporting for some member states.

The Commission on Global Health Risk Framework for the Future also expressed concerns over the self-assessment monitoring tool of the IHR, because questions are binary (yes/no) answers and recommended that WHO devise a regular independent mechanism to evaluate country performance against benchmarks (GHRF Commission 2015: 33). For example, a country can 'tick yes' for having a national public health legislation, but other dependent legislation (biosecurity, food safety, environmental health) may not be in place—thereby reducing overall the country's ability to manage health crisis or for the global community to understand and respond to capability and information gaps in that country (ibid.). Some countries continue to be slow or uneven in their reporting of IHR (2005) attributes. In 2013, one study showed that the African region was well below global averages across all attributes measures with no African state reporting full implementation (Kasolo et al. 2013: 11–13).

Biological Weapons Convention (BWC)

The second multilateral instrument relevant to our discussion here is the UN Security Council Resolution 1540 (2004), which calls on all 192 states to prohibit non-state actors from developing, acquiring, manufacturing, possessing, transporting, transferring or using nuclear, chemical or biological weapons and their delivery systems.

More importantly and specific to bio-threats only, the BWC has historically played the most significant role in preventing the weaponisation of biology. The BWC was established in 1972 and seeks to prohibit the development, production, acquisition, transfer, stockpiling and use of biological and toxin weapons (Gerstein 2013; Chevrier and Spelling 2016: 331–356). In 2001, there was an attempt by some member states to introduce a verification process, but this was vetoed by the US following inspection of Soviet sites under the Tripartite agreement between the Soviet Union, USA and the UK. The US arguing it could be difficult to certify that a state's biological program was merely defensive rather than offensive. The US also had concerns that inspection to labs could be disruptive or provide opportunity for industrial espionage against legitimately operating biotechnology companies (Gerstein 2013: 137). Historically there has been a mixed record by some 'Five Eyes' intelligence countries in assessing verification and therefore non-compliance of the BWC. Koblentz surveyed the role of intelligence (particularly HUMINT) in assessing the former Soviet Union's offensive bio-weapons program between 1971 and 1990 which resulted in an incomplete picture of Moscow's program (Koblentz 2009: 157). Additionally, as discussed in Chapter 2, in 2002 several 'Five Eyes' intelligence communities (US, UK and Australia) incorrectly assessed that Iraq had a mobile offensive bio-weapon capability. Intelligence collection on its own can either over or under-estimate such capabilities.

Between 5 yearly review conferences, several initiatives and activities have been introduced (confidence building measure, meetings of experts, information exchanges) to improve the effectiveness and the implementation of the Convention. However, state parties are only encouraged to implement relevant national legislation and other measures to prohibit prevent the development, production, stockpiling or transfer or use of bio weapons. How they precisely undertake measures is at the discretion of individual state parties. The BWC has been criticised for several reasons over the years. Some of this is warranted, while other criticisms seem to not take into account that the BWC is different from its chemical and nuclear counter proliferation counterparts. As Gerstein argues, 'material is the centre of gravity for nuclear discussions and intent being the center of gravity for biological issues' (Gerstein 2013: 176). Developing nuclear weapons leaves a large recognizable footprint, whereas the development of an offensive biological weapon requires virtually no specialised equipment (ibid.).

The first major criticism of the BWC is that it has no verification mechanism or any other mandatory provisions for monitoring compliance. A second complaint is that for many years (until 2006), it lacked an implementation capability to help states fulfil their obligations. Since 2006, the Convention has had a small three team Implementation Support Unit (ISU) based in the United Nations Office for Disarmament Affairs in Geneva which aims to 'assist, coordinate, and magnify the implementation efforts of the States Parties to help States Parties help themselves' (Lennane 2011: 85). In reality though, the ISU does not have 'capacity for analysis and coordination other than for the collection of the annually submitted confidence building measures, posting them to the website and organising and attending conferences' (Gerstein 2013: 173). Historically there has also been a low number of party states submitting their annual confidence building measures. Although the BWC ISU was able to report that a record number (81) annual confidence building measures were submitted in 2016, this only represented 45.5% of all 179 state parties submitting that year. Though the trend line seems to be going up from a low in 2014 of 19 (*BWC Newsletter* 2017: 3).

A third criticism of the BWC is that it has moved slowly since inception and further questions remain about its relevance strategically and operationally in preventing bio-threats and risks into the future. Such questions are likely fundamental to its long term viability. However despite shortcomings, the BWC has nonetheless created a normative institution for reducing the risk of biological or toxin weapons being used or developed by state and non-state actors (Lennane 2011: 85). More importantly, as developments in biotechnology continue at a pace, the BWC does provide a venue, where the security implications of dual-use technology can be assessed which will be critical in 'mitigating these emerging threats' (Gerstein 2013: 175). The BWC still does have an important role in reducing weaponisation of biology in the future, though its poor funding particularly of the ISU means that other multi-lateral measures are needed to amplify the work of the Convention.

The Proliferation Security Initiative and the Australia Group

In addition to the above historic/traditional proliferation arrangements of the BWC, other international regimes have been implemented such as the Australia Group (established in 1985) and the Proliferation Security Initiative (established in 2003). Both have a broader counter proliferation objectives beyond biological weapons to chemical and nuclear. The Australia Group 41 member countries have collaborated on the development of lists of technologies and materials that could be used in the development of chemical and biological weapons. Member countries then commit to monitor the export or transfer of these materials. The Australia Group maintains common control lists for dual use bio-equipment, technology, software, bio agents and plant and animal pathogens as the basis for promoting common standards and regulations (Australia Group Common Control List Handbook 2015). The Australia Group works in concert with the BWC. The PSI was a Bush Administration initiative that sought to supplement existing non-proliferation regimes, but seeks to enforce these by interdicting and seizing illegal weapons or missile technology in planes or ships carrying cargo. The PSI also includes intelligence sharing and joint operational activity (National Institute for Public Policy 2009).

Global Health Security Agenda (GHSA)

Turning the focus slightly away from multi-lateral counter proliferation measures, other multilateral initiatives have focused on improving global health security. In some respects the GHSA provides a bridge between traditional, narrow security approaches to biological weapons and a wider securitisation of global health. The GHSA was established in 2014 by the Obama Administration and is a multi-sectoral approach to global health security seeking to include governments, international organisations and non-government organisations. GHSA was set up in part to 'advance further the IHR implementation through focused activities to strengthen core capacities and to ensure a world safe and secure from global health threats posed by infectious disease; where we can prevent or mitigate the impact of naturally occurring outbreak and intentional or accidental releases of dangerous pathogens' (Heymann et al. 2015: 1889). GHSA is a refreshing approach not only because it seeks to establish a global framework and capacity to assess, measure and sustain advances in global preparedness for epidemic threats, but it also addresses biosecurity as a public health priority—thereby linking public health and health security, development, defense and agricultural sector (Cameron 2017). The underlining logic of GHSA suggests that the same attributes needed to prevent, detect and respond to deliberate use of a bio agent are those required to manage a natural or accidental outbreak of a biological agent. GHSA also includes 12 technical targets aligned to three areas: prevention, detection and response (Heymann et al. 2015: 1889). Like earlier initiatives, such as the US sponsored Global Health Initiative (GHI), which was discontinued by the Obama Administration in 2012 due a lack of financial and technical authority to leverage and coordinate multiple US agencies—the GHSA will need to secure ongoing funding beyond 2019 from major donors including the US. At a November 2017 GHSA ministerial meeting in Uganda, assembled governments signed onto an extension of the GHSA for another five years. US Secretary Tillerson had issued public support for continuing it, but at the time of writing no commitment by the US for future financial support (beyond FY 2019) has been made. GHSA holds promise, but in addition to ongoing funding challenges, those member states signed up to it will need to ensure effective governance is in place to align funding to global health priorities articulated by the WHO, World Bank, IMF and other donors in order to avoid duplication and promote an effective approach to international health security capabilities (Paranjape and Franz 2015; Schnirring 2017).

In summary, this discussion of multilateral security and global health initiatives demonstrates that there is a diverse number of stakeholders working in these sectors, which can play a role in preventing bio-threats and risks—whether they are natural pandemics or a malicious attack from a biological weapon. It's clear that the 'Five Eyes' intelligence communities have worked extensively with other member states in counter-proliferation institutions such as the BWC and the Australia Group for several decades, but what remains still under developed is how global health security stakeholders and intelligence communities can work more collaboratively for the mutual goal of global health security regardless of whether the risks are natural pandemics or result from a bio-terror attack or theft of a dangerous select agent from a lab. More trusting and formalised contact between both global health security stakeholders and those working in the security and intelligence communities can only be mutually beneficial to preventing major bio-threats and risks.

Stakeholders and Their Own Biosafety Procedures

The final cluster of stakeholders that can help prevent bio-threats and risks are of course those that specialise in biosafety and its promotion in their research institutes, biotechnology companies, universities and medical facilities. Promoting biosafety in environments that work with select agents and other facilities that work with less dangerous material which can still cause harm relies on consistently high risk management practices. In all 'Five Eyes' countries there has historically been in place biosafety risk management procedures and practices to prevent accidental infection, accidental release, or intentional misuse of biological substances. However, as noted in Chapter 2 in the last two decades the expansion in synthetic biology, biotechnology and biological science research has meant there are now more people working in more locations on dangerous pathogens—not just in well-regulated liberal democracies such as those in the 'Five Eyes' countries, but also in developing countries; where biosafety and biosecurity capabilities and practice may be less established such as parts of Africa, the Middle East,

Pakistan and former Soviet states (Gronvall et al. 2016; Shinwari et al. 2014). Just in terms of the scale of this expansion of facilities working with dangerous pathogens—in the US alone, there is thought to be thousands of BSL 3 labs and in China the number of such labs is increasing too (Nature Editorial 2014: 443).

The US and other 'Five Eyes' countries such as Canada have invested in cooperative engagement programs since 9/11 in several former Soviet Union states. The US Defense Threat Reduction Agency (DTRA) has lead efforts in Georgia to reduce bio-risk by securing/consolidating pathogens, training scientists in biosafety and biosecurity technology, regulation and detection. Likewise, the CDC has been involved in building public health capacity there as well as in Armenia and Azerbaijan (Bakanidze et al. 2010: 7). As important as building biosafety capacity is in developing countries, it is clear that much more still needs to be done to build biosafety capacity in 'Five Eyes' countries—including finding better ways to understand and manage comprehensively threats and risks in the biosciences environment.

Biosafety experts such as Salerno and Gaudioso argue for more comprehensive risk management systems across the global bioscience community 'to avoid an accident that jeopardizes the entire bioscience enterprise' (Salerno and Gaudioso 2015: xv). Their argument is that such a system would supplement existing national and international biosafety regulations by risk managing fully at an organisational and unit level every single potential incident rather than by generic risk hazard assessments that are currently done by most facilities today (ibid.: 201). Others have also called for more systematic tools and approaches for managing biosafety incidents in labs dealing with particular dangerous pathogens such as Marburg Virus (Dickmann et al. 2015). Still others have argued that while 'security awareness is high among employees who work with biological select agents and toxins, it is not pervasive across the entire life research community' (Grphyon Scientific 2016: 1014).

Such a statement does not seem to be hyperbole if one looks at some of the cases of biosafety and security lapses since 9/11 (GAO 2009, 2013). There have been several lapses at CDC between 2014 and 2016. In June 2014, dozens of workers in CDC could have been potentially exposed to live anthrax that hadn't been killed before being shipped from CDC's Bioterrorism Rapid Response and Advanced Technology (BRRAT) BSL 3 to a BSL 2 lab in its Bacterial Special Pathogens Branch. CDC investigations determined that at least 67 CDC staff members may have been exposed to viable anthrax cells or spores though no illness or deaths occurred (CDC 2014). The same report found several breaches of biosafety process and procedure including failures of policy, training, supervision, judgement and even scientific knowledge (ibid.). Similarly, biosafety lapses cases involving CDC labs occurred in January 2014 when an unintentional cross contamination strain of low pathogenic avian influenza A (H9N2) with a strain of highly pathogenic avian influenza A (H5N1) was shipped from CDC to the USDA (Schnirring 2014). Further biosafety breaches were detected in July 2014—this time at the National Institute of Health campus in Bethesda Maryland; where 6 viable smallpox vials were discovered improperly stored (Dennis and Sun 2014a). An additional five improperly stored vials were also found at the NIH—three were select agents (*Burkholderia pseudmomallei, Francisella tularensis and Yersinia pestis*) (Dennis and Sun 2014b). In the NIH cases despite their age, they were still viable organisms which could have caused illness. Their theft could have also posed a bio-threat and risk to the community.

Then after a hiatus where biological material was suspended being sent between BSL 3 and BSL 2 labs live transfers commenced again. After a further internal CDC review (CDC 2015a, b) some additional safety measures were put into place, however there was a subsequent lapse when a specimen of Chikungunya virus was shipped from a high secure lab in Fort Collins to a lower level one which had not been killed (Young 2015). Similarly, in 2015 the Pentagon shipped live anthrax spores from the Dugway Proving Ground in Utah to 9 states and one international location that were also meant to have been killed (Burns 2015). It was later found that Dugway and the US DOD had been shipping nationally and internationally live anthrax for more than 10 years—often without adequate safeguards. Other reports suggested that some samples were sent by Federal Express (Sisk 2016). Similarly in November 2016, the US HHS discovered that a private lab had 'inadvertently sent a toxic form of ricin to one of its training centres multiple times since 2011 putting training staff at risk' (GAO 2017: 1). Similar biosafety lapses have occurred in the UK resulting in 75 investigations since 2010 of government, university and hospital labs (Sample 2014).

As noted in Chapter 2, one possible bio-threat and risk pathway could be the theft of biological substances or information from a biosciences institution. Lapses in biosafety arrangements demonstrate, at least in some cases, biosecurity vulnerabilities that could make the theft or even infiltration of a threat actor into high containment lab easier. Thefts from labs have occurred in the past by an insider, and a motivated insider can compromise biosafety for a range of reasons. Bunn and Sagan's edited book *Insider Threats* provides a useful taxonomy for thinking about 'insider threats' (Bunn and Sagan 2016). They can be: self-motivated insiders, who at some point decide to become a spy or thief. Insiders can also be recruited insiders, who are already inside an organisation, but become convinced to become part of a plot. Finally, an infiltrated insider might be associated with some adversary of the organisation and join it with the purpose of carrying out a malicious act against it. Bunn and Sagan also refer to inadvertent or non-malicious actors, who pose a threat by making mistakes without really intending to do so—such as leaving a password lying around. Finally, the authors refer to a 'coerced insider', who remains loyal in intent, but knowingly assists in theft or sabotage to prevent hostile acts against themselves or their loved ones (ibid.: 4).

The insider threat that was posed by Bruce Ivins' activities in a high containment lab (that resulted in *Amerithrax* in 2001) demonstrates the potentially high threat and risks associated with an insider. The Ivins case provides a useful case study in how an organisation's security procedures and other organisational and cognitive biases can miss for several years risks posed by an insider threat actor (Stern and Schouten 2016: 74–102). Since the *Amerithrax* incident, significant investment has been made to close the biosafety vulnerabilities revealed by it.

Increasingly since 9/11 and *Amerithrax*, a number of policies, procedures and normative behaviour have developed in the scientific community to promote biosafety and biosecurity. These have ranged from safety regulation codes such as the US *Biosafety in Microbiological and Biomedical Laboratories (BMBL)* to more formal legislative and oversight regulations. The latter will be addressed in Chapter 8. There are also technical and policy improvements that can be made in securing both physical and remote access to labs including computer systems that house data, which are at risk of theft or being hacked (Gryphon Scientific 2016: 1014; Berger 2013: 113–127; Slayton et al. 2013: 51–70).

Leaving aside discussion of some of the formal legislative and regulatory instruments for promoting biosafety, the development and maintenance of effective risk management across the biosciences also relies on an organisational culture that treats biosafety and biosafety as an equal priority to other deliverables. A culture of accountability at all levels must also exist if effective risk management can prevent, identify and treat bio-threats and risks promptly. A rogue insider threat, who may have been assessed as appropriate to work with select agents and seems initially to follow all the relevant biosafety regulations and procedures could still pose a risk if they have not embraced the organisation's normative cultural biosafety values. It is critical then in order to stop opportunities for insider threats, that the organisation promote relevant biosafety cultural values as much as and perhaps more than adherence to formal biosafety regulations.

Risk management measures must of course be measured against the ability of scientists to carry out its functions. Effective engagement with local law enforcement and relevant domestic security intelligence organisations in each 'Five Eyes' country to help scientists build viable biosafety cultures will likely remain important in addition to internal organisation biosafety initiatives. Stern and Schouten provide a number of useful suggestions for improving policies and procedures that may help improve biosafety cultures across the biosciences enterprise (2016: 101–102). Two that I think would be helpful are, one: developing standard operating procedures for proactively identifying vulnerabilities including using 'red team' exercises to explore how systems could become exploited. In other words, what motivators (financial, psychological, religious, and political) might drive an insider threat and are there ways to assess the signs of such an evolving threat? The other is to 'ensure personnel reliability programs incorporate ongoing assessments of counterintelligence vulnerabilities, including vulnerabilities to self-ascribed whistle-blowers or attention seekers' (ibid.: 101).

Effective biosafety and biosecurity training is also crucial as the number of labs working with select agents or other dual use bio-agents proliferate globally, particularly in locations with fragile states. More consistent approaches to training will also be important so nations can be confident that as many scientists as possible regardless of the country or the context in which they work understand what bio-risks and threats may emerge and how to prevent or mitigate against them (Sture et al. 2012).

Disruption

As discussed above there are multiple stakeholders in the scientific community, global health security and biosafety fields that can play a critical role themselves in preventing bio-threats and risks as well as supporting the operational efforts of the intelligence community to prevent these. While prevention of bio-threats and risks is one critical dimension that stakeholders can play central roles another is disruption. Although the intelligence community can use a range of knowledge, technologies and methodologies from stakeholders in the scientific community, to prevent bio-threats and risks, we have to accept that it will not be possible to detect every criminal or terrorist act.

Nonetheless, some of the techniques, practices, technologies and knowledge available from stakeholders in the scientific community will still be useful to disrupting bio-threats and risks. In other words prevention may not always be possible yet measures can be put into place—which can detect threats early enough to reduce their impact. Similar to preventing bio-threats and risks, disrupting them will also rely on seeking advice from stakeholders involved in bio-surveillance, public health and biosafety research, amongst others on disrupting them as well. For example, as discussed earlier IARPA's commissioning of research into detecting signals of bioengineering changes (FELIX) may result in better capability for the intelligence community in not only preventing bioengineering changes that make it easier for terrorists to carry out attacks on populations, critical infrastructure or biotechnology companies, it could also help detect and disrupt the planning stages for such attacks. Additionally as noted earlier, if a high containment lab has a strong biosafety culture it is more likely that disruption of a bio-threat may be possible just by colleagues speaking up about suspicious activities in their working environment rather than any elaborate disruption knowledge and techniques, procedures the intelligence community might have in place to disrupt such threats. But knowledge, technologies, techniques and practice for disruption of bio-threats and risks cannot just come from scientific stakeholders in the biosciences, it should also come from other fields and practitioners working in other areas where successful disruption operations has taken place. These areas include criminology, policing, engineering, legislation, cyber, counter-intelligence amongst others.

In this section, we examine briefly what other stakeholders and discipline perspectives might the intelligence community learn from that can provide better capabilities for the disruption of bio-threats and risks. Are there lessons to be learnt from other stakeholders, disciplines or even other threat contexts that might be relevant to disrupting bio-threats that might not have been initially detected? Since 9/11, there are three stakeholder and discipline groups, which are investigating and applying disruption strategies to threats and risks and their knowledge might be relevant in disrupting threats and risks in the bio context. These are criminology, counter-terrorism and cyber. We will explore each briefly to see how stakeholders (researchers and practitioners) have developed disruption strategies in each and how they might be employed against bio-threats and risks.

Criminology

Insights from criminology and the practical application of disruption for crime prevention has provided a supplementary approach to traditional law enforcement approaches of prosecution against certain crimes through the courts. Disruption is not a new concept in criminology and law enforcement practice, though it can be difficult to define in all law enforcement contexts (Ratcliffe 2008: 204). Its meaning at least in the criminology/policing/law enforcement contexts can partly be traced back to broader desires—initially by UK law enforcement followed later by other 'Five Eyes' countries in the late 1990s and early 2000s to move law enforcement away from its traditional reactive mode to offending to one driven by intelligence. This concept of law enforcement or policing being intelligence driven or led gained significant traction in the criminology and policing literature (Walsh 2011; Ratcliffe 2016; Innes and Sheptycki 2004). It was driven initially in the UK by the desire for governments to maximise efficiencies and reducing costs by increasing the use of intelligence to drive strategic and operational decision-making. The implementation of intelligence led policing models into operational policing across 'Five Eyes' countries has had mixed results partly due to cultural, financial and leadership issues in agencies that have attempted to put intelligence at the centre of strategic and operational decision making in policing (Walsh 2011; Ratcliffe 2016). Nonetheless, despite historical challenges in adopting intelligence led approaches, increasing fiscal constraints and the ever increasing demands on law enforcement in managing both high volume crimes and complex operating environments in counter-terrorism, cyber and organised crime meant, at least in many national law enforcement agencies; a greater demand for an intelligence driven approach (Walsh 2011). This intelligence driven approach, which promulgated proactive disruption of crime strategies was in part an admission that not all crime could be prevented or the offenders prosecuted.

Additionally, in many law enforcement agencies such as the Australian Federal Police (AFP), the growing volumes of information collected have given intelligence a more central role in triaging the significance of information, value adding to it and guiding investigators to targets and operations that are high priority; or have the greater likelihood of successful prosecution outcomes. In complex organised crime cases such as transnational drug trafficking, people smuggling and even terrorism and cyber threats, which we discuss shortly—intelligence driven disruption strategies have become increasingly popular for many 'Five Eyes' law enforcement agencies. This has particularly been the case where it can be difficult to dismantle completely the organised crime group—or to even know the full extent of the group's network. Disruption operations that attempt to take down threat actors with key roles (e.g. facilitator, financier, and logistics) may nonetheless reduce the threat posed by the organised crime network even if the network continues to exist. Additionally, with some organised crime networks, it may be difficult to secure sufficient evidence for prosecution against a more serious offence such as drug importation, but there may be sufficient intelligence that can be used to make the criminal environment more hostile for the group's illicit enterprise by arresting key group members for lesser offenses such as unexplained wealth or migration irregularities. While disruption of crime does seem like a useful tool in preventing or reducing the impact of offenders, the criminology literature demonstrates it has been difficult to evaluate the effectiveness of intelligence driven disruption strategies. Ratcliffe cited an RCMP disruption attributes tool, which attempts to examine where the disruption activity is aimed at (core business, financial, personnel) and whether the kind of disruption for one or more of these attributes is high, medium or low in impact (Ratcliffe 2008: 207). However, such tools are largely subjective and qualitative—making it difficult to accurately measure the impact of intelligence driven disruption measures. The other concern about disruption strategies is that they may just cause displacement, where other criminal enterprises take the place of those removed by law enforcement or as Innes suggest, 'disrupting a network may just provide a vacuum for more dangerous offenders to step in' (Innes and Sheptycki 2004: 14). Finally, the literature suggest that employing effective disruption strategies rely on proactive collection and valid analysis that can led to both timely strategic and operational outcomes that in turn result in threat mitigation and harm minimisation.

So are there benefits for the intelligence community working on bio-threats and risks to investigating research and practice for disrupting threats in the organised crime context? The answer is a qualified 'yes'. Much of course depends on the nature of the threat and risk posed. Clearly as with any crime, it is hard to disrupt a bio-threat, when it's still in the head of the offender. However, we do know that criminal and terrorist acts don't just happen spontaneously. There usually involve predicate steps taken by the offender. Some of these might happen in very compressed periods while in other offences planning may take years. Either way, and regardless of whether these can be detected by the intelligence community, there is likely to be some signs in the predicate planning stages of an impending threat/risk that can provide the intelligence community opportunities for disruption. It is difficult to say in which bio-threat cases disruption strategies will be most successful. Much will depend on how quickly the intelligence community can collect and analyse information that may be indicative of an evolving bio-threat and risk. As discussed previously, good collection and analysis is contingent on having robust core intelligence processes in place and more importantly effective intelligence governance. Both are needed to ensure intelligence efforts are coordinated across multiple internal intelligence community stakeholders, with relevant knowledge—as well as ensuring information and expertise from external stakeholders (the scientific community) is available to provide earlier warning signs of an emerging bio-threat.

While it is important not to over-play the potential for success of the kind of disruption strategies used against traditional organised crime groups, there are likely bio-threat scenarios where disruption strategies may make a difference. Arguably, disruption of bio-threats could be on a continuum with the individual threat actor on one end and a sophisticated organised group on the other. At the individual level one could have the scenario of a lone terrorist actor or a mad/bad scientist. While it may seem difficult to get early warning of the malicious act of mad/bad scientist, we saw in the earlier discussion on 'insider threats' that it may be possible to disrupt their activity before you reach an *Amerithrax* style attack. Twenty/twenty is hindsight with the Bruce Ivins Amerithrax case, but the lessons learnt from this incident do provide guidance on the sources of collection and analysis required from within the intelligence and scientific communities to aid the disruption of this kind of bio-threat. It does not mean that all similar cases of 'insider threats' will be detected, prevented or disrupted, but a more careful collection and analysis of 'odd' behaviour or unusual security lapses by a scientist working in a high containment lab could reveal areas of vulnerabilities. Detection both of abnormal changes to an individual's psychological profile and/or in their working environment can provide opportunities for those vulnerabilities to be disrupted. At the other end of the bio-threat scale, a more organised bio-criminal or terrorist planned event may resemble in some respects other illicit criminal markets and networks (drugs, identity fraud, money laundering) and thereby present opportunities for disruption. Again this is not to suggest that disruption of organised bio-threat scenarios will be always be possible. As discussed in earlier chapters, since 9/11, even with state based WMD programs the intelligence community has had a mixed record in detecting them and uncovering the intention and capability of non-state actors to exploit dual use technology for malicious end remains difficult.

However, disruption could be useful in some bio-crimes where there is a bigger network of actors involved in the illicit business. For example, in crime scenarios where food suppliers are not registered legally to import food into a 'Five Eyes' country because it poses a biosecurity risk, there may be opportunities for parts of the intelligence community (particularly national law enforcement agencies) to work with agriculture, animal health, food regulatory agencies and relevant scientific stakeholders to disrupt illicit food suppliers from a country of concern. Equally there may be opportunities for disruption of activity from non-compliant biotechnology providers in a 'Five Eyes' country, who provide dual use equipment to a company overseas with a questionable profile that resides in a country vulnerable for terrorist infiltration.

Counter Terrorism

In addition to useful knowledge that can be gained from criminology and law enforcement practice there are also perspectives on disruption from contemporary counter terrorism studies that may have utility in the bio-threat and risk context. As noted above, since 9/11 law enforcement agencies across the 'Five Eyes' countries have been increasingly deploying disruption strategies in countering terrorism given the preservation of life demands an earlier interception of attacks preferably at the planning stage. As Innes suggest in the case of counter terrorism operations, one aim is to overtly disrupt planned attacks, which has many effects including sending a message to other terrorist groups that they may be next, reassuring the community and if possible deploying countering violent extremism (CVE) strategies in communities where future attacks may arise (Innes et al. 2017: 253). In the UK in particular, a key plank in its counter terrorism strategy has been disruption both at the strategic and tactical level. At the strategic level, disruption has involved a number of initiatives from arresting persons of interest, legislative action and enhanced surveillance (Innes et al. 2017: 265).

In addition to global influence of groups such as Al Qaeda and Islamic State, the growth in lone actor attacks—some 198 across the US and European countries from 1970s to late 2000s (Danzell and Montanez 2016: 136) has also been a significant catalyst for enacting further stringent legislative measures such as detention without trial and control orders (Walsh 2016). All 'Five Eyes' countries have also adopted further legislative changes that allow disruption of terrorist attacks by reducing thresholds law enforcement and intelligence agencies need for reasonable suspicion in order to access both electronic and human intelligence (HUMINT). Governments desire to do something to reduce the threat and risks posed by terrorists by creating increasingly proactive, flexible and permissive legislative environments has also raised concerns about the role of intelligence, secrecy and privacy. These issues will be discussed as they relate to the bio-threat and risk context in Chapter 8.

But legislation is only one plank in effective counter terrorism and the scale and pace of actual and potential terrorist attacks suggest other disruption strategies are required at the tactical level. Innes et al. suggest such strategies might include: 'prosecution against an individual or a network for offences other than those they were principally being investigated for and/or interfering with the operations of the criminal enterprise in cases where there is insufficient evidence to secure prosecution' (2017: 265). They add that, at the tactical level, disruption strategies can 'interfere with the ability of suspected adversaries to operate effectively and efficiently' (ibid.). Innes et al. suggests that tactical disruption functions at 'near event interdiction', which can mitigate or minimise harms associated with the actual or planned terrorism attack (ibid.). Other counter-terrorism disruption strategies in 'Five Eyes' countries have included the creation of CVE policies and interventions as well as the disruption or take down of social media venues advocating politically motivated violence or recruitment to jihadist groups.

Regardless of the complexity of post 9/11 terrorist attacks—such as the multi-site attacks in Paris 2015 orchestrated by a group; or the knife attack against two police officers in Australia in 2014 by one individual—disruption strategies employed by law enforcement and national security intelligence agencies are also likely to be usefully employed in the bio-threat and risk context. Just how useful strategic and tactical disruption strategies used in conventional counter-terrorism will be in the bio-threat context depends on the nature of the intent and capability of individual threat actor(s) and the risks posed by their actions. The effectiveness of disruption strategies in the bio-threat context like conventional terrorist attacks are contingent on a range of variables that are unique to that event. In the bio-threat context, leaving aside large levels of uncertainty about the future threat trajectory for bio-terrorism, effective disruption will rely on law enforcement and intelligence agencies understanding how the intention, capability and opportunities of threat actors operating in a particular environment—make an attack possible. Intention, capability and opportunities will differ along the threat continuum from individual to group and from state to non-state actor. For example, in the research facility, hospital or high containment laboratory environment, intention, capabilities and opportunities may be shaped by actors that are internal, external or an indirectly involved in the facility (Perman et al. 2013: 95). Threats can also be as Perman suggest overt or clandestine (ibid.). In some cases, if a scientist is motivated politically (for religious, environmental or political reasons) to commit an act of violence by using a biological agent it may be easier to disrupt their activities if they are public about their agenda. However, in the case of a clandestine plan it could be very difficult to disrupt an attack launched externally or internally in a contained lab.

Nonetheless, as we saw with historical cases of lone actor threats such as the Bruce Ivins *Amerithrax* incident there are likely predicate steps in the process to carrying out an attack which are revealable. Similarly, in the lesser known case of Dr. Larry Ford, who was suspected of murdering his business partner in a biotech company—the police subsequently found a cache of weapons, white supremacist writings and allegations that he attempted to infect six mistresses with biological agents (Perman et al. 2013: 94). Again even in cases of lone actors such as this whose attack planning is more clandestine; there may well be an abundance of 'warning intelligence' that if collected and assessed in time might be useful in disrupting a lone actor planned attack. While it can be difficult to disrupt a lone actor plot, more elaborate ones by a group of conspirators could in some circumstances provide greater opportunities for interception and disruption by law enforcement and intelligence agencies. This is because in plots involving multiple actors there are more stages before the attack can be carried out. Some stages such as communications, procuring supplies and transport also provide points of vulnerability, where threat actors can be exposed to authorities and disrupted. So an external threat such as a terrorist attack against a high containment laboratory might involve communications amongst group members, financing of the plan, purchasing of explosives and surveillance of the facility's perimeters. Each stage presents opportunities for disruption providing intelligence and information is available to law enforcement and intelligence agencies. Similarly a theft of intellectual property or biological material from a private sector biotechnology company might result from either an external criminal group; or state actor pressuring or paying an employee to steal information on their behalf. Again, intelligence may exist already about the criminal group or the compromised employee that provides opportunities for disruption.

In an ideal world of course, it would be desirable if all potential biothreat and risk scenarios could be prevented early in the intent stage, where they are mainly an idea in a perpetrator's head. Pre-employment screening, including criminal checks and select agent risk assessments will show up some individuals, who are not suitable to access and work with dangerous biological agents. This will have an early disruptive effect but it is not fool proof. People can lie about their circumstances in security suitability checks allowing them the ability to access and plan malevolent acts in a secure biological facility rather than just thinking about them. Once operating inside a facility—depending on the nature of the planned attack it can be very difficult for law enforcement and the intelligence community to respond quickly enough to disrupt the attack before its fully implemented. In all threat scenarios (simple to complex) in addition to the mandatory background checks for workers, each scientific institution needs to develop a full suite of threat assessments that can be updated regularly on different threat actors, including but not limited to: visitors, criminals, lone actor attacks (internal and external), terrorist and issued motived groups, international terrorists groups and foreign powers (Perman et al. 2013: 94). These threat assessments should be developed by an institution's internal security department in collaboration with local law enforcement. The relatively low number of threat scenarios that have taken place involving bio-agents since 9/11 will likely mean that there will be many intelligence gaps in assessing the intent, ability and opportunity of different threat types. However, providing baseline threat assessments will begin to build pictures of threats scenarios that should help promote better biosafety measures as well as opportunities to disrupt threats earlier should they begin to emerge.

In summary, law enforcement and intelligence agencies working on bio-threats and risks of the future can learn a lot from their counter terrorism colleagues. Since 9/11, countering terrorism continues to produce lessons for the law enforcement and intelligence communities on how more effectively to disrupt emerging terror plots before they are implemented. The knowledge gained from investigating conventional terrorism attacks that don't involve biology can help those working on future bio-threats and risks by seeing how to optimise the legislative, intelligence, investigative and community response to terrorism while also learning lessons from contemporary counter terrorism efforts. In particular, the increase in lone actor terrorist attacks in the west— often with short notice underscores that either an insufficient amount of intelligence or types of intelligence that cannot be revealed in court often exists. In these cases, other tactical disruption strategies are gaining traction amongst 'Five Eyes' countries to mitigate the threat and harm posed by terrorists. Similarly, given the complexity of threat scenarios that could arise from the exploitation of dual use biotechnology, it may be difficult in some cases to collect sufficient solid 'evidence' or use bio-forensics to attribute confidently for a conviction on bioterrorism or bio-criminal activity. Nonetheless, the various counter terrorism strategies discussed above point to ways threat actors may be disrupted on lesser offences while also providing a greater intelligence dividend on other individuals involved.

Cyber

The final knowledge area and stakeholder group that intelligence agencies and investigators working with bio-threat and risks may learn more from is cyber security. As Koblentz and Mazanec (2013) suggest there are a lot of common characteristics between biological and cyber weapons including but not limited to: difficulty of attribution and how multiple technologies can be used for offensive, defensive and civilian applications (421–425). Both authors argue because of these similarities there is likely a lot cyber can learn from how bio-threats have been managed historically. This is undoubtedly true, though in this section the focus will be the opposite—i.e. what can intelligence and investigative agencies working on bio-threats learn from the cyber threat and capability landscape? Even a cursory review of the literature suggest that there are a number of areas where current cyber research and practice could inform the 'Five Eyes' intelligence communities understanding of current and emerging bio-threats and risks. Space does not allow an exhaustive discussion on all of them, but there are three cyber areas in particular; where I believe those working with bio-threats and risks could benefit greatly from knowing more about in order to learn the lessons from the cyber context as well as identifying good intelligence and investigative practice. These areas are: the dark web, cyber terrorism and cyber espionage. I will discuss each briefly in turn.

Turning to the dark web environment first here we are referring to the content on the internet that is 'not indexed by standard search engines' (Weimann 2016: 196). Much of the dark web is hidden or blocked and can only be accessed by specialised browsers. Given the relative anonymity it provides, the dark web has seen the proliferation of child pornography, credit card fraud, identify theft, drugs and arms trafficking amongst other illicit offences. The dark web only emerged in recent years though law enforcement and intelligence agencies have made some in roads into its penetration and disruption. The FBI's shut down of the dark web site Silk Road, which operated between February 2011 and October 2013 was to that point the largest and most sophisticated anonymous online market place for illicit drugs (Zajácz 2017). New technological solutions are also being developed to better identify, collect and analyse illicit activity on the dark web, including DARPA's MEMEX software, which helps catalogue dark web sites (Weimann 2016: 203). Nonetheless, all 'Five Eyes' intelligence communities will need to continue to develop their collection, analytical and investigative capabilities in the dark web content to profile more accurately various illicit market places in order to orchestrate impactful disruption activity across multiple markets.

Although it is unknown, at least in an unclassified sense the extent to which illicit markets exist that could benefit bio-threat actors (criminals or terrorists), undoubtedly law enforcement and intelligence agencies, who are given a watching brief on emerging bio-threats and risk should be exploiting the dark web more for opportunities for disruption. A first step might be first to map the bio-terrorism literature and identify researchers, who have access to bioterrorism agents/disease research, domain, institutions, countries and emerging topics and trends in bio-terrorism agents/disease research. Chen shows how by using informatics research it might be possible to use knowledge mapping techniques, to analyse productivity status, collaboration status and emerging topics in the bio-terrorism domain (Chen 2011: 335–367). Additionally, other intelligence and investigative teams that are working on non-bio threats such as conventional terrorist attacks, terrorism financing, drug trafficking or even child sexual exploitation may come across offenders, who have links to others interested in exploiting dual use biological agents for malevolent objectives. So the work currently going on by intelligence agencies working on broader cyber security issues such as cyber-crime or cyber terrorism is directly relevant to improving collection and analysis against emerging bio-threats and risks.

Developments in the second area cyber-terrorism provides another opportunity for bio-threat intelligence and investigative teams to learn off their colleagues working on cyber threats. In the past we often think about the classical 'bio-terrorism' attack involving the aerolising and dispersal of a dangerous pathogen like Anthrax into a crowded place. This mode of attack may still be chosen in the future by a terrorist group (leaving aside for a minute the technical difficulties of such an attack). Though committed acts through cyber opens up other choices for a bio-attack. Cyber security specialist's knowledge of cyber terrorism is still developing. We have seen for example groups like the Taliban and IS increasingly use computers for recruitment, propaganda and communications, but it remains difficult to know empirically how many of the current virtual attacks such as ransomware can be attributed to terrorist or led to deaths or impacted critical infrastructure in significant ways. Such attacks could just as easily be attributed to cyber hackers (criminals) or state sponsored espionage both issues we will return to shortly (Riglietti 2017; Bernard 2017; Heickerö 2014).

Nonetheless, it is clear that terrorism groups are increasing their use of computers including the dark web given they know that intelligence communities are monitoring the surface internet and social media. In August 2014, Al-Aan TV reported a laptop belonging to a Tunisian member of IS captured in Syria contained thousands of documents from the dark web including 19 pages about making biological weapons in a way to impact the biggest number of people (Weimann 2016: 200). There have also been cases where IS has carried out a series of cyber-attacks, 'exclusively computer based, which in one instance even led to the disclosure of private information regarding US government officials, from private conversations to work and email addresses' (Riglietti 2017: 19).

The final area of cyber security that is useful for bio-threat intelligence and investigative teams to reflect on relates to cyber hacks and espionage. Putting hacks and espionage together is not meant to suggest that both are always linked—though we have seen in the Russian interference in the 2016 US presidential election they can be. China too is playing an increasingly sophisticated and aggressive cyber espionage strategy aimed at political interference and stealing intellectual property (Inkster 2015). There seems little doubt that the extent of hacking (unauthorised access to a computer or network) being perpetrated by state and non-state actors is on the rise and network vulnerabilities across the civil and military space remain.

In a recent article, FBI Assistant Special Agent in Charge (Chicago), Todd Carroll said the average time between an unauthorised user getting inside a network and the user being detected is 150 days—'a lifetime in cyber means'. Todd went on to say that 57% of business owners don't have a dedicated employee or vendor monitoring for cyber-attacks (Stone 2017). We have also seen in recent years the growth in malware and ransomware attacks across the globe. For example, in 2017 the Wannacry ransomware attack caused 230,000 infections across 124 countries (locking down banking, energy and manufacturing systems) (Schilling 2017). The dark web also provides terrorist and criminal groups opportunities to operate botnet campaigns in anonymity that can remotely operate networks of computers to commit attacks on other systems including critical infrastructure. Again there is insufficient space to provide a full survey of all the cyber hacking and espionage threats, and indeed what to do about them is beyond the scope of this chapter (Clarke and Knake 2010: 257–280).

Nonetheless the hacking attacks—whether they are state sponsored (espionage) or non-state actors (terrorists or criminals) provide another rich source of knowledge to be collected and assessed that can be used by those working on emerging bio-threats and risks. For example, it would seem unwise for bio-threat intelligence and investigative teams to not learn from the fast changing angles of cyber-attack from hackers given how the physical security of biological institutions, their intellectual property and the kinds of biological products produced in such facilities is reliant on secure cyber systems. We have seen in recent years the take down of government websites involving ransomware attacks on both government and private sector networks. Increasingly more information is being shared and stored via the Cloud. What would be the impact of a major ransomware attack that locks down the entire bio-surveillance capability of a public health authority such as CDC do to maintaining national health security? Could a cybercriminal group infiltrate the network of a major biodefense company steal IP and sell it to a terrorist group on the dark web? Could research stored via the Cloud on non-secure networks relating to the genetic sequences of pathogens be stolen by a terrorist group or state actor to engineer bio-weapons? (Blue Ribbon Project 2015: 44–46). In all the three areas discussed above, a fuller development of links between those working in the cyber intelligence collection and analysis streams, and those who might examine emerging bio-threats and risks is a necessary first step in bringing relevant knowledge and practice from cyber security to bio-threat stakeholders.

Treatment

In this final section the attention is turned to what kind of stakeholders play a role in treating bio-threats and risk? Second, in performing these roles, how can they help the 'Five Eyes' intelligence communities build better capability (knowledge, practice and technology) about treating actual or emerging bio-threats and risks? As we have seen so far the management of bio-threats and risks is potentially a crowded enterprise with many stakeholders (beyond the intelligence communities) playing critical roles. In this section, I have grouped them into three 'types of stakeholder': first responders, science and technology stakeholders and security stakeholders. These are not three distinct clusters of unique stakeholders that do not interact with each other. Depending on the nature of the bio-incident that has occurred, one would expect to see a close interaction amongst the various knowledge brokers and practitioners from each group. For example, a release of a synthetically manufactured select agent in an airport should result in the combined strategic and tactical contributions from first responders, engineers and security personnel rather each being delivered in isolation. An uncoordinated delivery of knowledge, practice and expertise to treat an unfolding bio-threat/risk from multiple stakeholders will not result in the best outcome for mitigating the risk or disrupting future potential of similar threats occurring.

Again as with previous sections, the focus here is not a deep exploration of the specific knowledge, practice or technology of all stakeholders involved potentially in the treatment of bio-risks. This would be an impossible task. Instead this section will explain briefly what each of the three broad stakeholder categories (first responders, science and technology and security) can do broadly to treat bio-risks (current or potential), what intelligence communities can learn from this in ways that extend their capabilities to manage bio-threats and risks.

First Responders

The label 'first responders' is a descriptor for a much broader range of stakeholders including: fire/hazmat, paramedics, emergency responders, health and hospital service providers. Each would play a different role in both responding to and treating a bio-incident depending on the type of biological hazard, their jurisdictional and legislative responsibilities and fiscal capacity. In all 'Five Eyes' countries with perhaps the exception of New Zealand (with a smaller population and only one national government) the complexity of response will be particularly governed by the overlapping roles that various local, state and federal first responders might play. Obviously in the US with multiple federal, state and local agencies, the coordination of first responder efforts to a bio-incident presents more challenges than other 'Five Eyes' countries such as Australia and the UK with less agencies and jurisdictions. There is not an abundance of academic literature on the role of first responders in treating bio-threats and risks. This lack of evidence makes it difficult to assess accurately what first responders can do to treat bio-threats and risks, what the challenges are and what the intelligence community can learn from these important stakeholders. There is however, some research available that can increase the intelligence communities' understanding of first responder capabilities to treat bio-threats and risks as well as illuminate some of the challenges in doing so. This research should provide at least a start to what the intelligence community can learn from first responders as they deploy their knowledge and practice to disrupt and treat bio-threats and risks.

9/11 and the *Amerithrax* incident provided a catalyst for law enforcement and public health agencies to work closer together to respond to an unfolding threat. Since *Amerithrax*, across the 'Five Eyes' countries further work has been done to better coordinate the work of law enforcement and public health agencies on treating bio-threats and risks. But such efforts have not involved routinely the broader spectrum of national security intelligence agencies, who have tended to play a more strategic and adhoc role compared to their law enforcement counterparts. Overall, policy, coordination and legislative efforts to bring first responders and members of the intelligence and law enforcement community together have had only mixed success for a number of reasons. In 2007, a study of how law enforcement and public health agencies in the US, Canada, UK and Ireland work together on bio-threat incidents identified several common barriers to improving multi-agency responses (Strom and Eyerman 2007). These included cultural, legal, structural, communication and leadership barriers (ibid.: 135). Ten years on from Strom and Eyerman's research, other researchers have made similar observations about the ability of first responders to manage effectively a bio-threat incident and to work with law enforcement and intelligence community on such tasks. But it's not just the capability issues raised above, other research points to other technical challenges to treating the impact of bio-threats and risks in the physical environment. For example, research by chemists and environmental engineers show that given the varying nature and strains of the bacteria—the science for assessing risk of exposure may not be able to provide a fully accurate risk assessment of a building's vulnerability or resilience to a bio-attack nor—in some cases whether first responders have effectively 'cleaned the environment up after exposure' (Canter 2007; Taylor et al. 2013). A lack of effectiveness in responding to a bio-threat incident in a local area obviously can have broader public sector implications in both treatment and preparedness of bio-risks. For example, Gerstein (2017: 86) citing a study by advocacy group Trust for America's Health reported that 26 states and DC scored 6/10 or lower on a scale for preparedness. Additionally, since 9/11 major disease outbreaks such as SARS and Ebola have also demonstrated fragility in parts of the world, including some 'Five Eyes' country's public health response capability, which remains a concern if there was a major bio-terrorist event.

The Blue Ribbon Study Project Report raised similar concerns about the capability of certain responders including those local, state and federal agencies that might be involved in decontaminating sites following a bio-incident. In the US, the report raised similar coordination issues between federal, state and local agencies in which first responder agency would take the lead in decontaminating and remediating environments and how other agencies would get involved to ensure the attack site was deemed safe for people to return (Blue Ribbon Study

Project 2015: 26). One underlying theme arising from the studies mentioned on first responder's roles in treating bio-threats and risks is that the intelligence community must share more information with emergency services on the nature of the threat they are meant to respond to. This is not to suggest that in all the 'Five Eyes' countries that no sharing is going on. My selected interviews with law enforcement and intelligence officials in each country did not give the impression that no sharing was going on with first responders. However it is clear if the local fire officers or emergency staff in a hospital are meant to better respond to a bio-incident they will need regular, consistent, reliable, real-time information and intelligence. This is vital to them safely securing the scene, or rapidly diagnosing and treating infected patients while also keeping themselves safe. Importantly too, the more intelligence they receive will likely be helpful in first responders preserving any relevant evidence from the scene that might be needed by the either the law enforcement and intelligence communities. Gerstein makes a valuable point when referring to improving bio-preparedness and response activities, when he suggests that first responders need to be seen as part of a complex system rather than each representing a series of programs (Gerstein 2017: 88).

In addition to the range of knowledge and practice the intelligence community can learn from first responders, arguably the biggest lesson they can learn is to seek to better understand the 'linkages among disparate disciplines (biodefense, public health, emergency management), government, industry, the scientific community and themselves to better support first responders' (ibid.). If the 'Five Eyes' intelligence communities were able to create the necessary national health security coordination arrangements suggested in Chapter 6 such as the health security coordination council and the national health security strategy, then through these institutions further intelligence sharing mechanisms could be established to improve information flow between the intelligence communities and first responders at federal, state and local levels. However, first further research is required to investigate how law enforcement and intelligence communities work currently with first responders to identify and as much as possible ameliorate the cultural, legal, communication and leadership barriers that persist.

Science and Technology

A second cluster of knowledge and stakeholders for treating bio-threats and risks could be loosely described as 'science and technology' stakeholders. In earlier sections, under the relevant headings (prevention and disruption), significant space was devoted to how our intelligence communities can learn from a range of stakeholders working across a diverse array of disciplines (including bio-surveillance, public health, biosafety, criminology, counter terrorism and cyber). In each of these disciplines, discussion included exploration of relevant science, technology and knowledge useful for the intelligence community in preventing and disrupting bio-threats and risks. Some of that discussion, for example bio-surveillance, biosafety and strengthening global health is also relevant to our focus here in treating bio-incidents. However, in this section the focus is not what the intelligence community can learn from stakeholders working in the above disciplines, but rather what they can learn from disciplines more removed from the biological sciences or relevant social sciences (e.g. engineering or security studies).

What can the intelligence community learn from physical, mechanical or environmental engineering? There are multiple roles engineering specialties could play and are playing in preventing, disrupting and treating bio-threats and risks. For one and historically, the US DOD has relied on engineers, microbiologists to provide advice on weaponisation of biological agents under a range of scenarios and conditions (state actor and terrorists threats). For example, even pre 9/11, between 1999 and 2000 DTRA funded Project Bacchus to see if a team of scientists and engineers, who allegedly did not have extensive experience in bio-weapons could make bio-weapon facility using just commercially available items. The objective was to see if the team could make anthrax successfully without the detection of the intelligence community, though it was later revealed that this team did have substantive technical knowledge and support throughout this project (Vogel 2013: 41–43). Engineers have also long been engaged in studying aerolisation dynamics, which has become increasingly a multi-disciplinary collaboration of environmental engineers, biomedical engineers, microbiologists, chemists and epidemiologists (Xu et al. 2011). Related to aerolisation studies has been the work of hardware and software engineers—many of whom came from the aerospace and automotive industries that have brought their skills into modelling bio-terrorism attacks to help first responders predict how airborne particles might move through sections of a city under certain weather and windflow conditions (Thilmany 2005).

Other engineering studies, sometimes referred to bio-protection studies have been important in the design of the heating ventilation and air conditioning (HVAC) systems used to resist biological contaminants. Much of this research became activated after the *Amerithrax* incident, and is designed at reducing the health consequences from airborne contaminants by augmenting heating and air conditioning systems (Ginsberg and Bui 2015). Another focus of engineering led research relates to improving the portability, speed and reliability of bio aerosol monitors for pathogens. One recent study has been working on a device that would be fully portable and automated—capable of detection of selected air-borne microorganisms on the spot—within 30 to 8 minutes depending on the genome and particular strain of the organism (Agranovski et al. 2017).

Security

In this last sub-section in our exploration of what other stakeholders may be useful in treating bio-threats and risks we turn our attention to the role of security officers. I am conscious in the discussion above regarding prevention and biosafety much was said about the role of security officers and managers in promoting biosecurity and biosafety across all sectors of the bio-sciences enterprise (e.g. research centres, hospitals, biotechnology companies, public and private labs). In this section, we focus instead on the role of security officers and managers across the broader economy—beyond biosciences. As argued in previous chapters, in addition to taking a one health perspective to bio-threats and risk, 'Five Eyes' intelligence communities and their law enforcement colleagues need to also understand the potential development of bio-threats and risks beyond the technical world of biotechnology and labs to include also in their wider social, economic and community contexts.

Hence in this section, we are referring to the role of security officers and companies that work across the international, national, state and local economies in each 'Five Eyes' country. Given the trajectory of most (if not all) future bio-threats is unknown, our intelligence communities need to be forging more formalised (less adhoc) relationships with security officers in a range of non-biotechnology industries (banking, mining, food supply, agriculture, critical infrastructure).

As Nalla and Wakefield (2014) argue several factors have increased the role of private security since the Second World War. Increased economic wealth, enhanced security technology (alarms, access control and CCTV), in addition to an increase in the control by a number of private sector companies of publicly accessible places have, amongst other factors all contributed to the growth in private sector security (ibid.: 727). While it is difficult to generalise 'as the functions of security officers/agencies are as varied as the organisations that employ them' (ibid.: 731), their functions and roles cut across many facets of each 'Five Eyes' nation to include office buildings, warehouses, shopping malls, education establishments, residential complexes and critical infrastructure. One often thinks of the classic scenario of a security guard standing in front of a physical gate, which is one role of many others which might also, depending on their functions include traffic control, surveillance, responding to emergencies, security vetting. In the security role of complex large companies, airports and electricity plants, it is likely that the security officers will have a deep understanding of their physical and virtual security environments and this kind of expert knowledge would be integral for them and the intelligence community gaining threat awareness, prevention, surveillance, disruption, treatment and recovery to bio threats and risks which may manifest in their operating environment.

Historically however, the relationship between intelligence communities (including law enforcement) and private sector security has not been optimal partially because a lack of trust between both (ibid.: 739). However, several studies on private and public sector security do show several areas of improvement across each 'Five Eyes' country. Some of these improvements have been initiated by governments such as in the UK making significant cuts to policing in the late 1990s and mid-2000s and seeking the private sector security sector to pick up more cheaply what were considered less core policing such as offender management and transfers of prisoners. In other cases, governments were interested in engaging with the private sector to extend their own security and intelligence collection capabilities with terrorism. Connors et al. (2000), Wakefield (2003), and Rigakos (2002) provide more detailed analysis of a range of factors that have been involved in building partnerships with private sector security companies in the US, UK and Canada respectively. 9/11 and of course subsequent terrorist attacks in many western countries has seen a more focused attempt by 'Five Eyes' countries to reach out to the private sector—including private sector security given many attacks occur in public places owned or managed by the private sector. Threats as well to public and privately owned critical infrastructure (aviation, power, water, and telecommunication) have also influenced 'Five Eyes' government's closer liaison with the private sector. For example in the US, DHS has established a private sector office to provide government advice on relevant security issues to the private sector as well as promoting public-private partnerships. In Australia, since 9/11 parts of the Australian intelligence community, particularly ASIO has developed closer links with the private sector. In 2004 Australia's Attorney General's Department created the Business-Government Advisory Group on National Security to provide a vehicle for the Government to discuss a range of national security issues and initiative with CEOs and senior business leaders (DPM &C 2015: 6). The group later (2014) evolved into the Australian Governments Industry Consultation on National Security (ibid.).

More recently (2017) the Australian Government released its strategy for protecting crowded places from terrorism. This significant policy document was developed in close partnerships with federal, state and local governments, the intelligence community and the private sector. The key objective being to assist owners and operators to increase the safety, protection and resilience of crowded places across Australia (ANZCTC 2017). An interesting aspect of this strategy is that it places the primary responsibility for protecting sites and people on private sector businesses. Similar policy articulations have been declared in the UK's counter-terrorism strategy (HMG 2011) and Canada's approach to counter-terrorism (Canadian Government 2011).

In summary, it's clear that various agencies of the 'Five Eyes' intelligence communities and their broader law enforcement counterparts have increased their liaison and implemented various initiatives with private sector industry. What is less clear is the nature and extent of these as they relate to the prevention, disruption and treatment of potential bio-threats and risks. Much is unknown, for example, about whether intelligence and law enforcement communities are actively working in partnership with the private sector beyond the classical threat typologies of basic terrorist's tactics, improvised explosive devices or vehicle born attacks. Given the low probability high impact nature of the evolving bio-threat environment, it is likely that many private sector companies (banking, shopping malls, mining, hotels) see little need to include bio-threats in their security risk management plans or indeed consult with intelligence and law enforcement communities on them.

While it is important not to be alarmist on low probability threats that are more likely on balance to effect the biosciences community rather than the broader private sector economy, it seems unwise for the latter not to consider the impact of such bio-threats on their operations and to at least have formalised dialogues on these with the intelligence community. But such a dialogue will in the future rely on several factors identified already by researchers coming together to develop more effective public-private crime prevention strategies. Prenzler and Sarre list several factors including: a common interest in reducing a specific crime, leadership, mutual respect, information sharing based on high levels of trust in confidentiality and formalised mechanisms for consultation and communications (Prenzler and Sarre 2014: 783).

Conclusion

This chapter surveyed the role of external stakeholders external (to the 'Five Eyes' intelligence communities) in preventing, disrupting and treating bio-threats and risks. Depending on the particular bio-threat a diverse array of stakeholders could provide knowledge, skills and capabilities to the intelligence community. The large number of disciplines and stakeholders with relevant technical knowledge suggest that they will continue to play a critical role in the prevention, disruption and treatment of bio-threats and risks. In many cases, such as in bio-surveillance, forensics and even engineering the scientific and technical stakeholders discussed here may play a greater role than the traditional intelligence and investigative response to managing bio-threats and risks.

The chapter also highlighted that although each 'Five Eye's intelligence community has a wealth of knowledge to tap into from stakeholders, however in most cases all stakeholder groups are faced with their own theoretical and practical limitations. Analysts and investigators working on bio-threats and risks need to understand these limitations while also seeking to build deeper and more formalised partnerships with scientific, technical and cross disciplinary stakeholders. In the final Chapter 8, we shift the focus away from the practice and processes involved in interpreting bio-threats and risks to oversight and accountability issues. Given the legislative, ethical and normative challenges modern intelligence practice faces, particularly in understanding the potential threat trajectory of synthetic biology, what role can oversight and accountability play in achieving the objectives of the intelligence communities in liberal democracies?

References

Agranovski, I. E., et al. (2017). Miniature PCR Based Portable Bioaerosol Monitor Development. *Journal of Applied Microbiology, 122*(1), 129–138. https://doi.org/10.1111/jam.13318.

ANZCTC, (2017). *Australia's Strategy for Protecting Crowded Places from Terrorism*. ANZCTC, Australian Government.

Australia Group. (2015). *Common Control List Handbook, Volume 2: Biological Weapons-Related Common Control Lists*. From www.defence.gov.au/export-controls/master/docs/AustGroupCommonControlListHandbaookVolIIpdf. Accessed March 12, 2017.

Bakanidze, L., et al. (2010). Biosafety and Biosecurity as Essential Pillars of International Health Security and Cross-Cutting Elements of Biological Non-Proliferation. *Biomed Central, 10*, 1–8.

Berger, K. (2013). Biosecurity in Research Laboratories. In R. Burnette (Ed.), *Biosecurity* (pp. 113–128). Hoboken, NJ: Wiley.

Bernard, R. (2017). These Are Not the Terrorist Groups You're Looking for: An Assessment of the Cyber Capabilities of Islamic State. *Journal of Cyber Policy, 2*(2), 255–265. https://doi.org/10.1080/23738871.2017.1334805.

Blue Ribbon Study Panel. (2015). *Blue Ribbon Study Panel on Biodefense. A National Blueprint for Biodefense: Leadership and Major Reform Needed to Optimise Efforts*. Washington, DC: Hudson Institute for Policy Studies.

Blue Ribbon Study Panel. (2017). *Biodefense Special Focus: Defense of Animal Agriculture*. Washington, DC: Blue Ribbon Study Panel.

Buehler, J., et al. (2004). Group CDCW. Framework for Evaluating Public Health Surveillance Systems for Early Detection of Outbreaks: Recommendations from the CDC Working Group. *MMWR Recommendations and Reports: Morbidity and Mortality Weekly Report, 53*, 1–11.

Bunn, M., & Sagan, S. (Eds.). (2016). *Insider Threats*. Ithaca, NY: Cornell University Press.

Burns, R. (2015). US Military Says It Mistakenly Shipped Live Anthrax Sample. From http://www.nbcnewyork.com/news/national-international/Pentagon-Shipped-Live-Anthrax-Samples–305221031.html. Accessed March 13, 2017.

BWC. (2017). *BWC Newsletter*. Geneva: United Nations.

Canadian Government. (2011). *Building Resilience Against Terrorism: Canada's Counter Terrorism Strategy*. Ottawa: Government of Canada.

Cameron, E. (2017, July 19). Biosecurity Imperative: An Urgent Case for Extending the Global Health Security Agenda. *Atomic Pulse*.

Canter, D. (2007). Addressing Residual Risk Issues at Anthrax Clean Up. How Clean Is Safe? *Journal of Toxicology and Environmental Health, Part A, 68*(11–12), 1017–1032.

CDC. (2014). *Report on the Potential Exposure to Anthrax*. Atlanta, GA: CDC.

CDC. (2015a). *90 Day Internal Review of the Division of Select Agents and Toxins*. Atlanta, GA: CDC.

CDC. (2015b). Report of the Advisory Committee to the Director, CDC Follow Up on CDC Progress.

Chen, H. (2011). *Bioterrorism and Knowledge Mapping Dark Web Exploring and Data Mining the Dark Side of the Web* (pp. 335–367). New York, NY: Springer.

Chevrier, M., & Spelling, A. (2016). The Traditional Tools of Biological Arms Control and Disarmament. In F. Lentzos (Ed.), *Biological Threats in the 21st Century* (pp. 331–356). London: Imperial College Press.

Clarke, R., & Knake, R. (2010). *Cyber War*. New York, NY: Ecco.

Collier, N. (2015). A Review of Web-Based Epidemic Detection. In S. Davies & J. Youde (Eds.), *The Politics of Surveillance and Response to Disease Outbreaks* (pp. 85–107). Surrey, UK: Ashgate.

Connors, E., et al. (2000). *Operation Cooperation, Guidelines for Partnerships Between Law Enforcement and Private Security Organisations.* Rockville, MD: Bureau of Justice Assistance.

Danzell, O., & Montanez, L. (2016). Understanding the Lone Wolf Phenomena: Assessing Current Profiles. *Behavioural Sciences of Terrorism and Political Aggression, 8*(2), 135–159.

Dennis, B., & Sun, L. (2014a, July 16). FDA Found More Than Smallpox Vials in Storage Room. *Washington Post.* From https://www.washington-post.com/national/health-science/fda-found-more-than-smallpox-vials-in-storage-room/2014/07/16/850d4b12-0d22-11e4-8341-b8072b1e7348_story.html?utm_term=.978241b9d1f8. Accessed March 14, 2017.

Dennis, B., & Sun, L. (2014b, September 5). More Deadly Pathogens, Toxins Found Improperly Stored in NIH and FDA Labs. *Washington Post.* From https://www.washingtonpost.com/national/health-science/six-more-deadly-pathogens-found-improperly-stored-in-nih-and-fda-labs/2014/09/05/9ff8c3c2-3520-11e4-a723-fa3895a25d02_story.html?utm_term=.4bc6ce160f62. Accessed March 14, 2017.

Dickmann, P., et al. (2015). Marburg Biosafety and Biosecurity Scale (MBBS): A Framework for Risk Assessment and Risk Communication. *Health Security, 13*(2), 88–95. https://doi.org/10.1089/hrs.2014.0065.

DPM &C. (2015). *Review of Australia's Counter Terrorism Machinery.* Department of Prime Minister and Cabinet, Australian Government.

Dzau, V., & Sands, P. (2016). Beyond the Ebola Battle Winning the War Against Future Epidemics. *New England Journal of Medicine, 375,* 203–204.

Eaves, E. (2017). IARPA Director Jason Matheny Advances Tech Tools for US Espionage. *Bulletin of the Atomic Scientists, 73*(2), 67–73.

GAO. (2009). *High Containment Laboratories: National Strategy for Oversight is Needed.* Washington, DC: GAO.

GAO. (2011). *Biosurveillance Non Federal Capabilities Should Be Considered in Creating a National Biosurveillance Strategy.* Washington, DC: GAO.

GAO. (2013). High Containment Laboratories: Assessment of the Nation's Need Is Missing. *Testimony Before The Subcommittee Emergency Preparedness, Response and Communications, Biosurveillance Observations on the Cancellation of Biowatch Gen-3 and Future Considerations for the Program,* 18 (2014).

GAO. (2016). *Testimony Before the Subcommittee on Emergency Preparedness Response and Communications, Committee on Homeland Security, House of Representatives.* Washington, DC: GAO.

GAO. (2017). *GAO High Containment Labs Coordinated Actions Needed to Enhance the Select Agent Program's Oversight of Hazardous Pathogens* (Vol. GAO 18–145). Washington, DC: GAO.

Geoghegan, J., & Holmes, E. (2017). Predicting Virus Emergencies and Evolutionary Noise. *Open Biology, 7*, 1–9.

Gerstein, D. (2013). *The Biological and Toxin Weapons Convention. National Security and Arms Control in the Age of Biotechnology.* Lanham, MD: Rowman and Littlefield.

Gerstein, G. (2017). Glaring Gaps: America Needs a Biodefense Upgrade. *Bulletin of the Atomic Scientists, 73*(2), 86–91.

GHRF Commission. (2015). *The Neglected Dimension of Global Security. A Framework to Counter Infectious Disease Crisis.* Washington, DC: Global Health Risk Framework for the Future Commission.

Ginsberg, M., & Bui, A. (2015). Bio Protection of Facilities. *Defense & Security Analysis, 31*(1), 4–21. https://doi.org/10.1080/14751798.2014.995335.

Gronvall, G., et al. (2016). National Biosafety Systems. UPMC Center for Health Security.

Gryphon Scientific. (2016). *Risk and Benefit Analysis of Gain of Function Research Final Report.* Takoma Park, MD: Gryphon Scientific, LLC.

Heickerö, R. (2014). Cyber Terrorism: Electronic Jihad. *Strategic Analysis, 38*(4), 554–565. https://doi.org/10.1080/09700161.2014.918435.

Heymann, D., et al. (2015). Global Health Security: The Wider Lessons from the West African Ebola Virus Disease Outbreak. *The Lancet, 385*, 1884–1901.

HMG. (2011). *CONTEST: The UK's Strategy for Countering Terrorism.* London: Her Majesty's Government.

Inkster, N. (2015). Cyber Espionage. *Adelphi Series, 55*(456), 51–82. https://doi.org/10.1080/19445571.2015.1181443.

Innes, M., & Sheptycki, J. (2004). From Detection to Disruption: Intelligence and the Changing Logic of Police Crime Control in the UK. *International Criminal Justice Review, 14*, 1–24.

Innes, M., et al. (2017). A Disruptive Influence? Preventing Problems and Counter Violent Extremism Policy in Practice. *Law and Society Review, 51*(2), 252–281.

Insinna, V. (2013). Government Biosurveillance to Include Social Media. *National Defense, 97*(710), 13.

Kasolo, F., et al. (2013). Implementation of the International Health Regulations (2015) in the African Region. *African Health Monitor, 18*, 11–13.

Kim, J., et al. (2015). Advances in Anthrax Detection: Overview of Bioprobes and Biosensors. *Applied Biochemistry and Biotechnology, 176*(4), 957–977.

Koblentz, G. (2009). *Living Weapons.* New York: Cornell University Press.

Koblentz, G., & Mazanec, B. (2013). Viral Warfare: The Security Implications of Cyber and Biological Weapons. *Comparative Strategy, 32*(5), 418–434. https://doi.org/10.1080/01495933.2013.821845.

Lennane, R. (2011). Biological Weapon Convention. In R. Katz & R. Zilinskas (Eds.), *Encyclopaedia of Bioterrorism Defense* (pp. 82–86). Hoboken, NJ: Wiley-Blackwell.

Marston, B., et al. (2017). Ebola Response Impact on Public Health Programs, West Africa 2014–2017. *Emerging Infectious Diseases Journal, 28*(Supplement), 25–31.

Mawudeku, A., et al. (2015). GPHIN Phase 3: One Mandate, Multiple Stakeholders. In S. Davies & J. Youde (Eds.), *The Politics of Surveillance and Response to Disease Outbreaks* (pp. 71–85). Surrey, UK: Ashgate.

MMWR. (2016). CDC's Response to the 2014–2016 Ebola Epidemic West Africa and the United States. *MMWR, Supplement, 65*(3), 1–106.

Nalla M.K., & Wakefield A. (2014). The Security Officer. In M. Gill (Ed.), *The Handbook of Security* (pp. 727–746). London: Palgrave Macmillan.

National Institute for Public Policy. (2009). The Proliferation Security Initiative: A Model for Future International Collaboration. *Comparative Strategy, 28*, 395–462.

Nature Editorial. (2014). Biosafety in the Balance. *Nature, 510*, 443.

O'Shea, J. (2017). Digital Disease Detection: A Systematic Review of Event-Based Internet Biosurveillance Systems. *International Journal of Medical Informatics, 101*(Supplement C), 15–22. https://doi.org/10.1016/j.ijmedinf.2017.01.019.

Paranjape, S., & Franz, D. (2015). Implementing the Global Health Security Agenda Lessons from the Global Health and Security Programs. *Health Security, 13*(1), 9–19.

Perman, B., et al. (2013). Basic Principles of Threat Assessment. In R. Burnette (Ed.), *Biosecurity. Understanding, Assessing, and Preventing the Threat* (pp. 89–90). Hoboken, NJ: Wiley.

Prenzler, T., & Sarre, R. (2014). The Role of Partnerships Security Management. In M. Gill (Ed.), *The Handbook of Security* (pp. 791–812). Basingstoke: Palgrave Macmillan.

Ratcliffe, J. (2008). *Intelligence Led Policing.* Collompton, UK: Willan.

Ratcliffe, J. (2016). *Intelligence Led Policing* (2nd ed.). Abingdon, UK: Routledge.

Reed, M. (2016). *The Research Impact Handbook.* Huntly, UK: Fast Track Impact Ltd.

Regalado, A. (2016, February 9). Top US Intel Official Calls Gene Editing a WMD Threat. *MIT Technology Review.*

Rigakos, G. (2002). *The Para Police.* Toronto: University of Toronto Press.

Riglietti, G. (2017). Defining the Threat: What Cyber Terrorism Means Today and What It Could Mean Tomorrow. *International Journal of Business and Cyber Security, 1*(2).

Robert Koch Institute. (2018). *Signale—Early Warning System.* Berlin: Robert Koch Institute. From https://www.rki.de/EN/Content/infections/epidemiology/signals/signals_node.html. Accessed March 15, 2018.

Salerno, R., & Gaudioso, J. (Eds.). (2015). *Laboratory Biorisk Management Biosafety and Biosecurity.* Boca Raton, FL: CRC Press.

Sample, I. (2014). Revealed: 100 Safety Breaches at UK Labs Handling Potentially Deadly Diseases. *The Guardian.* From https://www.theguardian.com/science/2014/dec/04/-sp-100-safety-breaches-uk-labs-potentially-deadly-diseases. Accessed March 15, 2017.

Schilling, J. (2017). Ransomware101-How to Face the Threat. *Petroleum Accounting and Financial Management Journal, 36*(2), 6–8.

Schnirring, L. (2014, August 15). CDC Probe of H5N1 Cross Contamination Reveals Protocol Lapses, Reporting Delays. *CIDRAP.* From http://www.cidrap.umn.edu/news-perspective/2014/08/cdc-probe-h5n1-cross-contamination-reveals-protocol-lapses-reporting-delays. Accessed March 15, 2017.

Schnirring, L. (2016, January 13). Pandemic Readiness Review Says $4.5 Billion a Year Needed. *CIDRAP.* From http://www.cidrap.umn.edu/news-perspective/2016/01/pandemic-readiness-review-says-45-billion-year-needed. Accessed March 15, 2017.

Schnirring, L. (2017). Secretary Tillerson Lauds Global Health Security Agenda. Minneapolis, MN: University of Minnesota (CIDRAP). Retrieved from http://www.cidrap.umn.edu/news-perspective/2017/10/secretary-tillerson-lauds-global-health-security-agenda.

Shaikh, A.T., Ferland, L., Hood-Cree, R., Shaffer, L., & McNabb, S. (2015). Disruptive Innovation Can Prevent the Next Pandemic. *Frontiers in Public Health, 3*(215). https://doi.org/10.3389/fpubh.2015.00215.

Shinwari, Z., Khalil, A., & Nasim, A. (2014). Natural or Deliberate Outbreak in Pakistan: How to Prevent or Detect and Trace Its Origin: Biosecurity, Surveillance Forensics. *Archivum Immunologiae et Therapiae Experimentalis, 62*(4), 263–275. https://doi.org/10.1007/s00005-014-0298-6.

Sisk, R. (2016). Army Probe of Anthrax Scandal Raises More Red Flags. *Military.Com.* Retrieved from http://www.military.com/daily-news/2016/01/13/army-probe-of-anthrax-scandal-raises-more-red-flags.html.

Slayton, J., et al. (2013). Physical Elements of Biosecurity. In R. Burnette (Ed.), *Biosecurity* (pp. 51–70). Hoboken, NJ: Wiley.

Sparrow, A. (2016). Who Isn't Equipped for a Pandemic or Bioterror Attack? The WHO. *Bulletin of the Atomic Scientists*. From https://thebulletin.org/who-isnt-equipped-pandemic-or-bioterror-attack-who9555.   Accessed March 15, 2017.

Stern, J., & Shouten, R. (2016). Lessons from the Anthrax Letters. In M. Dunn & S. Sagan (Eds.), *Insider Threats* (pp. 74–102). Ithaca and New York: Cornell University Press.

Stone, R. (2017). *The Week in Fintech: FBI Agent Says Cybersecurity Practices Need to Change*. New York: SNL Financial LC.

Strom, K., & Eyerman, J. (2007). Interagency Coordination in Response to Terrorism: Promising Practices and Barriers Identified in Four Countries. *Criminal Justice Studies, 20*(2), 131–147. https://doi.org/10.1080/14786010701396871.

Sture, J., Minehata, M., & Shinomiya, N. (2012). Looking at the Formulation of National Biosecurity Education Action Plans. *Medicine, Conflict and Survival, 28*(1), 85–97. https://doi.org/10.1080/13623699.2012.658628.

Taylor, J., et al. (2013). The Role of Protection Measures and their Interaction in Determining Building Vulnerability and Resilience to Bioterrorism. *Bioterrorism and Biodefense, 4*(1), 1–10.

Thilmany, J. (2005). Harms Way Engineering Software and Micro Technology Prepare the Defense Against Bioterrorism. *Mechanical Engineering CIME, 127*(8), 22–25.

Vogel, K. (2013). *Phantom Menace or Looming Danger?* Baltimore, MD: The Johns Hopkins University Press.

Wakefield, A. (2003). *Selling Security. The Private Policing of Public Space*. Cullompton and Devon: Willan.

Walsh, P. F. (2011). *Intelligence and Intelligence Analysis*. Abingdon, UK: Routledge.

Walsh, P. F. (2016). Australian National Security Intelligence Collection Since 9/11: Policy and Legislative Challenges. In K. Warby (Ed.), *National Security, Surveillance and Terror* (pp. 51–74). Cham, Switzerland: Springer International Publishing.

Weimann, G. (2016). Going Dark: Terrorism on the Dark Web. *Studies in Conflict & Terrorism, 39*(3), 195–206. https://doi.org/10.1080/1057610X.2015.1119546.

WHO. (2015). Ebola Virus Disease in West Africa—The First Nine Months of the Epidemic and Forward Projections. *The New England Journal of Medicine, 371*, 1481–1495.

Wilson, J. (2017). Signal Recognition During the Emergence of Pandemic Influenza Type A/H1N1: A Commercial Disease Intelligence Unit's Perspective. *Intelligence and National Security, 32*(2), 222–230.

Xu, Z., et al. (2011). Bioaerosol Science, Technology and Engineering: Past and Present. *Aerosol Science and Technology, 45*(1), 1337–1349.

Yan, S., et al. (2017). Utility and Potential of Rapid Epidemic Intelligence from Internet-Based Sources. *International Journal of Infectious Diseases, 63*(Supplement C), 77–87. https://doi.org/10.1016/j.ijid.2017.07.020.

Young, A. (2015, August 28). Labs Cited for 'Serious' Security Failures in Research with Bioterror Germs. *USA Today*. From http://www.usatoday.com/story/news/2015/08/28/lab-security-violation-bioterrorism-select-agent-regulation/32439491/. Accessed March 15, 2017.

Zajácz, R. (2017). Silk Road: The Market Beyond the Reach of the State. *The Information Society, 33*(1), 23–34. https://doi.org/10.1080/01972243.2016.1248612.

8

Oversight and Accountability

Like all threat and risk environments, the extent to which intelligence can support the disruption, prevention and treatment of bio-threats and risks is governed in each 'Five Eyes' country by several layers of federal, state/provincial and in some cases local legislation and regulation that determines how intelligence is collected, assessed and disseminated. A great deal of this legislation also relates to the oversight of intelligence in liberal democracies such as the 'Five Eyes' countries. Accordingly, one cannot understand the role intelligence can play in the future in managing bio-threats and risks without also a broad knowledge about the legislative, regulatory, oversight and accountability mechanisms that govern how intelligence capabilities can be applied against such threats and risks.

In this chapter, we will review the key legislative, regulatory, oversight and accountability issues that impact on how the 'Five Eyes' intelligence communities can support decision-makers in understanding current and emerging bio-threats and risks. Many of the current challenges are no different from those identified in other threat and risks contexts,

© The Author(s) 2018
P. F. Walsh, *Intelligence, Biosecurity and Bioterrorism*,
https://doi.org/10.1057/978-1-137-51700-5_8

though some are more specific to the application of intelligence capabilities to bio-threats and risks. After discussing each area (legislative, regulatory, oversight and accountability), I will provide some analysis of how current challenges may be addressed in order to promote better intelligence practice against bio-threats and risks.

Legislation

As with most threat and risk types (e.g. counter-terrorism, organised crime and cyber), there is a growing body of legislation within each 'Five Eyes' country that defines 'the functions of intelligence agencies and what they are allowed to do' in the prevention, disruption and treatment of bio-threats and risks (Walsh 2011: 218). There is almost an unlimited amount of legislation that could be relevant to defining how intelligence 'works' on bio-threats and risks. Indeed since 9/11, legislation drafted in the counter-terrorism context in each 'Five Eyes' country has as discussed in Chapter 7, promoted an increasingly flexible and proactive approach to intelligence collection, particularly electronic collection (telecommunications, internet and social media). Similar more permissive and flexible 'powers' have also been given to 'Five Eyes' intelligence communities in other areas such as illegal immigration and organised crime.

So understanding fully how legislation impacts on what intelligence agencies can and cannot do in the bio-threat and risk context, requires a detailed analysis of specific legislation enacted to promote biosafety and biosecurity—as well as how legislation enacted for the purposes of defining the authority and operation of intelligence in other threat and risk areas (e.g. counter-terrorism and organised crime) might also play a role in the bio-threat and risk context. Given the volume of legislation that could be specifically and potentially relevant to how each Five Eyes intelligence communities manage bio-threats and risk is extremely large and evolving, a better use of space in this section is to focus on a selection of bio-threat and risk specific and more general intelligence legislation that are most relevant to describing what intelligence agencies can do and are allowed to do in the bio-threat and risk contexts. The section will then highlight some of the impacts of legislation on intelligence practice and how legislative change raises broader concerns about privacy, human rights, judicial process and even the constitutionality of some new laws, particularly new counter-terrorism and intelligence laws.

Specific Biosafety, Biosecurity Legislation

In the US in addition to legislation there have been several presidential directives dating back to 1969, but these largely increased post 9/11 during the Bush Administration—notably including HSPD 4 (The National Strategy to Combat WMD 2002) and HSPD 10 (Biodefense for the 21st Century 2004). Later during the Obama Administration (PPD National Strategy for Countering Biological Threats 2009) was signed. There are several biosafety and biosecurity related legislation in the US that impacts either directly or indirectly on the work on the US IC. There are too many to discuss in detail but key ones are: The Biological Weapons Anti-Terrorism Act of 1989 and the Public Health Security and Bioterrorism and Response Act of 2002. Pre 9/11, the Biological Weapons Anti-Terrorism Act of 1989 was the main piece of legislation. The Biological Weapons Anti-Terrorism Act of 1989 was significant in implementing the BWC and introducing further measures to protect the US from bio-terrorism. In particular, it sought to do this by amending the Federal Crime Code to impose penalties on those who knowingly develop, acquire, transfer any bio-agent, toxin or delivery system for use as weapon or assist a foreign state or organisation to do so. It also provided extra-territorial jurisdiction for offences by or against US nationals. The Act was also one of the earliest biosecurity–bioterrorism related references to intelligence authorising the interception of wire, oral and electronic communications related to bio-weapon offenses under specified conditions.

The Public Health Security and Bioterrorism and Response Act of 2002 introduced a range of preparedness measures against bio-terrorism such as improving state, local and hospital preparedness as well as enhancing the role of agencies such as the US Department of Agriculture and Health and Human Services in bolstering controls on dangerous biological agents. Following the 2002 Act, later drafted legislation built on its control and regulation measures such as the Select Agent Program and Biosafety Improvement Act of 2009, which administers the handling of select agents in high containment labs, determines and reviews agents for the select agents program—as well as promoting guidelines for minimum biosafety and biosecurity training for relevant lab staff. Interestingly, the Select Agent Program was also developed under the PATRIOT Act the latter being though more associated with as discussed below the NSA's bulk metadata collection activities.

Similarly, in Australia, Canada, the UK and New Zealand, a tranche of biosecurity and bioterrorism related legislation has also been enacted—though less in number compared to the US. In Australia, the principal legislation dealing with public health surveillance, the conditions for working with and the listing of Security Sensitive Biological Agents (SSBAs) is the National Health Security Act 2007, which has been subsequently amended several times. This act also stipulates steps for monitoring compliance of individuals and organisations working with SSBAs as well as background check requirements on those working with them. However, much earlier than the enactment of the National Health Security Act 2007, the Australian Government passed the Weapons of Mass Destruction (Prevention and Proliferation) Act 1995, which like the US Biological Weapons Anti-Terrorism Act of 1989 prohibited the supply or export of goods that may be used to acquire, develop weapons capable of causing mass destruction. In Canada, the key health security legislation is the Human Pathogens and Toxins Act (HPTA) which came into force in 2015. The HPTA was also accompanied by regulations—the Human Pathogens and Toxins Act and its regulations (HPTR), though the later will be discussed in the following section on regulations. HPTA is similar in many ways to schedules of the National Health Security Act 2007 (Australia) in detailing compliance, licensing and background checks required for individuals and organisations working with SSBAs. Since 9/11, Canada has also amended its Criminal Code and the Public Safety Act 2002 to implement the BWC and in the case of the former law make it a criminal offence to intentionally cause serious risk to the health or safety of the public. The UK in contrast to all other 'Five Eyes' countries has one of oldest pieces of biosecurity/bioterrorism legislation with its enactment in 1974 of the Biological Weapons Act, which implemented the provisions of the BWC. After 9/11 however, the UK government enacted the Anti-Terrorism, Crime and Security Act (2001). Parts VI–IX of this Act were designed to build on controls originally set out in the original Biological Weapons Act 1974. The Anti-Terrorism Crime and Security Act's creation was influenced by growing concerns over WMD and bioterrorism, 9/11, the *Amerithrax* incident and intelligence assessments that Iraq had offensive biological weapons. These sections further delineated various offences related to terrorists using, acquiring or transferring 'noxious substances or things that which could endanger human life' (Walker 2005: 176–186). Part VII relates to arrangements for maintaining lists of controlled substances, including inspection regimes and the role of police in these and more broadly the issuing of warrants for violations of the Act (ibid.: 184).

In New Zealand, there are several acts that to a greater or lesser extent might play a role in managing bio-threats and risks including: the Health Act 1956, Epidemic Preparedness Act 2006, the Biosecurity Act 1993, the Hazardous Substances and New Organisms Act 1996, and the Civil Defence Emergency Management Act 2002. There are also associated regulations such as the Anthrax Prevention Regulations 1987 and the Health (Infectious and Notifiable Diseases) Regulations 2016.

Legislative Challenges

It is difficult to generalise across all 'Five Eyes' countries about what impact and challenges have arisen for their respective ICs based on the above brief survey of the main biosecurity, biosafety and bio-terrorism legislation. A full account of these would need to also include a larger sample of other related pieces of legislation not discussed here for brevity reasons. A more detailed study, however, is needed and should include how biosecurity and bio-terrorism related legislation in the agriculture, food, environmental, and animal health sectors intersects with the roles and functions of more long-standing statutes just discussed that deal with WMD and bio-terrorism. Such a study should also include an investigation of how various biosecurity acts have been applied against bio-criminal matters such as intellectual property theft, cyber-hacking or assault using a dangerous biological substance. Results of this work could then provide a baseline for understanding how a diverse suite of legislation impacts (positively and negatively) in enabling more effective intelligence activity against bio-threats and risks.

Leaving aside the need for further detailed examination of biosecurity, biosafety and bio-terrorism legislation, three general conclusions can be made about the key challenges confronting 'Five Eyes' intelligence communities ability to work with such legislation. The first challenge is that the diversity and rapid change of the bio-threat and risk environment has led to an increase number of legislation or amendments in existing laws. This has led to varying degrees a fragmented legislative approach to bio-threats and risks. This fragmentation is most obvious in the US, where multiple biosecurity, biosafety and bioterrorism specific legislation since 9/11 has led to an overlapping and sometimes duplicating legislative responses—where multiple agencies have both some authority and funding to manage an aspect of the bio-threat/risk landscape. This promotes within all agencies involved in this space (both non-intelligence and intelligence), a lack of clarity on how best they can operationalise their capabilities under various statutes in concert with each other (Blue Ribbon Report 2015).

In the case of the US, some legislative efforts in recent years were made to deal with this fragmentation. In 2014 (113th Session of Congress), a new bill was introduced to the House of Representatives (HR43034) as the WMD Prevention and Preparedness Act, which included a range of governance and coordination measures already discussed in Chapter 6 (e.g. development of a national bio-surveillance strategy and appointment of a senior national security council member to advise the president on biodefense). Interestingly, Title 2 of the Act included measures for improving intelligence coordination including the implementation of a national intelligence strategy for biological weapons, which would be integrated into a broader national intelligence strategy for WMD. The bill at time of writing, however still has not passed and has been referred to the House Subcommittee on Emergency Preparedness Response and Communications. It remains also unclear whether the bill's focus on WMD and not a broader health security risk approach as discussed in Chapter 6 would really improve Intelligence Governance challenges across the US IC—or how it can more effectively work with non IC members of the health security enterprise (public health, agriculture, local authorities and the private sector).

Leading on from the discussion of the WMD Prevention and Preparedness bill, the second broad challenge is the historical siloing of legislation that either seeks to deal with WMD issues, bio-terrorism, biosafety, bio-surveillance or emergency response rather than adopting more of a one health security approach to legislation. Not all legislation of course needs to be folded into the one 'super law' for managing bio-threats and risks. The management of different threats and risks across the one health spectrum (plant, animal, human) will still require specialised legislation in these different contexts, however further consideration on how the role of intelligence agencies can be better coordinated with the roles and responsibilities of other stakeholders (health, agriculture, emergency management) is required. The final challenge is assessing how the bio-safety, bio-terrorism and biosecurity legislation discussed here operate with broader intelligence related legislation which is the topic in the next section?

Other Intelligence Related Legislation

Equally and perhaps in some 'Five Eyes' countries even more diverse than the role and number of bio-safety, biosecurity and bio-terrorism legislation is the large amount of intelligence and counter-terrorism laws that have been passed since 9/11, which are also relevant to how the ICs of these countries might manage bio-threats and risks. Again space limitations preclude a detailed discussion of them all. In Australia alone, under the Howard Government (1996–2007), it has been estimated that there were more than 44 pieces of just counter-terrorism legislation passed in the decade since 9/11 (Williams 2011: 1144). A more detailed discussion of 'Five Eyes' intelligence related post 9/11 legislation can be found in Walsh (2011: 218–227).

Instead the focus here will be to highlight 'flagship' intelligence legislation in each 'Five Eyes' country since 9/11, particularly those that have provided their intelligence communities with greater collection capabilities/powers as well as legislation which has sponsored broader organisational reform. Exploring the role of legislation in bringing about enhanced collection capabilities and organisational reforms is critical to understanding how various acts have enabled or constrained the operations of each 'Five Eyes' country's intelligence community. This in turn is important in gaining insight into the challenges and opportunities that shape how each 'Five Eyes' intelligence community can operate in the future broadly and specifically on emerging bio-threats and risks. Turning to the US first, since 9/11 there are three significant pieces of legislation that are worth mentioning as each in their own way have arguably done more than any others to shape how the IC has operated as well as underscoring the ongoing challenges for agencies working a broad range of threats including bio-threats and risks. In turn these are: *Intelligence Reform and Terrorism Prevention Act 2004* (IRTPA), The US Patriot Act and the USA Freedom Act.

In 2004, the US Congress enacted the IRTPA to address the failures identified by the IC in the 9/11 Commission Report, which included insufficient information sharing between, for example, the CIA and FBI, and inadequate integration and coordination of their foreign and domestic intelligence collection efforts (9/11 Commission Report 2004: 353–360). One year earlier, the establishment of the Department of Homeland Security (DHS) represented an attempt to better coordinate collection efforts of both the foreign and domestic elements of the US intelligence enterprise. Though the enactment of IRPTA was meant to lead to several more historic and significant changes, including the creation of the Office of the Director of National Intelligence (ODNI) and sanctioning a new information sharing environment (ISE) involving major security organizations. In short, the creation of a Director of National Intelligence would now be responsible for coordinating and integrating the efforts of all 16 intelligence agencies together—thereby hopefully in the future addressing several points of IC failure identified in the 9/11 Commission and later the mistakes made in assessing Iraq's WMD capability in 2002–2003. While in recent years, particularly under the former DNI General Jim Clapper 's tenure (9 August 2010–20 January 2017) the DNI has been able to improve coordination and integration around missions, it is less clear how future DNIs with much less experience and respect across the IC will fare in being the leader of the IC. The IRTPA, like the creation of the CIA in 1947 was in the end a series of compromises—which gave the DNI lots of responsibilities, but no real authority to take control of the US IC or agency operational budgets, particularly those controlled by the Pentagon. In a sense, the IRTPA was meant to recast leadership in the US IC, but the ODNI's establishment and the compromises made have neutered the DNI's ability to set a fully integrated and authoritative agenda across the IC. Understanding the reforms possible under successive DNIs and their limitations is required by those who also want to see greater leadership by the US IC on how best to deal with emerging bio-threats and risks.

Equally important for understanding the many challenges around intelligence collection since 911 was the implementation of the Providing Appropriate Tools Required to Intercept and Obstruct Terrorism Act of 2001 (US PATRIOT Act) under the Bush Administration. The 'enactment of the USA PATRIOT Act represented the first foundation stone to a policy and legal framework, which enabled increasing degrees of latitude in US security intelligence and law enforcement intelligence collection' (Walsh 2017: 180). In particular, Section 215 of the Patriot Act allowed the government to apply for a court order (via the Foreign Intelligence Surveillance Court) compelling a person or entity to turn over records that may be relevant to a foreign intelligence investigation (ibid.). Since 2006, court orders under Section 215 were used to acquire large volumes of telephone metadata. This bulk data set was held by the NSA and could be queried by foreign intelligence investigators to identify links between terrorists and others that may be terrorists. Section 215 was continually extended by the Bush Administration rather than comprehensively reviewed and only in June 2015 was it amended following President Obama signing into law the USA Freedom Act (H.R. 2048). The Patriot Act raised a number of legal, policy, civil rights and privacy concerns and it was the exposure of the metadata program by the New York Times and NSA contractor Edward Snowden that influenced President Obama's enactment of the USA Freedom Act.

The USA Freedom Act was a compromise by law makers—some who did not want any changes to the Patriot Act less the US becomes vulnerable to more terrorists attacks and other law makers and civil rights lobbies that disapproved of the bulk storage of US citizen's communications metadata. The USA Freedom Act reauthorized some expired provisions of under Section 215 of the Patriot Act (e.g. collection of business records in national security investigations), but prohibited the bulk collection of data of American's telephone and internet metadata by the NSA or other US intelligence agencies (Walsh 2017: 180). Collection must now be linked to a specific selection term (SST) meaning and identifiable person not the mere bulk collection of data (ibid.).

In contrast to the US, where the post 9/11 legislative environment was dominated by the IRPTA and USA Patriot Act, other 'Five Eyes' countries such as Australia released a larger number of intelligence collection enabling legislation. As mentioned earlier the focus shortly after 9/11 in Australia, Canada, the UK and New Zealand was less on major structural reform of their ICs and more to a greater and varying degree on implementing less headline policy measures to improve intelligence coordination as well as 'providing their ICs with more flexible and proactive ('hunting') intelligence capabilities'. For a more a detailed discussion of how the major post 9/11 US intelligence and legislative reform approach differed other 'Five Eyes' countries see the comparison between the US and Australia in Walsh (2011: 159–165).

Given space is a premium, in the remaining part of this section I will mainly focus on a high level thematic discussion of key relevant intelligence legislation in other (non US) 'Five Eyes' countries. In Australia after 9/11 several policy responses, including independent government reviews were developed (e.g. the Smith Review) to strengthen the coordination efforts and capabilities of the IC (Walsh 2011, 2016: 51–74). However, in Australia arguably more so than any other 'Five Eyes' country, successive governments have steadily increased the both the number of legislation and the powers ascribed in them to various members of the Australian IC. In another publication in 2016, I provide a detailed discussion of relevant legislation implemented by various Australian governments since 9/11 so the reader looking for more detail can go to (Walsh 2016: 51–74).

One early (2003) legislative response to the growing concern of terrorism by the Howard (conservative) Government was to enhance intelligence collection capabilities by enacting the *Australian Security Intelligence Organisation Legislation Amendment (ASIO) (Terror) Act* 2003 *(Cth)*, which amended the previous *ASIO Act* 1979 *(Cth)* by introducing a questioning and detention warrant scheme. ASIO is Australia's domestic security intelligence agency. In simple terms, amendments to the *ASIO Act* allowed ASIO officers to detain and question persons not yet formally charged of a terrorism offence for a period of 24 hours when this could substantially assist in the collection of intelligence that is important in relation to a terrorism offence. Additionally, a person could be detained up to one week for questioning if there were reasonable grounds he or she may alert another person about an ASIO investigation, was a risk of not appearing for questioning, or could obstruct or destroy material that might be requested under warrant. These amendments proved controversial, with legal and human rights scholars claiming them to be potentially unconstitutional (Williams 2011).

Other legislative measures such as the *Anti Terrorism Act* 2004 *(Cth)* extended the questioning provision of 12 hours to 20, which increased the overall intelligence gathering capabilities of agencies under Division 2 (Section 23E) of the *Crimes Act* 1914 *(Cth)*. The other significant intelligence collection and counter terrorism response during the Howard years were control and preventative detention orders. Division 104 of the *Criminal Code* now allowed control orders against individuals not suspected of any criminal offence that may be subjected to restrictions (equivalent to house arrest). These measures were thought to be reasonably necessary to protect the public from terrorism. Views on the need for control orders varied at the time these reforms were introduced (see for example, McDonald 2007: 106; White 2007: 116–125). The preventative detention measures under Division 105 of the *Criminal Code*, allowed for an individual to be detained for up to 48 hours if there was a reasonable expectation this would prevent imminent terrorist acts or assist in preserving evidence relating to a recent terrorist act. The initial 48-hour period could be further extended under state law by 14 days.

More recently in Australia, there have seen further enhancements of collection and operational capability in Australia's IC (particularly AFP and ASIO) in 2014 with the passing of three more larger pieces of legislation: the National Security Legislation Amendment Act (2014), The Counter Terrorism Legislation Amendment (Foreign Fighters) Act (2014), and the Telecommunications (Interception and Access) Amendment (Data Retention) Act (2014). Further details on the specifics of each can be found in Walsh (2016: 51–74). In short, each provided more flexible and proactive powers to Australia's IC for example in the case of the National Security Legislation Amendment Act (2014) by lowering the threshold for issuing warrants. Interestingly, around the same time US law makers were debating the USA Freedom bill, which as noted above removed the ability of its IC to hold bulk metadata, in Australia the Telecommunications (Interception and Access) Amendment (Data Retention) Act (2014) enactment was bringing in new provisions whereby telecommunications and internet providers were required to store metadata up to a two year period (Walsh 2017: 181). Finally, in late 2016 and into 2017 two major policy landmarks were implemented by the Malcolm Turnbull (coalition) government, which will likely have profound changes in both the broader Australian IC and the legal framework under which it operates. The first was the commissioning of an independent intelligence review in late 2016 and the second was the establishment by the government of a new super ministry—the Department of Home Affairs. The new ministry came into operation in late 2017 and is a confederation of national security and law enforcement agencies (including ASIO, ACIC, AUSTRAC, Office of Transport Security, Immigration and Border Protection and the AFP). All of these agencies have their own multiple pieces of legislation, which outlines their roles, authorities in all operations, including their intelligence roles. The authors of the independent intelligence review Michael L'Estrange and Stephen Merchant called for a comprehensive review of the legal framework in which Australia's IC works. They described the historical adhoc approach to intelligence legislation as incremental and piece meal (L'Estrange and Merchant 2017: 89–111). At the time of writing, it is not certain when such a review will take place. It will be a major undertaking, but a necessary one given the major reforms currently underway in the Australian IC and within the new Department of Home Affairs.

Similarly in the UK and Canada there has been a growth in counter-terrorism and intelligence legislation aimed at providing quicker interception capabilities and more streamlined processes for doing so (ibid.). In the UK similar to Australia a Data Retention and Investigatory Powers Act was passed in 2014 and in Canada C51 or the Anti-terrorism Act was passed in June 2015. C-51 was partly but not wholly in response to lone wolf terror attacks in the country during this time and brought in sweeping changes not seen since Canada's Anti-Terror Act of 2001 (Walsh 2017: 182). For example, C-51 amended a series of Canada's intelligence and security related acts, including the CSIS Act, the Secure Air Travel Act, the Criminal Code and the Immigration and Refugee Protection Act (ibid.). There are a number of similarities between Canada's C-51 and Australia's 2014 Foreign Fighters Act particularly in measures for preventing citizens to leave to prescribed areas to commit acts of terror as well as penalties for advocacy of terrorism in public or online (Walsh 2016: 51–74).

Finally, New Zealand also followed other 'Five Eyes' intelligence countries early after 9/11 in expanding the definition of terrorism offences, penalties and powers for its IC by enacting the Terrorism Suppression Act 2002. This Act was criticised at the time by lawyers and civil liberty groups for defining too broadly what constitutes a terrorism act (Walsh 2011: 224). Looking at broader New Zealand intelligence legislation historically there have been a few major pieces, which have governed the roles, functions, powers and oversight of various agencies. The key ones have been: the Intelligence and Security Committee Act 1996 (established a parliamentary oversight committee), the Government Communications Security Bureau Act 2003 (governed the operations of New Zealand's sigint operations) and the New Zealand Secret Intelligence Service 1969 (which governed the operations of New Zealand's humint agency). Following in February 2016 a first ever major (Cullen and Reddy) review of New Zealand's intelligence community, the reviewers identified a number of deficiencies in the above current pieces of legislation. In particular there were inconsistencies identified in both the GCSB Act 2003 and the NZSIS Act 1969 over functions, roles, authorisations and accountability (Cullen and Reddy 2016: 2). The Cullen and Reddy intelligence review provided the impetus for the New Zealand Government passing the Intelligence and Security Act 2017, which seeks to more clearly place the objectives, duties, covert activities, authorisations and accountability of both New Zealand's two key intelligence agencies (GCSB and NZSIS) into the one Act.

From our brief tour above of the major legislative milestones that have guided intelligence operations since 9/11, it's clear there are multiple challenges to having fully effective legislative frameworks that can facilitate better intelligence practice—including appropriate safeguards, transparency and oversight mechanisms. In each 'Five Eyes' country there is a unique set of challenges, which have evolved based on that country's own particular political and law making processes.

Leaving aside the unique political, policy and legal responses to intelligence law making in each country, however, there a number of similar challenges discernible across the 'Five Eyes' countries. First, like other public policy making contexts, when there is a crisis, governments tend to respond quickly, which is understandable, but the enactment or amendment process of legislation in crisis situations or after major independent reviews as we saw earlier, frequently results in laws that either less well designed, or adhoc and incremental solutions. This can be seen in the development of counter-terrorism legislation in each country and in the implementation of major legislation such as the US IRTPA.

Second 'making good legislation' can be difficult in the post 9/11 security environment, where the rapid growth in technology at the disposal of the IC is also increasingly available to threat actors—particularly encrypted communications technologies. Additionally, while technological revolutions in data surveillance, data mining/matching and analytics technology has changed the way intelligence communities collect and analyse threats, it remains a challenge for law makers to proscribe authorities to use various technologies into law given the technologies are changing rapidly.

A third, common challenge in most 'Five Eyes' country's enactment of several pieces of legislation relates to difficulties in operationalising these correctly (lawfully) along with the fullest understanding of their ethical and accountability implications. There have been for example, cases in some 'Five Eyes' countries whereby intelligence agencies have been given greater or more flexible authorities yet demonstrated difficulty executing these in operations. Examples of the later point have been seen in Australia with the wrongful detention of a Mohammed Hanneef (Walsh 2011: 219–221), and Canada's application of legislation that led to the renditioning of Maher Arrar—as well as a wrongful adverse security finding against Adil Charkooui (ibid.: 230–231).

Meeting the Challenges

Each 'Five Eyes' country will naturally need to find their own path to overcoming the challenges and limitations posed by some legislation enacted since 9/11. In the above discussion, it's clear that some 'Five Eyes' countries–are more aware of the growing volume of fragmented and adhoc legislation in their own jurisdictions and the need to create clearer, less cluttered legal frameworks for their intelligence communities to operate from. As seen above, in 2017 New Zealand sought to create greater harmony and clarity across various acts that have historically governed its IC. Other '5 Eyes countries' are actively looking at similar harmonisation effort such as Australia and the UK.

However, managing emerging bio-threats and risks will require not just an auditing of the principle pieces of legislation that govern the roles, functions and authorities of each IC, but will also need a detailed review of the roles and authorities of ICs in biosafety, biosecurity and bioterrorism related laws as well. If 'Five Eyes' ICs are to more effectively contribute to the management of bio-threats and risks in the future, a detailed (and laborious) audit of both intelligence specific legislation and that more specific to biosafety, biosecurity and bioterrorism is required. This work is essential to identify overlapping duplicating biosafety, biosecurity and bioterrorism laws as a first step in working towards greater harmonisation of laws—that identifies where schedules, sections and regulations are not in concert with each other or are administratively difficult to oversee for the IC and other stakeholders to use. Of course as argued earlier in our discussion of public health stakeholders in Chapter 7 'Five Eyes', countries cannot improve their intelligence capabilities in managing bio-threats and risk on their own given global health is national health and vice versa.

National audits of existing legislation amongst the 'Five Eyes' clearly need to look for opportunities to harmonise relevant legislation within and across each country as well as eventually (hopefully) globally. As discussed in Chapter 7, there is now a crowded field of multilateral organisations (WHO/UN, World Bank, WTO), NGOs, and initiatives (GHSA)—each in their own way playing a role in global health governance. However, what is still lacking, is a truly global health law approach to effective multilateral cooperation. Some argue that 'state centrality of international law is the primary challenge to utilising law as an effective tool to advance global health problems' (Gostin and Taylor 2008: 53–63). Regardless, the impact of national biosafety, biosecurity and bioterrorism legislation on the prevention, disruption and treatment of bio-threats and risks is also clearly influenced and limited by fragmented, duplications and inconsistencies in areas of 'global health law making (ibid.).

Finally, bio-threats and risks cannot be ameliorated clearly by the mere passing of legislation as with any other kind of threat. Effective regulation is also critical to the prevention, disruption and treatment of bio-threats and risks which is the subject we now turn to. As too is robust oversight and accountability measures the final subject in this chapter.

Regulation Oversight and Accountability

Regulation

Before examining the role of oversight and accountability of 'Five Eyes' intelligence communities and how this impacts on their ability to prevent, disrupt and treat of bio-threats and risks, it is important first to define what we mean by regulation. Regulation theory and practice has gained momentum over the last three decades. It has been applied initially (and mainly) to the economic domain in regulating practice in financial services, consumer protection, transportation and communication to name a few (Sparrow 2001: 7). Overtime though, regulation practice has also developed in social sectors concerning health, safety, welfare, working conditions and the environment (ibid.). The net result of a wider number of regulatory sectors has been the emergence of a diverse multi-disciplinary field with regulation scholars and practitioners developing their own perspectives and means of 'what regulation is'—based on the sector of the economy or society they are focused on. Unsurprisingly then, no 'one size fits all' definition of regulation has emerged. Baldwin et al., however, in their handbook on regulation theory and practice do offer a generic definition which has its merits. Using Black's work, they define regulation as 'the intentional use of authority to affect behaviour of a different party according to set standards involving instruments of information gathering and behaviour modification' (Black cited in Baldwin et al. 2010: 12).

While no definition is perfect for understanding the diverse field of regulation in the bio-threat and risk sector, the one above has its merits because it's sufficiently broad yet not being overly legalistic. It also emphasises what regulations try to do, which is to modify behaviour. As discussed earlier in the legislation section, it is clear that a great deal of biosecurity, biosafety and bioterrorism related laws also include legally prescriptive regulations. For example, annexed to Canada's Human Pathogens and Toxins Act is the Human Pathogens Act Regulations, which stipulate mandatory measures related to issuing of licences for individuals/organisations working with select agents, notifications if an individual is going to increase the virulence or pathogenicity of human pathogens and other requirements related to security clearances and supervision. Yet as we shall see in this section not all regulatory requirements across the 'Five Eyes' countries are enshrined in legislation. Regulation can occur via different non legal instruments such as: policy, codes of conduct and self-regulation.

There is a large and diverse body of both legislative enabled regulatory mechanisms and more informal approaches to reducing bio-threat and risk across the biosecurity and bioterrorism sector. From a broader one health perspective of biosecurity, a comprehensive discussion of regulatory mechanisms would need to include a large number of issues including but not limited to: biosafety, agriculture and food security, importation/exportation biosecurity regulations, use of select agents, WMD counter-proliferation, animal and plant health, pharmaceuticals and dual use research. However, in the limited space here we will restrict our discussion of regulation to dual-use research of concern in the life sciences as this issue cuts across the entire one health continuum. It is also an area where each 'Five Eyes' IC continues to have a stake in how regulation mechanisms (formal legal or informal non legal) can help reduce bio-threats and risks.

In previous chapters, the potential security implications of dual use research was outlined. The exponential growth in synthetic biology, biotechnology and particular research such as gain of function projects, which have produced strains of dangerous pathogens has resulted in scientific advances but continue to raise national security concerns (see Tucker 2012; NAS 2016, 2017a, b). These concerns relate to whether advances in scientific knowledge and its dissemination might be exploited for malicious purposes by terrorists and criminals. Such concerns sit at one end of the debate about dual use research and at the other are members of the scientific community, who champion openness, transparency and communication of scientific knowledge. Since 9/11, and in the US in particular, debates have continued about how to address both national security concerns and the need for the scientific community to continue to carry out and disseminate research that may have legitimate benefits for the prevention or treatment of disease. The National Academies of Sciences, Engineering and Medicine's report on *Dual Use Research of Concern in the Life Sciences* provides a comprehensive summary of how policy and regulatory debates have developed since 9/11 to the present on this issue (National Academies of Sciences, Engineering and Medicine 2017: 30–44).

The National Academies report highlighted a number of deficiencies in the regulation and oversight of dual use research in the US which remain unresolved. Similar deficiencies have also been present to a greater or lesser extent in other 'Five Eyes' countries. In Australia, the 2001 experiment, which inadvertently made mouse pox (closely related to small pox) hyper-virulent sparked debates about how to improve oversight of this kind of dual use research. While some improvements have been made in the oversight of publicly funded research in Australia (e.g. the creation of an Australian Code for the Responsible Conduct of Research), the government seems to have largely devolved oversight to the research institutions themselves (Kamradt-Scott and Smith 2014).

More recently in 2016, a privately a funded research team at University of Alberta (Canada) recreated the horsepox virus (a close relative of small pox) from genetic pieces ordered in the mail. The research team stated they were interested in creating a better smallpox vaccine and cancer therapies, though there are concerns that the technique used could be misused to create smallpox which as noted earlier, was declared eradicated by the WHO in 1980. While there is some disagreement amongst scholars about the security implications of this experiment (Koblentz 2017; DiEuliis and James 2017), it has renewed debates about whether Canada's current regulatory regime for dual use research is sufficient.

The examples of mousepox, horsepox and other dual use research experiments discussed in previous chapters all underscore several deficiencies of a policy, regulatory and educational nature in the way dual use research of concern has been managed. From a policy perspective, the response in the US to managing dual use research has been fragmented. US policies do not comprehensively cover all dual use research. For example, non-government funded research by individuals or private sector institutions in the US or internationally are not bound by policies for conducting dual-use research (National Academies of Sciences, Engineering and Medicine 2017: 4–6). More recently in 2017, the US Health and Human Services Department issued new policy principles (known as the Framework) for guiding oversight of research involving enhanced potential pandemic pathogens (Koblentz and Klotz 2018). However the new guidelines do not apply to research conducted by other government departments or the private sector. Additionally, it remains unclear whether the current policy response includes all areas of biosecurity concern—especially those in emerging life sciences research areas (e.g. genome editing, gene drives, synthetic and systems biology) (ibid.: 5). Finally, there is no international organisation that completely owns the regulation of dual use research of concern and its dissemination.

Several international organisations and mechanisms including the WHO, the BWC, the Australia Group and UN Security Council have all played a role in policy debates over dual use research and may well be able to do so in the future (ibid.: 5).

Similarly, the regulatory and risk mitigation mechanisms have also been fragmented across the US and internationally in managing dual use research of concern. There remains little guidance on how to risk manage research of this kind, particularly guidance to journal editors on whether or how to publish dual use research of concern studies. Chapter 2 outlined several challenges with how dual use research publications relating to H5NI, polio, mouse pox and more recently horse pox were handled by advisory bodies such as the US National Science Advisory Board for Biosecurity (NSABB). The NSABB does not have a full mandate to provide comprehensive risk mitigation advice, legal or regulatory enforcement powers over the scientific community regarding the publication of dual use research of concern. The lack of a uniform, fully comprehensive advisory and regulatory body with a broad mandate makes it difficult potentially for scientists, publishers and research institutions to self-regulate or risk mitigate effectively against security concerns emanating from dual use research. Self-regulation and oversight advice however, has been also available from other institutions and processes. Interviews with officials across the 'Five Eyes' countries suggest that some law enforcement and intelligence agencies have played a role in providing security risk mitigation advice on dual use research of concern to the scientific community. Though in most cases, with the notable exception of the FBI WMD Directorate's outreach program (Hummel 2017), law enforcement and intelligence community engagements with the scientific communities of 'Five Eyes' nations on managing dual use research has been more informal and less frequent.

A third contributing factor to a fragmented regulatory approach to dual use research of concern since 9/11 has been a lack of consensus and approach on training scientists on the security implications of working with and publishing this kind of research. This has resulted in a lack of awareness of potential biosecurity concerns of dual use research. For many research institutions the focus in training seems to be biosafety—particularly promoting a safe work environment and accounting for dangerous pathogens rather than understanding the security implications of working and publishing dual use research of concern (ibid.: 7). More recently, improvements in training, including addressing biosecurity concerns have been made particularly in larger government funded research institutions, however training content and standards remain patchy and the overall approach is unsystematic across the life sciences sector.

Meeting the Challenges

The deficiencies including the fragmented approach to both the regulation and oversight of dual use research of concern across the 'Five Eyes' and more broadly internationally underscores the need for greater policy reflection on how to reform regulatory and oversight mechanisms in order to better manage this issue. Regulation theorist Malcom Sparrow citing Cary Coglianese argues that effective regulatory reform in its broadest sense needs to be framed across four major subject areas: *scope* i.e. what is the regulation meant to do—deregulation, re-regulation of emergent risks or markets, *nature*—consideration of alternative forms of regulation for example, tradeable permits in pollution controls and establishment of negotiated resolution procedures, *locus*—questions of centralisation or decentralisation, levels of regional or local autonomy relationship between federal and state law and finally *behaviour*—covers the strategies, tactics, policies, operational methods and culture of regulatory agencies (Sparrow 2001: 3). Arguably all four subject areas are relevant to considering how to build more effective regulation and oversight of dual use research of concern.

Also important to successful regulatory reform is how we can manage the volume and complexity of regulations, which in the biosecurity context (particularly in dealing with select agents) seem 'to have become a moving target causing institutions difficulty in implementing the new requirements before the regulations change again' (Gryphon Scientific 2016: 1015). Similarly, looking at the cost benefit equation of regulation and where should governments put most attention while retreating from other areas (Sparrow 2001: 21–22) seems critical to building better dual use research of concern regulation. For example, what can we learn from previous attempts by bodies such as the NSABB (e.g. the May 2016 report—*Recommendations for the Evaluation and Oversight of Proposed Gain of Function Research*) to issue guidance for gain of function research that might better inform biosecurity training programs or self-regulation procedures for the life sciences on the national security concerns of dual use research (NSABB 2016)? Leaving aside the good role the FBI has been playing in this space, how can each 'Five Eyes' intelligence community better work with the life sciences sector on dual use research concerns? What role can the private sector play in building on government regulation and compliance efforts?

There is growing evidence since 2009 with the establishment of the International Gene Synthesis Consortium (IGSC) that private companies synthetic biological products and services such as gene sequence orders are playing an industry led self-regulation role for screening their customers. The IGSC member companies vet customers (business, research institution or government agency) orders to determine whether the purchaser and the requested DNA sequence is legitimate against an extensive data base to make sure either is not a blacklisted organisation or DNA sequence. Unverifiable companies or request for sequences found not compliant with US federal and international guidelines are referred to regulatory authorities (IGSC 2018). In a recent press release the IGSC claims it currently represents approximately 80% of commercial synthesis worldwide so the work it is doing to promote self-regulation in a broader biosecurity context is clearly contributing to the oversight of dual use research of concern. Nonetheless, there are still a range of companies globally that are not part of IGSC that unscrupulous individuals and organisations can order synthetic biological products of concern. Such potential threat actors can also exploit cross jurisdictional weaknesses in regulatory and legislative mechanisms that currently exist globally to access DNA sequences that could be used to synthesise dangerous pathogens.

Finally, a full investigation of regulation and oversight in the dual use research area needs to consider the extent to which some local, national and international regulatory approaches are inflexible making them ineffective across a diverse life sciences sector. A 'one size fits all' approach to regulation may be unwise. As Sparrow notes 'we have seen in other sectors with rapid technological advances—'old rules are slow to go and new rules to address new risk are slow coming' (ibid.: 22). This seems to be the case where the NSABB has come under criticism for failing to include all research that could 'potentially be of concern within its definition of dual use research of concern, including unpredictable developments in the life sciences, such as the genome editing tool CRISPR/Cas9 or research in gene therapy.

There are also of course ethical dimensions to the legislative, regulatory and policy oversight of dual use research of concern (Miller and Selgelid 2008; Selgelid 2016). The increasing complexity of doing dual use research of concern, particularly GOF research requires further empirical investigation that can assess what ethical risks arise across the entire spectrum of synthetic biological research. It is not a simplistic question that some research projects are inherently ethically unacceptable while others are acceptable. The growing complexity of GOF and research using gene editing in different research contexts will likely reveal different ethical dilemmas of varying risk levels rather than a crystal clear indication of research that should be 'off limits'. Selgelid's 2016 ethical analysis of GOF research, commissioned by the US NIH underscores the ethical complexity and argues for an ethical decision-making framework including principles such as proportionality, risk minimisation, justice, evidence and others as a better way for policy makers and scientists to assess the ethical risks associated with GOF research (Selgelid 2016: 5).

It should be clear from the discussion above on legislation and regulation that both enable 'Five Eyes' countries in varying ways to disrupt, prevent and treat of bio-threats and risks. Yet in both cases (legislation and regulation), several challenges were identified which impact on the ways intelligence capabilities can be applied against bio-threats and risks.

In summary, there are political, institutional and ethical challenges arising from how legislative and regulatory mechanisms have been applied by 'Five Eyes' countries and these will continue to influence the role their intelligence communities can play in managing bio-threats and risks.

As discussed in Chapter 6 many of these challenges can only be addressed at the political leadership and Intelligence Governance levels. There is also limitations to how legislation or regulation can be used by intelligence agencies to disrupt, prevent and treat bio-threats and risks. Given the dynamic nature of synthetic biology and biotechnology it is unlikely that optimal legislative and regulatory responses can ever be completely realised. It may be by improving the oversight/accountability environment in which 'Five Eyes' intelligence work—some of these legislative and regulatory challenges can be addressed. This in turn could improve intelligence capabilities applied to bio-threats and risk in ways that are both more effective yet promote ethical approaches to intelligence in liberal democracies such as the 'Five Eyes' countries. In the final section, we will turn to a brief discussion of the role and challenges in oversight and accountability mechanisms within the 'Five Eyes' countries and how these may impact on the disruption, prevention and treatment of bio-threats and risks.

Oversight and Accountability

Leaving aside the complexity surrounding the legislative, regulatory and ethical oversight of dual use research, the extent to which each 'Five Eyes' country can effectively manage bio-threats and risks is also related to how intelligence communities exercise their authorities and powers lawfully, procedurally, and ethically. Given each 'Five Eyes' country is a liberal democracy, their intelligence communities need to be accountable for their actions to national governments and ultimately their tax paying citizens. Ideally, good internal and external oversight and accountability mechanisms should promote efficacious, cost effective and efficient intelligence support against threats in each 'Five Eyes' country, including bio-threats and risks. Such support of course also must not undermine democracy or the rights of individuals in liberal democracies.

Oversight and accountability mechanisms can be understood by classifying these into: *internal—ministerial and parliamentary—and external* (Walsh 2011: 228). Internal oversight and accountability of intelligence practice obviously starts with leadership and managerial review of activities at the agency and broader intelligence community levels. Each 'Five Eyes' country and each intelligence agency within the five countries have their own approaches to internal oversight so it is difficult to generalise or in limited space discuss them all. For example, in the US most intelligence and security agencies have an Inspector General that can assess and monitor internal issues which may present lawful, ethical, fiscal and personnel concerns (ibid.). In other 'Five Eyes' countries heads of intelligence agencies are also bound by statutory limitations to powers and are required to report regularly to ministers and to parliament.

Ministerial oversight then becomes the next level of accountability over intelligence practice. Since 9/11, along with either several new pieces or amended legislation, ministers in each 'Five Eyes' country have been given new authorities to prescribe the work of intelligence agencies as well as oversight powers. For example, in the UK, Australia, Canada and New Zealand ministers generally have powers in issuing warrants for the interception of communications and covert activities, though these powers are carefully controlled by relevant legislation—and in the case of the UK, Canada and New Zealand subjected to further reviews by judicial commissioners (ibid.).

An important additional component of ministerial oversight has been the development over the last several decades of independent executive oversight positions that provide another layer of checks and balances and 'can provide confidence that the agency is not being politically misused' (Gill and Phythian 2006 cited in Walsh 2011: 228). In the US, the Department of Justice Office of Inspector General has an independent investigative and auditing role for justice portfolio agencies such as the FBI. Similarly in Canada, the Inspector General of CSIS has traditionally had an independent review of CSIS (ibid.: 228–229). Similarly in both Australia and New Zealand there are also Inspector-Generals of Intelligence and Security (IGIS).

The IGIS in Australia has always had powers to launch independent of government routine investigations into Australian intelligence agencies, whereas the IGIS in New Zealand has only more recently in 2013 been given these powers in legislative amendments to the Inspector General of Intelligence and Security Act 1996. In the case of New Zealand, the roles of the IGIS have further been clarified along with the roles of functions of all the country's intelligence agencies in the 2017 Intelligence and Security Act. Canada also has an independent review agency the Security Intelligence Review Committee (SIRC), though traditionally it has only had oversight CSIS rather than other Canadian agencies with an intelligence function. Its inquiries also into CSIS operations have been retrospective compared to those of Australia's IGIS (ibid.: 229).

However, at the time of writing a major piece of legislation has been tabled in the Canadian parliament to create a body called—the National Security and Intelligence Review Agency (NSIRA), which will replace SIRC, the office of the CSE Commissioner as well as the national security review complaints investigations functions of the Civilian Review and Complaints Commission which oversees the RCMP's national security activities. The NSIRA will have independent review powers beyond CSIS to all agencies who use intelligence.

The final plank in internal oversight and accountability are the various parliamentary (and congressional) committees that oversee matters of intelligence, including policy, legislative, administrative and financial issues. We will deal with the US congressional oversight committees separately as they operate differently from other 'Five Eyes' countries. Australia, the UK and New Zealand have long had intelligence oversight committees with traditionally either no or limited access to classified material or sensitive details about intelligence operational activity (Walsh 2011: 229–230). But in all three cases, these committees have slowly been given a greater role in monitoring certain aspect of their intelligence communities. A key area has in each country has been the review of a growing suite of intelligence and counter-terrorism legislation enacted. For example, since 2014 the Australian Parliamentary Joint Committee on Intelligence and Security (IGIS) has played a constructive bipartisan role in improving several intelligence and counter-terrorism pieces of legislation including: The Counter

Terrorism Legislation Amendment (Foreign Fighters) Act (2014) and the Telecommunications (Interception and Access) Amendment (Data Retention) Act (2014) (Walsh 2017: 181). In the case of Canada, which traditionally has not had a dedicated parliamentary committee for solely overseeing intelligence, the Trudeau Liberal Government enacted in June 2017 the National Security and Intelligence Committee of Parliamentarians whose members are all security cleared and can receive any information by a department to review unless it is an ongoing operation; or that the appropriate minister determines that the review would be injurious to national security.

In contrast to the other 'Five Eyes' countries, the US congressional oversight committees—the Senate Select Intelligence Committee and the House Permanent Select Committee on Intelligence have historically operated differently. The Congressional committees have several oversight powers including, but not limited to: budgetary oversight, hearings (over intelligence policies, capabilities, and programs), senior intelligence staff nominations and covert action. Additionally, Senate and House members in both committees have security clearances enabling them the ability to view intelligence and intelligence programs—though in some cases sensitive material is not uniformly shared to all members and may go only to committee leadership. This has caused friction among committee members and the broader Congress periodically as was the case when some members declared they had not been briefed about enhanced (coercive) interrogation techniques orchestrated under the Bush Administration (Lowenthal 2012: 232).

Loch Johnson—a senior US scholar in intelligence studies, particularly on oversight and accountability issues has for several decades looked closely at how both congressional intelligence committees have operated. He provides a useful and novel taxonomy (ostriches, cheerleaders, lemon-suckers and guardians) to help explain their operations since the mid-1970s (Johnson 2018: 20). Johnson argues that law-makers have a tendency to play one of four major roles as 'spy watchers' though sometimes transitioning back and forth to the other roles (ibid.). Ostriches display little interest in accountability, have a low turn out to committee meetings and in general are disengaged. In contrast, cheer leaders advocate for the intelligence community—defending it against the media regardless of the circumstances and avoid engaging in deep introspection of intelligence activities. The third role—lemon suckers are innately hostile and suspicious of all activities carried out by the US IC. Lemon suckers see the IC as 'immoral, law breaking and or incompetent' (ibid.). Finally, the guardians are in Johnson's words 'both partners and critics of the spy agencies'. They can help explain and commend the performance of the IC to the public yet are not afraid to chastise the community when mistakes are made (ibid.: 21). The hope of history was that law makers would act primarily as guardians though in reality both congressional committees have become increasingly politicised and partisan– arguably more so since 9/11 where the accountability over various intelligence issues such as the 9/11 failures, WMD assessments pre Iraq invasion, coercive interrogation, Snowden and bulk metadata collection has not necessarily translated into balanced oversight or systemic improvements in the IC.

The final dimension of oversight and accountability includes *external review* and includes a range of stand-alone independent organisations and ad hoc commissions and inquiries which have oversight functions. The independent inquiries as noted in earlier chapters have usually be commissioned by governments at points of actual or perceived critical intelligence failure such as 9/11, intelligence assessments into the WMD capability of the Iraq regime or more recently in 2013 the impact of the Snowden leaks across all 'Five Eyes' countries. There are far too many examples of particular external reviews to discuss here and a reader keen to delve deeper has plenty of sources (Walsh 2011: 230–233; Johnson 2017; Gill 2016; Goldman and Rascoff 2016)

Conclusion

It's clear from the above discussion that the evolution of legislation, regulation and oversight/accountability mechanisms across the 'Five Eyes' countries presents a number of challenges for intelligence practice post 9/11. From a legislative perspective, there are challenges for governments and their ICs in crafting new legislative powers that are proportionate yet effective against constantly changing threat trajectories in issues such as terrorism, cyber and other transnational issues such as illicit goods trafficking. Responding, legislatively to the exponential growth in biotechnology and the potential for its growing misuse likewise will remain difficult. Similarly, trying to strike the optimal balance for the regulation of dual use research of concern that facilitates legitimate growth and research in the biological enterprise sector will require further reflection by governments, industries and 'Five Eyes' intelligence communities. If some of the challenges to building better legislative and regulatory responses are addressed then intelligence communities can be more enabled to prevent, disrupt and treat future bio-threats and risks. This will of course require better intelligence governance within and across intelligence agencies as discussed in Chapter 6. Finally, this chapter argued that with the public trust dividend of intelligence communities is low and with the growing number of actual and perceived intelligence failures since 9/11, the continued ability for 'Five Eyes' intelligence communities to manage lower probability high impact biological enabled threats also requires more effective, less fragmented approaches to oversight and accountability.

References

9/11 Commission. (2004). *The 9/11 Commission Report: Final Report of the National Commission on Terrorist Attacks upon the United States*. Washington, DC: 9/11 Commission.

Baldwin, R., Cave, M., & Lodge, M. (Eds.). (2010). *The Oxford Handbook of Regulation*. Oxford: Oxford University Press.

Blue Ribbon Study Panel. (2015). *Blue Ribbon Study Panel on Biodefense. A National Blueprint for Biodefense: Leadership and Major Reform Needed to Optimise Efforts*. Washington, DC: Hudson Institute for Policy Studies.

Cullen, M., & Reddy, P. (2016). *Intelligence and Security in a Free Society. Report of the First Independent Review of Intelligence and Security in New Zealand*. Wellington.

DiEuliis, D., & James, G. (2017). Why Gene Editors Like CRISPR/Cas May Be a Game Changer for Neuro Weapons. *Health Security, 15*(3), 296–307.

Gill, P. (2016). *Intelligence Governance and Democratisation: A Comparative Analysis of the Limits of Reform*. Abingdon, UK: Routledge.

Goldman, Z., & Rascoff, S. (Eds.). (2016). *Global Intelligence Oversight*. Oxford: Oxford University Press.

Gostin, L., & Taylor, A. (2008). Global Health Law: A Definition and Grand Challenges. *Public Health Ethics, 1*(1), 53–63. https://doi.org/10.1093/phe/phn005.

Gryphon Scientific. (2016). *Risk and Benefit Analysis of Gain of Function Research Final Report*. Takoma Park: Gryphon Scientific, LLC.

Hummel, K. (2017). A View from the CT Foxhole: Edward You, FBI WMD Directorate. *Biological Countermeasures Unit. CTC Sentinel, 10*(7), 9–12.

IGSC. (2018). *International Gene Synthesis Consortium Updates Screening Protocols for Synthesising DNA Products and Services* [Press release]. From https://www.prnewswire.com/news-releases/international-gene-synthesis-consortium-updates-screening-protocols-for-synthetic-dna-products-and-services-300576867.html?tc=eml_cleartime. Accessed March 15, 2017.

Johnson, L. (2017). *National Security Intelligence*. Cambridge, MA: Polity Press.

Johnson, L. (2018). *Spy Watching. Intelligence Accountability in the United States*. New York: Oxford University Press.

Kamradt-Scott, A., & Smith, F. (2014). Antipodal Biosecurity? Oversight of Dual Use Research in the United States and Australia. *Frontiers in Public Health, 2*(142), 1–3.

Koblentz, G. (2017). The De Novo Synthesis of Horse Pox Virus: Implications for Biosecurity and Recommendations for Preventing the Re-emergence of Smallpox. *Health Security, 15*(6), 620–628.

Koblentz, G., & Klotz, L. (2018). New Pathogen Research Rules: GOF, Loss of Clarity. *Bulletin of the Atomic Scientists*.

L'Estrange, M., & Merchant, S. (2017). *Independent Intelligence Review*. Canberra: Commonwealth of Australia.

Lowenthal, M. (2012). *Intelligence from Secrets to Policy*. Thousand Oaks, CA: CQ Press.

McDonald, G. (2007). Control Orders and Preventative Detention—Why Alarm is Misguided. In A. Lynch, et. al. (Eds.), *Law and Liberty in the War on Terror* (pp. 106–115). Annandale and Sydney: Federation Press.

Miller, S., & Selgelid, M. (2008). Ethics and the Dual-Use Dilemma in the Life Sciences. In F. Allhoff (Ed.), *Physicians at War: The Dual-Loyalties Challenge* (pp. 195–211). Dordrecht: Springer Netherlands.

NAS. (2016). *Gain of Function Research. Summary of the Second Symposium*. Washington, DC: National Academy of Sciences.

NAS. (2017a). *A Proposed Framework for Identifying Potential Biodefense Vulnerabilities Posed by Synthetic Biology Interim Report*. Washington, DC: National Academy of Sciences.

NAS. (2017b). *Human Genome Editing*. Washington, DC: Science Ethics and Governance.

National Academies of Sciences, Engineering and Medicine. (2017). *Dual Use Research of Concern in the Life Sciences. Current Issues and Controversies*. Washington, DC: National Academies of Science.

NSABB. (2016). *Recommendations for the Evaluation and Oversight of Proposed Gain of Function Research*. Washington, DC: National Science Advisory Board for Biosecurity.

Selgelid, M. (2016). Gain-of-Function Research: Ethical Analysis. *Science and Engineering Ethics, 22*(4), 923–964. https://doi.org/10.1007/s11948-016-9810-1.

Sparrow, M. (2001). *The Regulatory Craft, Controlling Risk, Solving Problems and Managing Compliance*. Washington, DC: Brookings Institution Press.

Tucker, J. (Ed.). (2012). *Innovation, Dual Use and Security*. Cambridge, MA: The MIT Press.

Walker, C. (2005). Biological Attack, Terrorism and the Law. *Terrorism and Political Violence, 17*(1–2), 175–200. https://doi.org/10.1080/09546550590520663.

Walsh, P. F. (2011). *Intelligence and Intelligence Analysis*. Abingdon, UK: Routledge.

Walsh, P. F. (2016). Australian National Security Intelligence Collection Since 9/11: Policy and Legislative Challenges. In K. Warby (Ed.), *National Security, Surveillance and Terror* (pp. 51–74). Cham: Springer International Publishing.

Walsh, P. F. (2017). Securing State Secrets. In R. Dover, H. Dylan, & M. Goodman (Eds.), *The Palgrave Handbook of Security, Risk and Intelligence* (pp. 177–194). London: Palgrave Macmillan.

White, M. (2007). A Judicial Perspective—The Making of Preventative Detention Orders. In A. Lynch, et al. (Eds.), *Law and Liberty in the War on Terror* (pp. 116–127). Annandale, Sydney: Federation Press.

Williams, G. (2011). A Decade of Australian Anti-terror Laws. *Melbourne University Law Review, 35*, 1137–1151.

9

Conclusion

This book had four objectives:

1. To provide an assessment of the contemporary (post 2001) and emerging biosecurity and bioterrorism threat environment.
2. Evaluate the role of intelligence in supporting tactical, operational and strategic decision-making on contemporary and emerging bio-threats.
3. Explore the effectiveness of intelligence processes and capabilities for decision-making support on bio-threats.
4. Understand how intelligence can assist in both the management of unfolding and emerging bio-threats.

The preceding chapters went some way to addressing these objectives, however further detailed research is required to comprehensively answer each. Turning to objective 1 first, Chapter 2 surveyed the bio-threat and risk landscape by focusing on two thematic threat clusters: *theft from biology facilities* and *dual use research of concern*. Within each of these clusters, it remains difficult to determine or anticipate how the bio-threat and risk environment will

© The Author(s) 2018
P. F. Walsh, *Intelligence, Biosecurity and Bioterrorism*,
https://doi.org/10.1057/978-1-137-51700-5_9

actually evolve. The chapter tried to provide a balanced view of how threats and risks might be assessed. Much depends on what theoretical and analytic heuristics policy makers, analysts and researchers bring to framing bio-threats and risks. Neither a technological determinist perspective nor complete ignoring of the conditions under which threats and risks may evolve is helpful. Chapter 5 also discussed several analytical frameworks and methodologies from a diverse suite of cross disciplinary fields that may help in better understanding potential bio-threat and risk trajectories. In summary, Chapter 2 provided a brief characterisation of the threat environment, but this work should only be seen as a start. All 'Five Eyes' intelligence communities in close collaboration with the research community will need to build a more evidence based approach to assessing the post 9/11 bio-threat environment.

The second objective (the role of intelligence in supporting decision-making on contemporary and emerging bio-threats), was addressed in Chapters 3, 4, and 5. It was clear from the discussion in each chapter, that intelligence has always played a role in helping decision-makers understand bio-threats and risks. In some instances, that role has not been arguably as effective as it might have been, such as the intelligence assessments provided on Iraq's WMD program. Though in other cases, for example, the *Amerithrax* investigation the role of intelligence has been more helpful. Chapters 3–5 also chronicled the many remaining challenges to the tasking and coordination, collection and analysis of intelligence, which combined constrain the ability of intelligence communities to provide an optimal role in managing bio-threats and risks.

For example, Chapter 3 discussed how the tasking and coordination of intelligence on bio-threats and risks was often adhoc, and decision-makers were distracted by a range of other more priority threats and risks (such as Russia, China, Cyber and conventional terrorism). As argued in Chapter 3, this is understandable to some extent given bio-threats and risks are for the most part likely to be low probability-high impact in nature. Nonetheless, a more sustained focus on bio-threats and risks by our intelligence communities is warranted to better understand (even if never completely), which threat trajectories are more likely than others. One has to be careful when drawing on analogies, but we can still see how each 'Five Eyes' intelligence community is still playing 'catch-up' in building up its capabilities to manage cyber. I wonder if the current lack of high level political tasking attention on potential threats emanating from biotechnology will see a similar scenario playing out in our intelligence enterprises. Finally, Chapter 3 argued that part of the problem with the current adhoc and low tasking by decision-makers on bio-threats and risks was that better risk and threat methodologies are needed to aid decision-makers about how they should task their limited intelligence collection and analytical resources.

Chapter 4 discussed both 'traditional' intelligence collection platforms (sigint and humint) and other scientific approaches (e.g. forensics and epidemiology). The discussion showed how the validation of sources has been difficult historically in bio-threat and risk cases. The intentional and malevolent use of biological substances, which are dual use in nature do not leave the same 'footsteps' that can be collected for nuclear and chemical weapons. There are no easy solutions to improving collection against bio-threats and risks though again it's clear that the intelligence community's traditional platforms may even be (at least initially) redundant in detecting some threats. Hence, and as underscored several times in all chapters, the intelligence community will need to gain a deeper understanding of specialised scientific knowledge and techniques that could help fill in the many gaps about bio-threats and risks. Good collection of course is not just about access to specialised knowledge and technology. As noted in Chapter 6 effective collection is also dependent on good leadership and the skilful leveraging of the right kind of resources at the right time.

Chapter 5 argued that several improvements also need to be made to the analytical processes as well as equipping analysts with the right continuing professional development strategies to work on bio-threats and risks. In terms of analytical processes, for one, a broader understanding of the range of potentially useful methodologies (interpretivists and empirical) is required. Analysts like a lot of other professions—often for expediency can get stuck in responding to tasks using the same mind-sets and techniques. This can encourage all sorts of cognitive biases such as: status-quo, confirmation or systematic bias. Chapters 5 and 7 introduced a range of analytical methodologies and insights from scientific and social scientific disciplines that may be useful in challenging bias. Given the complexity of potential bio-threats and risks, analysts working in this field in the future will need a broader perspective in order to improve the quality of the 'evidence' used in assessments. A deeper mining of knowledge from other disciplines will also improve interpretations of bio-threat actor behaviour and what factors might change understandings of threat and risk.

Regarding professional development for analysts working on bio-threat and risk issues, as we saw in Chapter 5—what analysts need or what their line managers think they need may not be the same thing. Since 9/11, progress has been made in moving analysts towards a professional role but debates still abound in the broadest sense about how to educate and train them—let alone what skills and competencies they need to work in specialised areas such as synthetic biology and biotechnology. Further research will be required to provide more informed evidence about what skills the next generation of bio-threat and risk analysts need. As with most of the preliminary findings in this book, better answers on the professionalization of bio-threat and risk analysts can only come with researchers working with the intelligence community.

Chapter 6 pivoted away from the second objective in the book and sought to address the third—namely whether intelligence processes and capabilities were effective in managing bio-threats and risks. The chapter referred to external governance (political leadership) and internal governance challenges (at the head of community or agency level), which impact on the overall effectiveness of intelligence processes and capabilities. Both the external and internal governance issues are difficult and unlikely to be resolved completely in the short to medium term (2018–2023). As noted in Chapter 3, bio-threats and risk are a low priority for 'Five Eyes' governments. Money goes where priorities are and so the leadership of our intelligence communities are also largely not focused on these threats and risks either.

Again, as noted in previous chapters, Chapter 6 did not seek to artificially inflate the significance of largely still unknown bio-threats and risks. More evidence is required to better calibrate threat and risk areas, but this is not possible if there is poor intelligence governance of these issues in the 'Five Eyes' intelligence communities. You don't know what you don't know without a concerted strategic leadership approach to finding it out. The political leadership and the leadership of each intelligence community needs to be more engaged in trying to identify evidence about bio-threats and risks in more strategic, proactive and coordinated ways. As Chapter 6 argues, what is required is mechanisms that can provide a more centralised and coordinated response to health security in each 'Five Eyes' intelligence community. Several suggestions were made about how this could be done including via the creation of health security coordination councils chaired by a senior politician and a national health security strategy for each 'Five Eyes' country. A national biodefense strategy has been promised by the Trump Administration but this seems to be putting the cart before the horse without first establishing a health security coordination council. It is hard to say whether all 'Five Eyes' countries will adopt any time soon these much needed external intelligence governance measures to help the policy and intelligence enterprise better focus on priorities and match funding to these.

Chapter 6 also discussed other key enabling activities of intelligence capability (ICT, human resources and research) and how challenges in each of these were precluding our intelligence communities playing more effective roles in managing bio-threats and risks. While external intelligence governance is largely up to the government of the day, the intelligence community leadership in each 'Five Eyes' country can address to some extent the many key enabling activity challenges raised in Chapter 6. Again this requires leadership within our intelligence communities—which if history is any judge can be lacking or ineffective when dealing with complex emerging threats.

While Chapter 6 argued that improved capabilities should translate into a more effective role for our intelligence communities in managing bio-threats and risks, it was also clear from the discussion that intelligence support to decision-making will always have its limits. In the future it may well be that in the prevention, disruption or treatment of many potential bio-threats and risks, the actual role of the intelligence community may be smaller than other stakeholders outside it. Hence Chapter 7 surveyed a myriad of stakeholders outside of intelligence communities (global health, crimi-nologists, engineers, cyber experts and first responders), who to varying degrees can play a role in the prevention, disruption and treatment of bio-threats and risks.

Chapter 7 discussed what knowledge, skills and methodological approaches some stakeholders have to offer the intelligence community and how those working in the law enforcement and national security context need to more effectively reach out and collaborate with them. The discussion did not to imply that each 'Five Eyes' intelligence com-munity had no history of reaching out to multiple stakeholders when dealing with bio-threats and risks. Instead what was argued for was a more strategic approach to collaboration—right across the core intel-ligence processes and the key enabling activities that support all intel-ligence processes. Given it will be often difficult to find and arrest bio-threat actors at the moment of offence due to the dual use of biol-ogy and the vastness of the biosciences enterprise, good strong relation-ships with multiple stakeholders will be essential to disrupting threats and risks in the future.

Finally Chapter 8 provided insights that stretch across all four of the book's objectives. In particular, it argued that neither legislation, reg-ulation or accountability mechanisms on their own will provide effec-tive, legal and ethical intelligence support to managing bio-threats and risks. Again further research is required to understand how legislation, regulation and accountability measures can be harnessed more effec-tively in ways that avoids the current fragmented approach to oversight of the biosciences. It's also clear from Chapter 8 that further policy work is required particularly in the oversight of dual use research of concern and that the intelligence community will need to continue to play a critical role in this work.

Future Outlook (2023 and Beyond)

The nature of the bio-threat and risk environment five years from now remains impossible to know with any confidence. This book has tried to put some stakes in the ground as to some of the issues which may drive the threat and risk environment, but no one really knows what will emerge. As noted in previous chapters, there remain large gaps in knowledge about whether some dual use research of concern might be exploited by criminals or terrorists. Indeed some of this knowledge, perhaps even most will remain 'unknowable'. As we have seen, the history of intelligence applied against bio-threats and risks has at best been mixed and at worst not sufficiently reliable. It may well be that in the future our intelligence communities will continue to get it wrong on the significance of some bio-threats and risks. But five years from now each 'Five Eyes' country will still need to play a role in at least trying to understand how elements of the bio-threat and risk trajectory may pan out even if the 'whole' is not knowable. Playing this role more effectively, if not perfectly, will require our intelligence communities overcoming many of the key challenges detailed in this book. These include amongst other things: improving intelligence governance in conjunction with a more scientific (evidence based) approach to preventing, disrupting and treating threats and risks. While there are never (unfortunately) any complete guarantees with intelligence, concerted efforts to address the challenges documented in the preceding chapters will hopefully make the inevitable intelligence failures less frequent and consequential.

References

9/11 Commission. (2004). *The 9/11 Commission Report: Final Report of the National Commission on Terrorist Attacks upon the United States*. Washington, DC: 9/11 Commission.

ACIC. (2016). *ACIC 2016–17 Annual Report*. Canberra: Commonwealth of Australia.

Agranovski, I. E., et al. (2017). Miniature PCR Based Portable Bioaerosol Monitor Development. *Journal of Applied Microbiology, 122*(1), 129–138. https://doi.org/10.1111/jam.13318.

Alibek, K. (1999). *Biohazard: The Chilling True Story of the Largest Covert Biological Weapons Program in the World—Told from the Inside by the Man Who Ran It*. New York: Random House.

Allison, G. (1971). *Essence of Decision: Explaining the Cuban Missile Crisis*. Boston: Little Brown and Co.

ANZCTC. (2017). *Australia's Strategy for Protecting Crowded Places from Terrorism*. ANZCTC: Australian Government.

Aras, G., & Crowther, D. (2010). *A Handbook of Corporate Governance and Social Responsibility*. Farnham, UK: Taylor and Francis.

Australia Group. (2015). *Common Control List Handbook, Volume 2: Biological Weapons—Related Common Control Lists*. From www.defence.gov.au/export-controls/master/docs/AustGroupCommonControlListHandbaookVolIIpdf. Accessed March 12, 2017.

© The Editor(s) (if applicable) and The Author(s) 2018
P. F. Walsh, *Intelligence, Biosecurity and Bioterrorism*,
https://doi.org/10.1057/978-1-137-51700-5

Bakanidze, L., et al. (2010). Biosafety and Biosecurity as Essential Pillars of International Health Security and Cross-Cutting Elements of Biological Non-proliferation. *Biomed Central, 10*, 1–8.

Baker, K. (2009). The Meaning and Practice of Biosecurity. *International Journal of Risk Assessment and Management, 12*(2/3/4), 121–146.

Baldwin, R., Cave, M., & Lodge, M. (Eds.). (2010). *The Oxford Handbook of Regulation*. Oxford: Oxford University Press.

Balmer, B. (2001). *Britain and Biological Warfare. Expert Advice and Science Policy, 1930–65*. Basingstoke, UK: Palgrave Macmillan.

Bamford, B. (2002). Biological Warfare: The Threat in Historical Perspective. *Medicine, Conflict and Survival, 18*(2), 120–137.

Battelle. (2014). *Battelle/Bio State Bioscience, Jobs, Investments and Innovation*. Columbus, OH: Battelle.

Baxendale, R. (2017, July 18). Australia to Get Super Home Affairs Ministry. *The Australian*.

Bean, H. (2007). The DNI's Open Source Center: An Organizational Communication Perspective. *International Journal of Intelligence and Counterintelligence, 20*(2), 240–257.

Berger, K. (2013). Biosecurity in Research Laboratories. In R. Burnette (Ed.), *Biosecurity* (pp. 113–128). Hoboken, NJ: Wiley.

Bernard, K. (2013). Health and National Security: A Contemporary Collision of Cultures. *Biosecurity and Bioterrorism: Biodefense Strategy, Practice and Science, 11*(2), 157–162.

Bernard, R. (2017). These Are Not the Terrorist Groups You're Looking for: An Assessment of the Cyber Capabilities of Islamic State. *Journal of Cyber Policy, 2*(2), 255–265. https://doi.org/10.1080/23738871.2017.1334805.

Betts, R. (1978). Analysis, War and Decision: Why Intelligence Failures Are Inevitable? *World Politics, 31*(1), 61–89.

Bhattacharjee, Y. (2009). News of the Week. Paul Keim on His Life with the FBI During the Amerithrax Investigation. *AAAS, 323*, 1416.

Blair, D. (2009). *Annual Threat Assessment of DNI for the Senate Select Committee on Intelligence*. Washington, DC: ODNI. From file:///C:/Users/DrPatrickF/Downloads/ADA517101.pdf. Accessed March 13, 2017.

Blue Ribbon Study Panel. (2015). *Blue Ribbon Study Panel on Biodefense. A National Blueprint for Biodefense: Leadership and Major Reform Needed to Optimise Efforts*. Washington, DC: Hudson Institute for Policy Studies.

Blue Ribbon Study Panel. (2016). *Biodefense Indicators One Year Later. Events Outpacing Federal Efforts to Defend the Nation*. Arlington, VA: Potomac Institute for Policy Studies.

Blue Ribbon Study Panel. (2017). *Biodefense Special Focus: Defense of Animal Agriculture*. Washington, DC: Blue Ribbon Study Panel.

Bombardt, J. (2000). *Contagious Disease Dynamics for Biological Warfare and Bioterrorism Casualty Assessments*. Alexandria, VA: U.S. Department of Defense.

Bravata, D., et al. (2004). Systematic Review: Surveillance Systems for Early Detection of Bioterrorism Related Diseases. *Annals of Internal Medicine, 40*(11), 910–924.

Budowle, B., & Williamson, P. C. (2009). *Microbial Forensics Wiley Encyclopaedia of Forensic Science*. John Wiley & Sons, Ltd.

Buehler, J., et al. (2004). Group CDCW. Framework for Evaluating Public Health Surveillance Systems for Early Detection of Outbreaks: Recommendations from the CDC Working Group. *MMWR Recommendations and Reports: Morbidity and Mortality Weekly Report, 53,* 1–11.

Bunn, M., & Sagan, S. (Eds.). (2016). *Insider Threats*. Ithaca, NY: Cornell University Press.

Burchill, S., et al. (Eds.). (1996). *Theories of International Relations*. Basingstoke, UK: Palgrave Macmillan.

Burnette, R. (Ed.). (2013). *Biosecurity Understanding, Assessing, and Preventing the Threat*. Hoboken, NJ: Wiley.

Burns, R. (2015). *US Military Says It Mistakenly Shipped Live Anthrax Samples*. From http://www.nbcnewyork.com/news/national-international/Pentagon-Shipped-Live-Anthrax-Samples–305221031.html. Accessed March 13, 2017.

Burr, J. (2012). The Mad (and Not So Mad) Scientist Next Door: A Holistic Approach to Addressing Do-it-Yourself Biology. *Journal of Biosecurity, Biosafety and Biodefense Law, 3*(1), 2154–3186, ISSN (Online). https://doi.org/10.1515/2154-3186.1035.

Butler, R. (2004). *Review of Intelligence on Weapons of Mass Destruction: Implementation of Its Conclusions*. London: HMSO.

BWC. (2017). *BWC Newsletter*. Geneva: United Nations.

Cameron, E. (2017, 19 July). Biosecurity Imperative: An Urgent Case for Extending the Global Health Security Agenda. *Atomic Pulse*.

Campbell, S. H. (2011). A Survey of the U.S. Market for Intelligence Education. *International Journal of Intelligence and Counterintelligence, 24*(2), 307–337. https://doi.org/10.1080/08850607.2011.548207.

Canadian Government. (2011). *Building Resilience Against Terrorism: Canada's Counter Terrorism Strategy*. Ottawa: Government of Canada.

Canter, D. (2007). Addressing Residual Risk Issues at Anthrax Clean Up. How Clean Is Safe? *Journal of Toxicology and Environmental Health, Part A, 68*(11–12), 1017–1032.

Carlson, R. (2003). The Pace and Proliferation of Biological Technologies. *Biosecurity and Bioterrorism: Biodefense Strategy, Practice, and Science, 1*(3), 203–214. https://doi.org/10.1089/153871303769201851.

Carus, S. (2001). *Bioterrorism and Biocrimes: The Illicit Use of Biological Agents Since 1900.* Washington, DC: National Defense University.

Carus, S. (2017). Occasional Paper 12. A Short History of Biological Warfare: From Pre-history to the Twenty-First Century. *Center for the Study of Weapons of Mass Destruction.* Washington, DC: National Defense University.

Caskey, S., & Sevilla-Reyes, E. (2015). Risk Assessment. In R. Salerno & J. Gaudioso (Eds.), *Laboratory Biorisk Management* (pp. 45–63). Boca Raton, FL: CRC Press.

Cass, S. (1999). Researcher Charged with Data Theft. *Nature Medicine, 5,* 474. https://doi.org/10.1038/8350.

Caves, J., & Carus, W. (2014). The Future of Weapons of Mass Destruction: Their Nature and Role in 2030 (Occasional Paper No. 10, pp. 1–75). *Center for the Study of Weapons of Mass Destruction.* Washington, DC: National Defense University.

CDC. (2014). *Report on the Potential Exposure to Anthrax.* Atlanta, GA: CDC.

CDC. (2015a). *90 Day Internal Review of the Division of Select Agents and Toxins.* Atlanta, GA: CDC.

CDC. (2015b). Report of the Advisory Committee to the Director, CDC Follow Up on CDC Progress.

Center for Biosecurity of UPMC. (2011). *US Government Judgments on the Threat of Biological Weapons: Official Assessments, 2004–2011* (pp. 1–26). Baltimore, MD: Center for Biosecurity of UPMC.

Center for Biosecurity of UPMC. (2012). *The Industrialization of Biology and its Impact on National Security.* Baltimore, MD: Center for Biosecurity of UPMC.

Chen, H. (2011). Bioterrorism and Knowledge Mapping *Dark Web Exploring and Data Mining the Dark Side of the Web* (pp. 335–367). New York, NY: Springer.

Chertoff, M. (2017). A Public Policy Perspective of the Dark Web. *Journal of Cyber Policy, 2*(1), 26–38. https://doi.org/10.1080/23738871.2017.1298643.

Chevrier, M., & Spelling, A. (2016). The Traditional Tools of Biological Arms Control and Disarmament. In F. Lentzos (Ed.), *Biological Threats in the 21st Century* (pp. 331–356). London: Imperial College Press.

Chhotray, V., & Stoker, G. (2008). *Governance Theory and Practice: A Cross-Disciplinary Approach.* London, UK: Palgrave Macmillan.

Christley, R., et al. (2005). Infection in Social Networks: Using Network Analysis to Identify High Risk Individuals. *American Journal of Epidemiology, 162*(10), 1024–1031.

Christopher, G., et al. (1997). Biological Warfare: A Historical Perspective. *Journal of the American Medical Association, 278*(5), 412–417.

Chyba, C. (2006). Biotechnology and the Challenge to Arms Control. *Arms Control Today, 36,* 11–17.

CIDRAP. (2017). *Secretary Tillerson Lauds Global Health Security Agenda.* Retrieved from http://www.cidrap.umn.edu/news-perspective/2017/10/secretary-tillerson-lauds-global-health-security-agenda.

Clapper, J. (2016, February 9). Statement for the Record. *Worldwide Threat Assessment of the US Intelligence Community. Armed Services Committee.* Washington, DC: ODNI.

Clarke, R., & Knake, R. (2010). *Cyber War.* New York, NY: Ecco.

Collier, N. (2015). A Review of Web-Based Epidemic Detection. In S. Davies & J. Youde (Eds.), *The Politics of Surveillance and Response to Disease Outbreaks* (pp. 85–107). Surrey, UK: Ashgate.

Connell, N. (2017). The Challenge of Global Catastrophic Biological Risks. *Health Security, 15*(4), 345–346.

Connors, E., et al. (2000). *Operation Cooperation, Guidelines for Partnerships Between Law Enforcement and Private Security Organisations.* Rockville, MD: Bureau of Justice Assistance.

Corbyn, Z. (2015, May 10). *Crispr: Is It a Good Idea to Upgrade? The Observer.* Retrieved fromhttp://newsrule.com/crispr-is-it-a-good-idea-to-upgrade-our-dna/.

Coulthart, S. (2016). Why Do Analysts Use Structured Analytic Techniques? An In-depth Study of an American Intelligence Agency. *Intelligence and National Security, 31*(7), 933–948. https://doi.org/10.1080/02684527.2016.1140327.

Crawford, D. (2007). *Deadly Companions.* Oxford: Oxford University Press.

Crumpton, H. (2012). *The Art of Intelligence: Lessons from a Life in the CIA's Clandestine Service.* New York: Penguin Publishing Group.

Cullen, M., & Reddy, P. (2016). *Intelligence and Security in a Free Society. Report of the First Independent Review of Intelligence and Security in New Zealand.* Wellington.

Dando, M. (2005). The Bioterrorist Cookbook. *Bulletin of the Atomic Scientists, 61*(6), 34–39. https://doi.org/10.1080/00963402.2005.11460936.

Danley, L. (2012). Duties and Difficulties of Investigating and Prosecuting Biocrimes. *Journal of Biosecurity, Biosafety and Biodefense Law, 3.*

Danzell, O., & Montanez, L. (2016). Understanding the Lone Wolf Phenomena: Assessing Current Profiles. *Behavioural Sciences of Terrorism and Political Aggression, 8*(2), 135–159.

DARPA. (2017). *DARPA Building the Safe Genes Toolkit.* From https://www.darpa.mil/news-events/2017-07-19. Accessed March 14, 2017.

Davies, S., & Youde, J. (Eds.). (2015a). *The Politics of Surveillance and Response to Disease Outbreaks.* Surrey, UK: Ashgate.

Davies, S., & Youde, J. (2015b). Surveillance, Response, and Responsibilities in the 2005 International Health Regulations. In S. Davies & J. Youde (Eds.), *The Politics of Surveillance and Response to Disease Outbreaks* (pp. 9–23). Surrey, UK: Ashgate.

Dennis, B., & Sun, L. (2014a, July 16). FDA Found More Than Smallpox Vials in Storage Room. *Washington Post.* From https://www.washington-post.com/national/health-science/fda-found-more-than-smallpox-vials-in-storage-room/2014/07/16/850d4b12-0d22-11e4-8341-b8072b1e7348_story.html?utm_term=.978241b9d1f8. Accessed March 14, 2017.

Dennis, B., & Sun, L. (2014b, September 5). More Deadly Pathogens, Toxins Found Improperly Stored in NIH and FDA Labs. *Washington Post.* From https://www.washingtonpost.com/national/health-science/six-more-deadly-pathogens-found-improperly-stored-in-nih-and-fda-labs/2014/09/05/9ff8c3c2-3520-11e4-a723-fa3895a25d02_story.html?utm_term=.4bc6ce160f62. Accessed March 14, 2017.

Dickmann, P., et al. (2015). Marburg Biosafety and Biosecurity Scale (MBBS): A Framework for Risk Assessment and Risk Communication. *Health Security, 13*(2), 88–95. https://doi.org/10.1089/hrs.2014.0065.

DiEuliis, D., & James, G. (2017). Why Gene Editors Like CRISPR/Cas May Be a Game Changer for Neuro Weapons. *Health Security, 15*(3), 296–307.

DOD. (2016). *The Department of Defense Chemical and Biological Defense Program Annual Report to Congress.* Washington, DC.

DOJ. (2010). *The United States Department of Justice. Amerithrax Investigative Summary.* Washington, DC.

DPM &C. (2015). *Review of Australia's Counter Terrorism Machinery.* Department of Prime Minister and Cabinet: Australian Government.

Dunn, L., & Arnold, A. (2010). *WMD Forecasting in Historical and Contemporary Perspective.* Fort Belvoir, VA: Advanced Systems and Concepts Office.

Dzau, V., & Sands, P. (2016). Beyond the Ebola Battle Winning the War Against Future Epidemics. *New England Journal of Medicine, 375,* 203–204.

Eaves, E. (2017). IARPA Director Jason Matheny Advances Tech Tools for US Espionage. *Bulletin of the Atomic Scientists, 73*(2), 67–73.

Edge, J., & Hoffman, S. (2015). Strengthening National Health Systems Capacity to Respond to Future Global Pandemics. In S. Davies & J. Youde (Eds.), *The Politics of Surveillance and the Response to Disease Outbreaks* (pp. 157–179). Surrey, UK: Ashgate.

Editorial. (2014). Biosafety in the Balance. *Nature, 510,* 443.

Elbe, S. (2010). Pandemic Security. In J. Burgess (Ed.), *The Routledge Handbook of New Security Studies* (pp. 163–173). Abingdon: Routledge.

Elbe, S. (2011). Pandemics on the Radar Screen: Health Security, Infectious Disease and the Medicalisation of Insecurity. *Political Studies, 59,* 848–866.

Elliott, S. (2007). The Threat from Within: Trade Secret Theft by Employees. *Nature Biotechnology, 25*(3), 293–295. https://doi.org/10.1038/nbt0307-293.

Ellis, P. D. (2014). Lone Wolf Terrorism and Weapons of Mass Destruction: An Examination of Capabilities and Countermeasures. *Terrorism and Political Violence, 26*(1), 211–225. https://doi.org/10.1080/09546553.2014.849935.

Fish, R. (2017, March 2). 2017 PHEMCE Review: Accomplishments and Future Areas of Opportunity. *Global Biodefense.* From https://globalbiodefense.com/2017/03/02/rebecca-fish-phemce-review-accomplishments-opportunities/. Accessed March 15, 2017.

Flood, P. (2004). *Report of the Inquiry into Australian Intelligence Agencies.* Canberra: Australian Government Printing Office.

Fouchier, R., et al. (2013). Gain-of-Function Experiments on H7N9. *Science.* https://doi.org/10.1126/science.1243325.

Friedman, D. (2015). Towards WMDFZ in the Middle East: Biological Confidence Building Measures. In H. Muller & D. Muller (Eds.), *WMD Arms Control in the Middle East. Prospects, Obstacles and Options* (pp. 176–180). Farnham, UK: Ashgate.

Frumkin, D., Wasserstrom, A., Budowle, B., & Davidson, A. (2011). DNA methylation-based forensic tissue identification. *Forensic Science International: Genetics, 5*(5), 517–524. http://dx.doi.org/10.1016/j.fsigen.2010.12.001.

Gronvall, G., et al. (2016). National Biosafety Systems. UPMC Center for Health Security.

GAO. (2005). Critical Infrastructure Protection. DHS Faces Challenges in Fulfilling Cybersecurity Responsibilities. Washington, DC: GAO.

GAO. (2009). *High Containment Laboratories: National Strategy for Oversight is Needed.* Washington, DC: GAO.

GAO. (2011a). Cybersecurity Human Capital Initiatives Need Better Planning and Coordination. Washington, DC: GAO.

GAO. (2011b). Defense Department Cyber Efforts: DOD Faces Challenges in Its Cyber Activities. Washington, DC: GAO.

GAO. (2011c). *Biosurveillance Non Federal Capabilities Should Be Considered in Creating a National Biosurveillance Strategy.* Washington, DC: GAO.

GAO. (2013). High Containment Laboratories: Assessment of the Nation's Need Is Missing. *Testimony Before the Subcommittee Emergency Preparedness, Response and Communications, Biosurveillance Observations on the Cancellation of Biowatch Gen-3 and Future Considerations for the Program*, 18 (2014).

GAO. (2016). *Testimony Before the Subcommittee on Emergency Preparedness Response and Communications, Committee on Homeland Security, House of Representatives.* Washington, DC: GAO.

GAO. (2017a). *Bio Forensics DHS Needs to Conduct A Formal Capability Gap Analysis to Better Identify and Address Gaps.* Washington, DC: GAO.

GAO. (2017b). *Biodefense Federal Efforts to Develop Biological Threat Awareness.* Washington, DC: GAO.

GAO. (2017c). *GAO High Containment Labs Coordinated Actions Needed to Enhance the Select Agent Program's Oversight of Hazardous Pathogens* (Vol. GAO 18–145). Washington, DC: GAO.

Garcia, M. (2006). Risk Management. In M. Gill (Ed.), *The Handbook of Security* (pp. 509–531). Basingstoke: Palgrave Macmillan.

Geissler, E., & Moon, van Courtland J. (Eds.). (1999). *Biological and Toxin Weapons: Research, Development and Use from the Middle Ages to 1945.* New York: Oxford University Press.

Gentry, J. (2015). Has the ODNI Improved US Intelligence Analysis? *International Journal of Intelligence and Counterintelligence, 28,* 637–661.

Geoghegan, J., & Holmes, E. (2017). Predicting Virus Emergencies and Evolutionary Noise. *Open Biology, 7,* 1–9.

George, D. (2017). How Should We Define Global Catastrophic Biological Risks? *Health Security, 15*(4), 339–340.

George, R., & Bruce, J. (Eds.). (2014). *Analyzing Intelligence National Security Practitioner's Perspectives.* Washington, DC: Georgetown University Press.

Gerstein, D. M. (2010). *Bioterror in the 21st Century: Emerging Threats in a New Global Environment*. New York: Naval Institute Press.

Gerstein, D. (2013). *The Biological and Toxin Weapons Convention. National Security and Arms Control in the Age of Biotechnology*. Lanham, MD: Rowman and Littlefield.

Gerstein, G. (2017a). Federal Research and Development for Agricultural Biodefense. Testimony Presented Before the House Science, Space and Technology Committee, Subcommittee on Research and Technology. Santa Monica: RAND.

Gerstein, G. (2017b). Glaring Gaps: America Needs a Biodefense Upgrade. *Bulletin of the Atomic Scientists, 73*(2), 86–91.

GHRF Commission. (2015). *The Neglected Dimension of Global Security. A Framework to Counter Infectious Disease Crisis*. Washington, DC: Global Health Risk Framework for the Future Commission.

GHRF Commission. (2016). The Neglected Dimension of Global Security. A Framework to Counter Infectious Disease Crisis. US: GHRF Commission.

Gill, P. (2016). *Intelligence Governance and Democratisation: A Comparative Analysis of the Limits of Reform*. Abingdon, UK: Routledge.

Gill, P., & Phythian, M. (2012). *Intelligence in an Insecure World*. Cambridge: Polity Press.

Ginsberg, M., & Bui, A. (2015). Bio Protection of Facilities. *Defense & Security Analysis, 31*(1), 4–21. https://doi.org/10.1080/14751798.2014.995335.

Goldman, Z., & Rascoff, S. (Eds.). (2016). *Global Intelligence Oversight*. Oxford: Oxford University Press.

Gonçalves, B., et al. (2013). Human Mobility and the Worldwide Impact of Intentional Localized Highly Pathogenic Virus Release. *Scientific Reports, 3*, 810. https://doi.org/10.1038/srep00810, https://www.nature.com/articles/srep00810#supplementary-information.

Goodman, M., & Hessel, A. (2013). The Bio-Crime Prophecy: DNA Hacking the Biggest Opportunity Since Cyber Attacks. *Wired*. From http://www.wired.co.uk/article/the-bio-crime-prophecy. Accessed March 14, 2017.

Gordis, L. (2009). *Epidemiology* (4th ed.). Philadelphia, PA: Saunders Elsevier.

Gostin, L., & Taylor, A. (2008). Global Health Law: A Definition and Grand Challenges. *Public Health Ethics, 1*(1), 53–63. https://doi.org/10.1093/phe/phn005.

Grabo, C. (2004). *Anticipating Surprise Analysis for Strategic Warning*. Lanham, MD: University Press of America.

Graham, B., & Talent, J. (2008). *World at Risk: The Report of the Commission on the Prevention of WMD Proliferation and Terrorism*. New York: Vintage Books.

Gronvall, G. (2012). *Preparing for Bioterrorism*. Baltimore, MD: Center for Biosecurity of UPMC.

Gryphon Scientific. (2016). *Risk and Benefit Analysis of Gain of Function Research Final Report*. Takoma Park: Gryphon Scientific, LLC.

Harris, S. (2014). *Lady Al Qaeda: The World's Most Wanted Woman*. From http://foreignpolicy.com/2014/08/26/lady-al-qaeda-the-worlds-most-wanted-woman/. Accessed March 15, 2017.

Hayden, M. (2016). *Playing to the Edge*. New York: Penguin Press.

Heickerö, R. (2014). Cyber Terrorism: Electronic Jihad. *Strategic Analysis, 38*(4), 554–565. https://doi.org/10.1080/09700161.2014.918435.

Helm, P. (2015). Risk, Resilience: Strategies for Security. *Civil Engineering and Environmental Systems, 32*(1–2), 100–117.

Heuer, R. (1999). *Psychology of Intelligence Analysis*. Washington, DC: Center for the Study of Intelligence.

Heuer, R., & Pherson, R. (2010). *Structured Analytical Techniques for Intelligence Analysis*. Washington, DC: CQ Press.

Heymann, D., et al. (2015). Global Health Security: The Wider Lessons from the West African Ebola Virus Disease Outbreak. *The Lancet, 385*, 1884–1901.

Hirschfeld, K. (2017). Failing States as Epidemiologic Risk Zones. *Health Security, 15*(3), 288–295.

Hitz, F. (2015). Human Source Intelligence. In L. Johnson & J. Wirtz (Eds.), *Intelligence: The Secret World of Spies* (4th ed., pp. 107–119). New York: Oxford University Press.

HMG. (2011). *CONTEST: The UK's Strategy for Countering Terrorism*. London: Her Majesty's Government.

Horton, R. (2017). Offline: Global Health Security—Smart Strategy or Naive Tactics. *The Lancet, 389*, 892.

HSC. (2005). The Human Security Centre: Human Security Report. Oxford.

Hulnick, A. (2002). The Downside of Open Source Intelligence. *International Journal of Intelligence and Counterintelligence, 15*(4), 565–579.

Hummel, K. (2017). A View from the CT Foxhole: Edward You, FBI WMD Directorate, Biological Countermeasures Unit. *CTC Sentinel, 10*(7), 9–12.

IGSC. (2018). *International Gene Synthesis Consortium Updates Screening Protocols for Synthesising DNA Products and Services* [Press release]. From https://www.prnewswire.com/news-releases/international-gene-synthesis-consortium-updates-screening-protocols-for-synthetic-dna-products-and-services-300576867.html?tc=eml_cleartime. Accessed March 15, 2017.

Inglesby, T., & Haas, B. (2017, November 21). Ready for a Global Pandemic? The Trump Administration May Be Woefully Underprepared. *Foreign Affairs*.

Inglis, T., et al. (2011). Forensic Investigation of Biological Weapons Use. In J. Gall & J. Payne-James (Eds.), *Current Practices in Forensic Medicine* (pp. 17–42). Chichester, UK: Wiley.

Inkster, N. (2015). Cyber Espionage. *Adelphi Series, 55*(456), 51–82. https://doi.org/10.1080/19445571.2015.1181443.

Innes, M., & Sheptycki, J. (2004). From Detection to Disruption: Intelligence and the Changing Logic of Police Crime Control in the UK. *International Criminal Justice Review, 14,* 1–24.

Innes, M., et al. (2017). A Disruptive Influence? Preventing Problems and Counter Violent Extremism Policy in Practice. *Law and Society Review, 51*(2), 252–281.

Insinna, V. (2013). Government Biosurveillance to Include Social Media. *National Defense, 97*(710), 13.

Inspectors General DOJ, & DHS. (2017). *Review of Domestic Sharing of Counter Terrorism Information.* Washington, DC: Office of Inspector General, Department of Homeland Security.

James, A., Phythian, M., Wadie, F., & Richards, J. (2017). The Road Not Taken: Understanding Barriers to the Development of Police Intelligence Practice. *The International Journal of Intelligence, Security, and Public Affairs, 19*(2), 77–91. https://doi.org/10.1080/23800992.2017.1336395.

Johnson, L. (2015). A Conversation with James R. Clapper Jr., The Director of National Intelligence in the United States. *Intelligence and National Security, 30*(1), 1–25.

Johnson, L. (2017). *National Security Intelligence.* Cambridge, MA: Polity Press.

Johnson, L. (2018). *Spy Watching. Intelligence Accountability in the United States.* New York: Oxford University Press.

Johnson, L., et al. (2014). An INS Special Forum: Implications of the Snowden Leaks. *Intelligence and National Security, 29*(6), 793–810.

Johnson, L., & Wirtz, J. (Eds.). (2015). *Intelligence: The Secret World of Spies.* New York: Oxford University Press.

Kahn, L. (2016, August 1). The Unintentional Exotic-Pet Bioattack on US Shores. *Bulletin of the Atomic Scientists.*

Kambouris, M. (2017). Mobile Stand Off and Stand in Surveillance Against Biowarfare and Bioterrorism Agents. In P. Karampelas & T. Bourlai (Eds.), *Surveillance in Action* (pp. 241–255). Cham: Springer.

Kamradt-Scott, A., & Smith, F. (2014). Antipodal Biosecurity? Oversight of Dual Use Research in the United States and Australia. *Frontiers in Public Health, 2*(142), 1–3.

Kasolo, F., et al. (2013). Implementation of the International Health Regulations (2015) in the African Region. *African Health Monitor, 18,* 11–13.

Kim, J., et al. (2015). Advances in Anthrax Detection: Overview of Bioprobes and Biosensors. *Applied Biochemistry and Biotechnology, 176*(4), 957–977.

Klotz, L., & Sylvester, E. (2009). *Breeding Bio Insecurity: How US Biodefense Is Exporting Fear, Globalizing Risk and Making Us All Less Secure*. Chicago: University of Chicago.

Klovdahl, A. (1985). Social Networks and the Spread of Infectious Diseases: The AIDS Example. *Social Science and Medicine, 21*(11), 1203–1216.

Koblentz, G. (2009). *Living Weapons*. New York: Cornell University Press.

Koblentz, G. (2010). Biosecurity Reconsidered. *International Security, 34*(4), 96–132.

Koblentz, G. (2012). From Biodefence to Biosecurity: The Obama Administration's Strategy for Countering Biological Threats. *International Affairs, 88*(1), 131–148.

Koblentz, G. (2017). The De Novo Synthesis of Horse Pox Virus: Implications for Biosecurity and Recommendations for Preventing the Re-emergence of Smallpox. *Health Security, 15*(6), 620–628.

Koblentz, G., & Klotz, L. (2018, February 26). New Pathogen Research Rules: GOF, Loss of Clarity. *Bulletin of the Atomic Scientists*.

Koblentz, G., & Mazanec, B. (2013). Viral Warfare: The Security Implications of Cyber and Biological Weapons. *Comparative Strategy, 32*(5), 418–434. https://doi.org/10.1080/01495933.2013.821845.

Koblentz, G., & Tucker, J. (2010). Tracing an Attack: The Promise and Pitfalls of Microbial Forensics. *Survival, 52*(1), 159–186. https://doi.org/10.1080/00396331003612521.

Kuntz, C., Salerno, R., & Jacobs, E. (2013). *A Biological Threat Prevention Strategy* Washington, DC: CSIS.

Kupferschmidt, K. (2017). Lab Made Smallpox Is Possible, Study Shows. *Science, 357*(6347), 115–116. https://doi.org/10.1126/science.357.6347.115.

Lakoff, A. (2015). Real Time Bio Politics: The Actuary and the Sentinel in Global Public Health. *Economy and Society, 44*(1), 40–59.

Lakoff, A., & Collier, S. (Eds.). (2008). *Biosecurity Interventions*. New York: Colombia University Press.

Lee, M. (2017, January 5). Julian Assange's Claim That There Was No Russian Involvement in Wikileaks Emails. *The Washington Post*. From https://www.washingtonpost.com/news/fact-checker/wp/2017/01/05/julian-assanges-claim-that-there-was-no-russian-involvement-in-wikileaks-emails/?utm_term=.bee-14c837aef. Accessed March 15, 2017.

Leitenberg, M. (1999). Aum Shinrikyo's Efforts to Produce Biological Weapons: A Case Study in the Serial Propagation of Misinformation. *Terrorism and Political Violence, 11*(4), 149–158. https://doi.org/10.1080/09546559908427537.

Leitenberg, M. (2005). *Assessing the Biological Weapons and Bioterrorism Threat.* Carlisle, PA: Strategic Studies Institute of the U.S. Army War College.

Leitenberg, M. (2009). *Assessing the Threat of Biological Weapons. Bioterrorism: A Public Policy Issue.*

Lennane, R. (2011). Biological Weapon Convention. In R. Katz & R. Zilinskas (Eds.), *Encyclopaedia of Bioterrorism Defense* (pp. 82–86). Hoboken, NJ: Wiley-Blackwell.

L'Estrange, M., & Merchant, S. (2017). *Independent Intelligence Review.* Canberra: Commonwealth of Australia.

Leuprecht, C., et al. (2017). Hezbollah's Global Tentacles: A Relational Approach to Convergence with Transnational Organised Crime. *Terrorism and Political Violence, 29*(5), 902–921.

Life Technologies. (2012, 10 January). *Life Technologies Introduces the Benchtop Ion ProtonTM Sequencer; Designed to Decode a Human Life Genome in One Day for $1,000.* Press release at http://www.lifetechnologies.com/content/ lifetech/us/en/home/about-us/news-gallery/press-releases/2012/life-techologies-itroduces-the-bechtop-io-proto.html.

Lowenthal, M. (2012). *Intelligence from Secrets to Policy.* Thousand Oaks, CA: CQ Press.

Lucero, C., et al. (2011). Biosurveillance Applications. *BMC Medical Informatics, 11,* 1–12.

Lynch, A., MacDonald, E., & Williams, G. (Eds.). (2007). *Law and Liberty in the War on Terror.* Annandale and Sydney: Federation Press.

Maher, B. (2012). The Biosecurity Oversight. *Nature, 485,* 431–434.

Marrin, S. (2009). Training and Educating U.S. Intelligence Analysts. *International Journal of Intelligence and Counterintelligence, 22*(1), 131–146. https://doi.org/10.1080/08850600802486986.

Marrin, S. (2011). *Improving Intelligence Analysis: Bridging the Gap Between Scholarship and Practice.* Abingdon, UK: Routledge.

Marrin, S. (2012). *Improving Intelligence Analysis: Bridging the Gap Between Scholarship and Practice.* Abingdon, UK: Routledge.

Marston, B., et al. (2017). Ebola Response Impact on Public Health Programs, West Africa 2014–2017. *Emerging Infectious Diseases Journal, 28*(Supplement), 25–31.

Martin, A. (2018, February 27). Legislation Aims to Boost Accountability, Collaboration of DHS Fusion Centers. *Homeland Preparedness News.*

Mawudeku, A., et al. (2015). GPHIN Phase 3: One Mandate, Multiple Stakeholders. In S. Davies & J. Youde (Eds.), *The Politics of Surveillance and Response to Disease Outbreaks* (pp. 71–85). Surrey, UK: Ashgate.

May, L., et al. (2009). Beyond Traditional Surveillance: Applying Syndromic Surveillance to Developing Settings—Opportunities and Challenges. *BMC Public Health, 9*(1), 242. https://doi.org/10.1186/1471-2458-9-242.

McConnell, J. (2008). *Annual Threat Assessment of DNI for the Senate Select Committee on Intelligence*. Washington, DC: ODNI.

McDonald, G. (2007). Control Orders and Preventative Detention—Why Alarm Is Misguided. In A. Lynch, et. al. (Eds.), *Law and Liberty in the War on Terror* (pp. 106–115). Annandale and Sydney: Federation Press.

McGurry, J. (2017). Volleyball Games Appear to Take Place at North Korean Nuclear Test Site. *The Guardian*. From https://www.theguardian.com/world/2017/apr/20/north-korea-volleyball-nuclear-test-site-punggye-ri. Accessed March 15, 2017.

McLeish, C., & Nightingale, P. (2007). Biosecurity, Bioterrorism and the Governance of Science: The Increasing Convergence of Science and Security Policy. *Research Policy, 36*(10), 1635–1654. https://doi.org/10.1016/j.respol.2007.10.003.

McNeil, W. (1998). *Plagues and Peoples*. New York: Anchor Books.

Mearsheimer, J. (2001). *The Tragedy of Great Global Power Politics*. New York: Norton.

Mercado, S. (2014). Open Source Intelligence. In L. Johnson & J. Wirtz (Eds.), *Intelligence: The Secret World of Spies* (4th ed., pp. 120–129). New York: Oxford University Press.

Miller, S., & Selgelid, M. (2008). Ethics and the Dual-Use Dilemma in the Life Sciences. In F. Allhoff (Ed.), *Physicians at War: The Dual-Loyalties Challenge* (pp. 195–211). Dordrecht: Springer Netherlands.

Millet, P., & Snyder-Beattie, A. (2017). Existential Risk and Cost Effective Biosecurity. *Health Security, 15*(4), 373–383.

MMWR. (2016). CDC's Response to the 2014–2016 Ebola Epidemic West Africa and the United States. *MMWR, Supplement, 65*(3), 1–106.

Morgenthau, H. (1967). *Politics Among Nations* (4th ed.). New York: Knopf.

Muller, H., & Muller, D. (Eds.). (2015). *WMD Arms Control in the Middle East, Prospects, Obstacles and Options*. Surrey, UK: Ashgate.

Murch, R. (2003). Microbial Forensics: Building a National Capacity to Investigate Bioterrorism. *Biosecurity and Bioterrorism: Biodefense Strategy, Practice and Science, 1*(2), 1–5.

Nalla, M. K., & Wakefield, A. (2014). The Security Officer. In M. Gill (Ed.), *The Handbook of Security* (pp. 727–746). London: Palgrave Macmillan.

NAS. (2006). *Globalization, Biosecurity and the Future of the Life Sciences*. Committee on Advances in Technology and the Prevention of their

Application to Next Generation Biodefense Threats. National Research Council. Washington, DC: National Academies Press.

NAS. (2016). *Gain of Function Research. Summary of the Second Symposium.* Washington, DC: National Academy of Sciences.

NAS. (2017a). *A Proposed Framework for Identifying Potential Biodefense Vulnerabilities Posed by Synthetic Biology Interim Report.* Washington, DC: National Academy of Sciences.

NAS. (2017b). *Human Genome Editing. Science Ethics and Governance.* Washington, DC: The National Academies Press.

National Academies of Sciences, Engineering and Medicine. (2017). *Dual Use Research of Concern in the Life Sciences. Current Issues and Controversies.* Washington, DC: National Academies of Science.

National Institute for Public Policy. (2009). The Proliferation Security Initiative: A Model for Future International Collaboration. *Comparative Strategy, 28,* 395–462.

National Security Council. (2009). *National Strategy for Countering Biological Threats.* Washington, DC.

Nature Editorial. (2014). Biosafety in the Balance. *Nature, 510,* 443.

Nature Editorial. (2017). Gene-Drive Technology Needs Thorough Scrutiny. *Nature, 552,* 6.

Nelson, M., et al. (2014). An Overview of Biosecurity in Australia. *Australian Journal of Forensic Sciences, 46*(4), 383–396. https://doi.org/10.1080/00450 618.2014.882986.

Neville, S. (2013, May 28). Horsemeat Lasagne Scandal Leaves Findus Reputation in Tatters. *The Guardian.* From https://www.theguardian.com/business/2013/feb/08/horsemeat-lasagne-scandal-findus-reputation. Accessed March 15, 2017.

NIC. (2002). *Iraq's Continuing Programs for Weapons of Mass Destruction: Key Judgments.* Washington, DC. From http://nsarchive.gwu.edu/NSAEBB/NSAEBB129/nie.pdf. Accessed March 15, 2017.

Nicolaides, C., et al. (2012). A Metric of Influential Spreading During Contagion Dynamics Through the Air Transportation Network. *PLOS One, 7*(7), 1–10.

Nightingale, C., & Martin, P. (2004). Biosecurity, Bioterrorism and the Governance of Science. *Research Policy, 36,* 1635–1654.

NRC. (2004a). *Biotechnology Research in an Age of Terrorism.* Washington, DC: National Academies.

NRC. (2004b). *Seeking Security: Pathogens, Open Access, and the Genome Databases.* Washington, DC: The National Academies Press.

NRC. (2006). *Globalization, Biosecurity and the Future of the Life Sciences.* Washington, DC: Institute of Medicine and National Research Council.

NSABB. (2016). *Recommendations for the Evaluation and Oversight of Proposed Gain of Function Research*. Washington, DC: National Science Advisory Board for Biosecurity.

Obama, B. (2010). *National Security Strategy*. Washington, DC: The White House.

Office of Inspectors General DOD, CIA, NSA, ODNI, & DOJ. (2009). *Report on the President's Surveillance Program Volume 1*. Washington, DC.

Office of Inspectors General DOJ, & DHS. (2017). *Review of Domestic Sharing of Counter Terrorism Information*. Washington, DC: Office of Inspector General, Department of Homeland Security.

Office of Science and Technology. (2017). *Recommended Policy Guidance for Departmental Development of Review Mechanisms for Potential Pandemic Pathogen Care and Oversight (P3CO)*. Washington, DC.

Omand, D., et al. (2012). Introducing Social Media (SOCMINT) Intelligence. *Intelligence and National Security, 27*(6), 801–823.

O'Leary, Z. (2007). *The Essential Guide to Doing Your Research*. London: Sage Publications.

Oppel, R., et al. (2010, January 4). Attacker in Afghanistan Was a Double Agent. *The New York Times*. From http://www.nytimes.com/2010/01/05/world/asia/05cia.html. Accessed March 15, 2017.

O'Shea, J. (2017). Digital Disease Detection: A systematic Review of Event-Based Internet Biosurveillance Systems. *International Journal of Medical Informatics, 101*(Supplement C), 15–22. https://doi.org/10.1016/j.ijmedinf.2017.01.019.

Ouagrham-Gormley, S. (2012). Barriers to Bioweapons: Intangible Obstacles to Proliferation. *International Security, 36*(4), 80–114. https://doi.org/10.1162/ISEC_a_00077.

Ouagraham-Gormley, S. (2017, July 18). Potemkin or Real? North Koreas's Biological Weapons Program. *Bulletin of the Atomic Scientists*.

Paranjape, S., & Franz, D. (2015). Implementing the Global Health Security Agenda Lessons from the Global Health and Security Programs. *Health Security*, 9–19.

Perman, B., et al. (2013). Basic Principles of Threat Assessment. In R. Burnette (Ed.), *Biosecurity. Understanding, Assessing, and Preventing the Threat* (pp. 89–90). Hoboken, NJ: Wiley.

Petro, J., & Carus, S. (2005). Biological Threat Characterisation Research: A Critical Component of National Biodefense, Biosecurity, and Bioterrorism. *Biodefense Strategy, Practice and Science, 3*, 295–308.

Pita, R., & Gunaratna, R. (2009). Revisiting Al-Qaeda's Anthrax Program. *CTC Sentinel, 2*(5), 10–13.

Prenzler, T., & Sarre, R. (2014). The Role of Partnerships in Security Management. In M. Gill (Ed.), *The Handbook of Security* (pp. 791–812). Basingstoke: Palgrave Macmillan.

Randerson, J. (2006, May 28). Revealed: The Lax Laws That Could Allow the Assembly of Deadly Virus DNA. *The Guardian*. From https://www.theguardian.com/world/2006/jun/14/terrorism.topstories3. Accessed March 15, 2017.

Rappert, B., & Gould, C. (Eds.) (2009). *Biosecurity. Origins, Transformations and Practices*. Basingstoke: Palgrave Macmillan.

Ratcliffe, J. (2008). *Intelligence Led Policing Collompton*. UK: Willan.

Ratcliffe, J. (2016). *Intelligence Led Policing* (2nd ed.). Abingdon, UK: Routledge.

Redmond, P. (2015). The Challenges of Counterintelligence. In L. Johnson & J. Wirtz (Eds.), *Intelligence the Secret World of Spies* (4th ed., pp. 305–316). New York: Oxford University Press.

Reed, M. (2016). *The Research Impact Handbook*. Huntly, UK: Fast Track Impact Ltd.

Regalado, A. (2016, February 9). Top US Intel Official Calls Gene Editing a WMD Threat. *MIT Technology Review*.

Regis, E. (1999). *The Biology of Doom. The History of America's Secret Germ Warfare Project*. New York: Henry Hold and Company.

Rigakos, G. (2002). *The Para police*. Toronto: University of Toronto Press.

Riglietti, G. (2017). Defining the Threat: What Cyber Terrorism Means Today and What It Could Mean Tomorrow. *International Journal of Business and Cyber Security, 1*(2).

Riley, K. (2018, February 28). Blue Ribbon Study Panel on Biodefense Warns Congress Against Delaying Federal Funds Tied to Comprehensive Strategy. *Homeland Preparedness News*.

Risen, J., & Lichtblau, E. (2005). Bush Lets US Spy on Callers Without Courts. *The New York Times*. From http://www.nytimes.com/2005/12/16/politics/bush-lets-us-spy-on-callers-without-courts.html. Accessed March 15, 2018.

Robert Koch Institute. (2018). *Signale—Early Warning System*. Berlin: Robert Koch Institute. From https://www.rki.de/EN/Content/infections/epidemiology/signals/signals_node.html. Accessed March 15, 2018.

Rosenau, W. (2001). Aum Shinrikyo's Biological Weapons Program: Why Did It Fail? *Studies in Conflict and Terrorism, 24*, 283–301.

Rovner, J. (2013). Intelligence in the Twitter Age. *International Journal of Intelligence and Counterintelligence, 26*(2), 260–271.

Rudner, M. (2009). Intelligence Studies in Higher Education: Capacity-Building to Meet Societal Demand. *International Journal of Intelligence and Counterintelligence, 22*(1), 110–130. https://doi.org/10.1080/0885060080 2486960.

Ryan, J., & Glarum, J. (2008). *Biosecurity and Bioterrorism.* Burlington, MA: Elsevier.

Salama, S., & Hansell, L. (2005). Does Intent Equal Capability? Al Qaeda and Weapons of Mass Destruction. *Nonproliferation Review, 12*(3), 615–653.

Salerno, R. (2015). Three Recent Case Studies. The Role of Biorisk Management. In R. Salerno & J. Gaudioso (Eds.), *Laboratory Biorisk Management. Biosafety and Biosecurity* (pp. 191–202). Boca Raton, FL: CRC Press.

Salerno, R., & Gaudioso, J. (Eds.). (2015). *Laboratory Biorisk Management Biosafety and Biosecurity.* Boca Raton, FL: CRC Press.

Sample, I. (2014). Revealed: 100 Safety Breaches at UK Labs Handling Potentially Deadly Diseases. *The Guardian.* From https://www.theguardian.com/science/2014/dec/04/-sp-100-safety-breaches-uk-labs-potentially-deadly-diseases. Accessed March 15, 2017.

Schilling, J. (2017). Ransomware 101-How to Face the Threat. *Petroleum Accounting and Financial Management Journal, 36*(2), 6–8.

Schnirring, L. (2014, August 15). CDC Probe of H5N1 Cross Contamination Reveals Protocol Lapses, Reporting Delays. *CIDRAP.* From http://www.cidrap.umn.edu/news-perspective/2014/08/cdc-probe-h5n1-cross-contamination-reveals-protocol-lapses-reporting-delays. Accessed March 15, 2017.

Schnirring, L. (2016, January 13). Pandemic Readiness Review Says $4.5 Billion a Year Needed. *CIDRAP.* From http://www.cidrap.umn.edu/news-perspective/2016/01/pandemic-readiness-review-says-45-billion-year-needed. Accessed March 15, 2017.

Schnirring, L. (2017). Secretary Tillerson Lauds Global Health Security Agenda. Minneapolis, MN: University of Minnesota (CIDRAP). Retrieved from http://www.cidrap.umn.edu/news-perspective/2017/10/secretary-tillerson-lauds-global-health-security-agenda.

Selgelid, M. (2016). Gain-of-Function Research: Ethical Analysis. *Science and Engineering Ethics, 22*(4), 923–964. https://doi.org/10.1007/s11948-016-9810-1.

Senate, U. S. (2014). *Report of the Senate Select Committee of Intelligence of the CIA'S Detention and Interrogation Program.* Washington, DC: Senate Select Committee on Intelligence.

Shaikh, A.T., Ferland, L., Hood-Cree, R., Shaffer, L., & McNabb, S. (2015). Disruptive Innovation Can Prevent the Next Pandemic. *Frontiers in Public Health, 3*(215). https://doi.org/10.3389/fpubh.2015.00215.

Shea, D. (2006). The National Biodefense Analysis and Countermeasure Center: Issues for Congress *CRS Report* (Vol. RL32891). Washington, DC: Congressional Research Service, The Library of Congress.

Shinwari, Z., Khalil, A., & Nasim, A. (2014). Natural or Deliberate Outbreak in Pakistan: How to Prevent or Detect and Trace Its Origin: Biosecurity, Surveillance Forensics. *Archivum Immunologiae et Therapiae Experimentalis, 62*(4), 263–275. https://doi.org/10.1007/s00005-014-0298-6.

Silberman, L., & Robb, C. (2005). *Commission on the Intelligence Capabilities of the US Regarding Weapons of Mass Destruction. Report to the President of the United States.* (pp. 1–501). Washington, DC.

Sims, J., & Gerber, B. (2009). *Vaults Mirrors and Masks Rediscovering US Counterintelligence.* Washington, DC: Georgetown University Press.

Sisk, R. (2016). Army Probe of Anthrax Scandal Raises More Red Flags. *Military. Com.* Retrieved from http://www.military.com/daily-news/2016/01/13/army-probe-of-anthrax-scandal-raises-more-red-flags.html.

Slayton, J., et al. (2013). Physical Elements of Biosecurity. In R. Burnette (Ed.), *Biosecurity* (pp. 51–70). Hoboken, NJ: Wiley.

Sparrow, A. (2016). Who Isn't Equipped for a Pandemic or Bioterror Attack? The WHO. *Bulletin of the Atomic Scientists.* From https://thebulletin.org/who-isnt-equipped-pandemic-or-bioterror-attack-who9555. Accessed March 15, 2017.

Sparrow, M. (2001). *The Regulatory Craft, Controlling Risk, Solving Problems and Managing Compliance.* Washington, DC: Brookings Institution Press.

Spiers, E. (2010). *A History of Chemical and Biological Weapons.* London: Reaktion Books.

SSCI. (2004). *Report on the US Intelligence Community's Pre War Intelligence Assessments on Iraq.* Washington, DC: US Senate.

Stattner, E., et al. (2011). Diffusion in Dynamic Social Networks: Application in Epidemiology. In A. Hameurlain, et al. (Eds.), *Database and Expert Systems Applications* (pp. 559–573). Heidelberg: Springer-Verlag GMBH.

Stern, J. (2002). Dreaded Risks and Control of Biological Weapons. *International Security, 27*(3), 89–123.

Stern, J., & Shouten, R. (2016). Lessons from the Anthrax Letters. In M. Dunn & S. Sagan (Eds.), *Insider Threats* (pp. 74–102). Ithaca, NY: Cornell University Press.

Stone, A. (2016). Need for FirstNet Greater Than Ever, First Responders Say. *Emergency Management.*

Stone, R. (2017). The Week in Fintech: FBI Agent Says Cybersecurity Practices Need to Change. New York: SNL Financial LC.

Strom, K., & Eyerman, J. (2007). Interagency Coordination in Response to Terrorism: Promising Practices and Barriers Identified in Four Countries. *Criminal Justice Studies, 20*(2), 131–147. https://doi.org/10.1080/14786010701396871.

Sture, J., Minehata, M., & Shinomiya, N. (2012). Looking at the Formulation of National Biosecurity Education Action Plans. *Medicine, Conflict and Survival, 28*(1), 85–97. https://doi.org/10.1080/13623699.2012.658628.

Suk, J., et al. (2011). Dual Use Research and Technological Diffusion. Reconsidering the Bioterrorism Threat Spectrum. *PLoS Pathogens, 7*(1), 1–3.

Taylor, J., et al. (2013). The Role of Protection Measures and Their Interaction in Determining Building Vulnerability and Resilience to Bioterrorism. *Bioterrorism and Biodefense, 4*(1), 1–10.

Tenet, G. (2007). *At the Center of the Storm: My Years at the CIA.* New York: Harper Collins.

The Government of Canada. (2013). *Canadian Biosafety Standards and Guidelines for Facilities Handling Human and Terrestrial Animal Pathogens, Prions, and Biological Toxins.* Ottawa.

Thilmany, J. (2005). Harms Way Engineering Software and Micro Technology Prepare the Defense Against Bioterrorism. *Mechanical Engineering CIME.*

Trevett, C. (2013, May 28). Fonterra Chief Gets 'Frank and Thorough Grilling'. *New Zealand Herald.*

Tucker, J. (Ed.). (2000). *Toxic Terror: Assessing Terrorist Use of Chemical and Biological Weapons.* Cambridge: Harvard University Press.

Tucker, J. (Ed.). (2012). *Innovation, Dual Use and Security.* Cambridge, MA: The MIT Press.

Tucker, J., & Koblentz, G. (2009). The Four Faces of Microbial Forensics. *Biosecurity and Bioterrorism: Biodefense Strategy, Practice, and Science, 7*(4), 389–397. https://doi.org/10.1089/bsp.2009.0043.

Tumpey, T. M., et al. (2005). Characterization of the Reconstructed 1918 Spanish Influenza Pandemic Virus. *Science, 310*(5745), 77–80. https://doi.org/10.1126/science.1119392.

Turnbull, M. (2015). *National Security Statement.* Parliament House, Canberra. From https://www.pm.gov.au/media/2015-11-24/national-security-statement. Accessed March 15, 2017.

UNMOVIC. (2007). *Compendium of Iraq's Prescribed Weapons Programmes in the Chemical, Biological and Missile Areas* (pp. 765–1030). New York: United Nations.

US Army. (2008). *Army Regulation 50–1. Biological Surety.* Washington, DC: US Department of Defense.

Van Cleave, M. (2007). *Counter Intelligence and National Security.* Washington, DC: National Defense University.

Vanier, M. (2017, April 30). NBAF Update the Lab as a Buffer Against Catastrophic Outbreaks. *The Mercury.* From http://themercury.com/ articles/nbaf-update-the-lab-as-a-buffer-against-catastrophic-outbreaks. Accessed March 15, 2017.

Vogel, K. (2008). Biodefense. In A. Lakoff & S. Collier (Eds.), *Biosecurity Interventions* (pp. 227–255). New York: Columbia University.

Vogel, K. (2013a). Intelligent Assessment: Putting Emerging Biotechnology Threats in Context. *Bulletin of the Atomic Scientists, 35*(1), 45–54.

Vogel, K. (2013b). Necessary Interventions. Expertise and Experiments in Bioweapons Intelligence Assessments. *Science, Technology and Innovation Studies, 9*(2), 61–88.

Vogel, K. (2013c). *Phantom Menace or Looming Danger?* Baltimore, MD: The Johns Hopkins University Press.

Vogel, K., & Knight, C. (2014). Analytic Outreach for Intelligence: Insights from a Workshop on Emerging Biotechnology Threats. *Intelligence and National Security,* 1–18. https://doi.org/10.1080/02684527.2014.887633.

Vogel, K., et al. (2015). Editorial: Biosecurity and Dual-Use Research: Gaining function—At What Cost? *Frontiers in Public Health, 3.* https://doi. org/10.3389/fpubh.2015.00013.

Voronova-Abrams, M. (2011). Biosecurity 2.0: Enduring Threats in the Former Soviet Union. *Bulletin of the Atomic Scientists, 67*(4), 78–90. https:// doi.org/10.1177/0096340211413752.

Wakefield, A. (2003). *Selling Security. The Private Policing of Public Space.* Cullompton, Devon: Willan.

Walker, C. (2005). Biological Attack, Terrorism and the Law. *Terrorism and Political Violence, 17*(1–2), 175–200. https://doi.org/10.1080/09546550590 520663.

Walsh, P. F. (2011). *Intelligence and Intelligence Analysis.* Abingdon, UK: Routledge.

Walsh, P. F. (2012). *Submission and Testimony to Inquiry into the Use of Criminal Intelligence, by Joint Parliamentary on Law Enforcement* (Final Report). Australian Parliament, Canberra. Retrieved from http://www.aph. gov.au/parliamentary_business/Committees/Senate_Committees?url=le_ ctte/criminal_intelligence/submission.htm.

Walsh, P. F. (2014). Managing Intelligence and Responding to Emerging Threats: The Case of Biosecurity. In M. Gill (Ed.), *The Handbook of Security* (pp. 837–854). Basingstoke: Palgrave Macmillan.

Walsh, P. F. (2015). Building Better Intelligence Frameworks Through Effective Governance. *International Journal of Intelligence and Counterintelligence, 28*(1), 123–142. https://doi.org/10.1080/08850607.2014.924816.

Walsh, P. F. (2016). Australian National Security Intelligence Collection Since 9/11: Policy and Legislative Challenges. In K. Warby (Ed.), *National Security, Surveillance and Terror* (pp. 51–74). Cham, Switzerland: Springer International Publishing.

Walsh, P. F., & Miller, S. (2016). Rethinking 'Five Eyes' Security Intelligence Collection Policies and Practice Post Snowden. *Intelligence and National Security, 31*(3), 345–368.

Walsh, P. F. (2017a). Drone Paramilitary Operations Against Suspected Global Terrorists: US and Australian Perspectives. *Intelligence and National Security, 32*(4), 429–433.

Walsh, P. F. (2017b). Making Future Leaders in the US Intelligence Community: Challenges and Opportunities. *Intelligence and National Security, 32*(4), 441–459. https://doi.org/10.1080/02684527.2016.1253920.

Walsh, P. F. (2017c). Teaching Intelligence in the Twenty-First Century: Towards an Evidence-Based Approach for Curriculum Design. *Intelligence and National Security, 32*(7), 1005–1021. https://doi.org/10.1080/02684527.2017.1328852.

Walsh, P. F. (2017d). Securing State Secrets. In R. Dover, H. Dylan, & M. Goodman (Eds.), *The Palgrave Handbook of Security, Risk and Intelligence* (pp. 177–194). London: Palgrave Macmillan.

Walsh, P. F., & Miller, S. (2016). Rethinking 'Five Eyes' Security Intelligence Collection Policies and Practice Post Snowden. *Intelligence and National Security, 31*(3), 345–368.

Waltz, K. (1979). *Theory of International Politics*. New York: Random House.

Watts, J., & Stewart, H. (2003, April 22). Asia Unable to Mask SARS Cost. *The Guardian*.

Weimann, G. (2016). Going Dark: Terrorism on the Dark Web. *Studies in Conflict & Terrorism, 39*(3), 195–206. https://doi.org/10.1080/1057610x.2015.1119546.

Wein, L., & Liu, Y. (2005). Analyzing a Bioterror Attack on the Food Supply: The Case of Botulinum Toxin in Milk. *Proceedings of the National Academy of Sciences of the United States of America, 102*(28), 9984–9989. https://doi.org/10.1073/pnas.0408526102.

Wendt, A. (1999). *Social Theory of International Politics*. Cambridge: Cambridge University Press.

White, M. (2007). A Judicial Perspective—The Making of Preventative Detention Orders. In A. Lynch, et al. (Eds.), *Law and Liberty in the War on Terror* (pp. 116–127). Annandale and Sydney: Federation Press.

WHO. (2015a). Ebola Virus Disease in West Africa—The First Nine Months of the Epidemic and Forward Projections. *The New England Journal of Medicine, 371,* 1481–1495.

WHO. (2015b). WHO Draft Resolution Preparedness Geneva: WHO.

Williams, G. (2011). A Decade of Australian Anti-Terror Laws. *Melbourne University Law Review, 35,* 1137–1151.

Williams-Jones, B., Olivier, C., & Smith, E. (2014). Governing 'Dual-Use' Research in Canada: A Policy Review. *Science and Public Policy, 41*(1), 76–93. https://doi.org/10.1093/scipol/sct038.

Willman, D. (2017, September 11). Judge Bars Public from Trial Over Homeland Security Contract for Device to Detect Bioterrorism. *The Los Angeles Times.* From http://www.latimes.com/nation/la-na-dhs-gag-order-20170911-story.html. Accessed March 15, 2017.

Wilson, J. (2017). Signal Recognition During the Emergence of Pandemic Influenza Type A/H1N1: A Commercial Disease Intelligence Unit's Perspective. *Intelligence and National Security, 32*(2), 222–230.

Wilson, J., et al. (2009). Media Reporting of the Emergence of the 1968 Influenza Pandemic in Hong Kong: Implications for Modern Day Situational Awareness. *Disaster Medicine and Public Health Preparedness.*

Xu, Z., et al. (2011). Bioaerosol Science, Technology and Engineering: Past and Present. *Aerosol Science and Technology, 45*(1), 1337–1349.

Yam, A. (2013, May 28). Memories Still Too Raw for Chinese Parents to Trust Baby Formula. *South China Morning Post.* From http://www.scmp.com/news/china/article/1273375/memories-still-too-raw-chinese-parents-trust-baby-formula. Accessed March 15.

Yan, S., et al. (2017). Utility and Potential of Rapid Epidemic Intelligence from Internet-Based Sources. *International Journal of Infectious Diseases, 63*(Supplement C), 77–87. https://doi.org/10.1016/j.ijid.2017.07.020.

Youde, J. (2015). Biosurveillance as National Policy: The United States' National Strategy for Biosurveillance. In S. Davies & J. Youde (Eds.), *The Politics of Surveillance and Response to Disease Outbreak* (pp. 137–157). Surrey, UK: Ashgate.

Young, A. (2015, August 28). Labs Cited for 'Serious' Security Failures in Research with Bioterror Germs. *USA Today.* From http://www.usatoday.com/story/news/2015/08/28/lab-security-violation-bioterrorism-select-agent-regulation/32439491/. Accessed March 15, 2017.

Young, A. (2016, September 30). CDC Lab Shipped Virus Without Following Key Safety Steps. *USA Today*. From http://www.usatoday.com/story/news/2016/09/30/cdc-lab-shipped-virus-without-following-key-safety-steps/91343102/. Accessed March 15, 2017.

Zajácz, R. (2017). Silk Road: The Market Beyond the Reach of the State. *The Information Society, 33*(1), 23–34. https://doi.org/10.1080/01972243.2016.1248612.

Zanders, J. (2015). Biological and Chemical Weapons and the Prospective Disarmament Process in the Middle East. In H. Muller & D. Muller (Eds.), *WMD Arms Control in the Middle East* (pp. 149–157). Surrey, UK: Ashgate.

Zegart, A. (2007). *Spying Blind*. Princeton, NJ: Princeton University Press.

Index

Printed in the United States
By Bookmasters